House of Houses

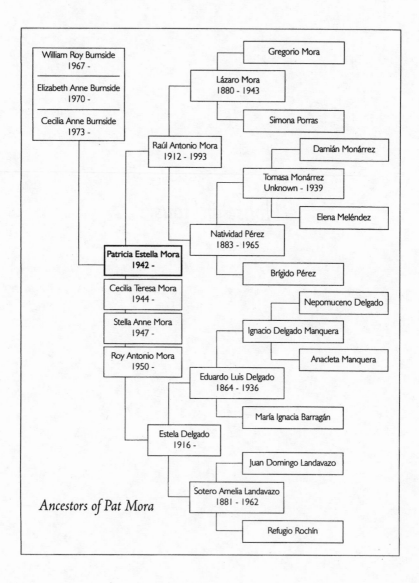

Ancestors of Pat Mora

- William Roy Burnside 1967 -
- Elizabeth Anne Burnside 1970 -
- Cecilia Anne Burnside 1973 -

- Patricia Estella Mora 1942 -
- Cecilia Teresa Mora 1944 -
- Stella Anne Mora 1947 -
- Roy Antonio Mora 1950 -

Raúl Antonio Mora 1912 - 1993

Lázaro Mora 1880 - 1943
- Gregorio Mora
- Simona Porras

Natividad Pérez 1883 - 1965

Tomasa Monárrez Unknown - 1939
- Damián Monárrez
- Elena Meléndez

Brígido Pérez

Estela Delgado 1916 -

Eduardo Luis Delgado 1864 - 1936

Ignacio Delgado Manquera
- Nepomuceno Delgado
- Anacleta Manquera

María Ignacia Barragán

Sotero Amelia Landavazo 1881 - 1962
- Juan Domingo Landavazo
- Refugio Rochín

Pat Mora

HOUSE OF HOUSES

*For Dianne,
Welcome to
my house!
Pat Mora
June 2003*

Beacon Press · Boston

Beacon Press
25 Beacon Street
Boston, Massachusetts 02108-2892

Beacon Press books are published under the auspices of
the Unitarian Universalist Association of Congregations.

A portion of "Abril lluvioso/Rainy April"
previously appeared in *Prairie Schooner*
as "A Walk with My Father."

02 01 00 99 98 97   8 7 6 5 4 3 2 1

Text design by Christopher Kuntze.

Library of Congress Cataloging-in-Publication Data

Mora, Pat.
    House of houses / Pat Mora.
      p. cm.
    ISBN 0-8070-7200-1 (cloth)
    ISBN 0-8070-7201-X (paper)
    1. Mora, Pat—Childhood and youth.   2. Women poets, American—20th
century—Biography.   3. Mexican American families—New Mexico.
4. New Mexico—Social life and customs.   I. Title.
    PS3563.073Z468   1997
    811'.54
    [B]—DC20   96-43948

For my children, niece, and nephews,

BILL, LIBBY, CISSY,

NIKI, GIL, & CHRISTOPHER,

who continue the story

Contents

Me in a dress Aunt Carmen made.

Refugio Rochín, my maternal great-grandmother, known as Doña Cuca.

My kind and patient maternal grandmother, Sotero Amelia Landavazo, whom we called Mamande.

The man on the left of this photo from the Mexican Revolution of 1910 is José Landavazo, my maternal great-uncle, who was separated from Mamande at childhood.

Mamande at an outdoor gathering (far right). In every photo she seems pensive.

*Wedding portrait of my maternal grandparents, Sotero Amelia
Landavazo and Eduardo Luis Delgado, Mamande and Papande.*

Mamande holding me (left), Aunt Nina (center), and Mother holding my sister, Cecilia.

My mother, Estela Delgado, held by her mother who is hiding behind the pillow.

Ygnacia Delgado, my maternal aunt, whom we called Lobo.

Mother holding hands with my favorite uncle, the wonderful storyteller, Uncle Lalo.

Soledad Mora, whom we call Aunt Chole, the eldest of my paternal aunts.

My parents, Estela and Raúl Mora, standing by our rock home.

Mother expecting me.

*My mother as a child and her father,
Papande.*

Acknowledgments

I WISH TO EXPRESS my deepest thanks to all the relatives who answered my many questions. In particular I wish to thank my mother, Estela Mora, my uncle, Eduardo Delgado, my aunts, Soledad Mora and Carmen Delgado, and my guardian angel in this life, my sister, Stella Mora Henry, for all their patience in answering my innumerable nosey questions and for entrusting the stories of their lives to me so openly. I've quoted their notes and cards, not wanting to alter how they wrote their thoughts. No member of my family asked to review or approve any part of this family memoir which says it all.

The year my husband and I spent at the School of American Research in Santa Fe was a boon to this book, set in my native Southwest. I am grateful to Dr. Doug Schwartz and the staff of the School for their cheerfulness and kindness.

I appreciate the faith my editor, Deborah Chasman, had in the book's concept, her careful readings of the work, and her ability to see and hear what I couldn't. I am also grateful to her assistant, Tisha Hooks, the copyeditor, George Lang, and to all the unseen and unsung staff at Beacon Press, *gracias, gracias.*

My husband, Vern Scarborough, read the entire manuscript and patiently listened to months of fretting. *La esperanza no engorda pero mantiene.* Thanks, Vern, for sustaining me with your hope.

My family has been curious yet patient. I am indebted to each of them and to all who came before, our *antepasados.*

House of Houses

Ut rosa flos florum, sic est domus ista domorum.

As the rose is the flower of flowers, so is this,
> the house of houses.

"How can you still be hungry if you're dead?" Aunt Chole sing-songs her question in the high pitch she reserves for birds, children, spirits. "Ay, *mi Raúl, querido*, what do you want?"

"I'll get him something, Tía," I say. In my dreamhouse my father returns, dark-skinned, balding, filling the room. "What do you want, Daddy? Coffee?"

"Sure, honey." He shuffles across the red tiled floor to the small corner fireplace in his old slippers and warms his hands, rubs them together, the pleasure of flesh on flesh, "*ah, ah.*" He shuffles toward the refrigerator of the large, family kitchen in his pajamas, reaches for the tin of cookies we keep for him, plain sugar cookies he and I both like. He sits with us at the blue kitchen table, and in his rough, teasing mode asks his sister who sees only shadows, our oldest living relative, "*¿Y tú cómo estás? No me digas que estás enferma otra vez,*" entreating her not to say she's sick again.

Aunt Chole laughs, knows him well. "Ay, Raúl, you know I haven't been sick in years." She coughs.

"*Anda, anda.* Now don't get dramatic. Are you putting honey on the tip of your tongue? Get her some honey, Patsy," he says using my childhood name, seeing me both in the past and in the present.

"I did, Daddy. It's in her tea, but I'll add some wood to the fire so she'll stay warm."

"Get her more honey. If not she'll drive us crazy with her coughing." My father grins slyly at me.

Aunt Chole shakes her head at her brother, the man unchanged even by his own funeral. *"Ay, Raúl. Como eres malo."* The parrot echoes, *"Ay, Raúl. Como eres malo,"* a reprimand the macaw hears often in this house.

My father chuckles, munches his cookies and sips his coffee, smiles at me. "How are you doing, honey? Everything all right?"

I want to say: how can it be all right if you're dead? How can it be that I will never again lean on your chest, feel your arms encircling, protecting, like the house? But I don't. I continue making the mix for the birds of this family house. I chop apples and carrots to stir with seeds. Like my father, I tease to stave off tears.

"I was reading to Aunt Chole from Lobo's missal about the saint days this week, like the feast of San Telesforo. Now there's a name for a grandchild. We could call him Telly. I'm always finding names for unborn grandchildren, Daddy. I found great saints' names for a group of male triplets—Polycarp, Pancratius, and Paphnutius—Polly, Panny, and Paphy. I'm already partial to Paphy. We could opt for the names of St. Richard of Luca's children, of course, Willibald, Wunibald, and Walburga."

My father smiles vaguely while Aunt Chole slips inside herself, to her private world. I serve her more tea, resolve to listen more, speak less. I want to tell her about the medical report on NPR this morning, that some persons who are blind perceive light without their awareness, that this perception regulates their internal clock, keeps it from drifting gradually into another time zone. But she will cry if I ask: do you feel light? Her sorrows on the tip of her tongue.

How much does our body know that we know not? Can it be cajoled to release its secrets?

"I'm writing a book about us," I say. "About the family."

"Make me handsome and strong. Just look at these muscles. I could still beat anybody up. Just let them try anything, honey." My father flexes, this ever bold spirit.

I struggle to sketch the home we inherited, adobe body to house the spirits I gather, living and dead; mud refuge whose outer skin, the exterior wall, offers the pleasure of being encircled by earth, the poetry of place. Between its layers, the outer and inner walls, grow piñon pines, Mexican elders, yucca, a giant mesquite that arches above the children's swings in the front courtyard.

Far more confident with words than a paintbrush, I make myself draw, spread paper on the kitchen table to see what I'll see, play with colored pens to create the wood double doors that open to reveal the hidden: the one-story Mexican house and its central garden, hushed in snow today, not paradise, but a space, in Gaston Bachelard's words, of "protected intimacy." Walls to create silence, water to create music, says architect Luis Barragán, so I draw the old fountain, symbol of life in an arid land; the four paths leading from it to the *portal*, the covered porch that borders the square garden, and the doors that open from the porch into the family rooms; the courtyard, porch, house, blocks nesting like bodies inside one another.

To the left of the outside wall, I sketch the garage, prickly pear and claret-cup cactus sprouting from its roof; out back shade and fruit trees—cottonwoods, *moras*, apricots, figs; the small bridge over the *acequia*, the irrigation canal; and on the right, the greenhouse and the road down to the river.

The house knows the sound of el Río Grande, river that for centuries wandered through this Chihuahua desert, largest desert in North America, old ocean bed where millions of years ago, land emerged from water, mountains rose. Oceans became seas, seas dried to lakes, and lakes evaporated into basins and *playas*. Water creatures—oysters, clams, coral—hardened in the sea of sand, wordless geological history.

Brown women and men knew this river, washed in it, planted with it, played in it, slept with its voice, long before *conquistadores*, historians, and politicians divided the land into countries and states, directed the river to become a border. Those ancient desert dwellers created shelter, shaped places for protection and privacy, as other humans have, whether in tundra or rainforests, built huts, hogans, igloos, tents, cabins, cottages, yurts; built houses of rock, wood, bamboo, bricks, adobe. Believing houses to be living, some feed them, bury caches to appease the hungry spirit *de la casa*.

In this landscape, Indians and Spaniards shaped space from what their hands touched—mud, straw, water—and the house grew out of the desert; a house of paradox, rooted, built on bedrock, yet the adobe hovers near the Río Grande between El Paso and Santa Fe. Jung, who understood the psychological implications of space shaping, referred to the house he built as "a confession of faith in stone." Is this our adobe confession? Through generations, sun, wind, rain, hands, voices, and dreams create and alter this place pregnant with possibilities in a landscape as familiar to me as my body. What does the house, the body, know?

My father points to the words, *Ut rosa flos florum, sic est domus ista domorum.* "What does that say?"

"It's Latin, a sentence I read in *Natural History*. It means: as the rose is the flower of flowers, so is this the house of houses."

My father smiles, after a pause asks, "You're not going to put your drawings in the book are you?"

I punch him in the arm.

He laughs. "Is my name in the book?"

"Poetry in the raw . . . untranslatable," Auden said of proper names. Though much in this house is imagined, how could I not use the family names, the stories I've heard, read, followed, stories from the interior, the private space a family creates and inhabits, in which time loses its power and past∞present braid as they do within each of us, in *our* interior. The clock ticks, the present becoming past, a current that like the wind resists control, drifts or gusts through our doors at will, bringing with it whatever it gathered, a dead bird, a butterfly.

Lobo, another of the transparent souls who moves comfortably through this, their house, enters the kitchen. Lobo: maternal aunt, Ignacia Delgado, who called us her *lobitos*, her four little wolves, when she'd knock on our front door after work, becomes through the years Lobo, wolf-mother, born the month of the Wolf Moon; Lobo, the sound of the word a sweet love call so unlike harsh-sounding Nacha, her name to others.

"Who's Nacha?" we tease in the bratty years.

"Nacha," Lobo smiles as she turns down our beds, "she is a ghost."

This aunt who died in 1983 is like us all, a creature of contradictions who while she frowns at men's bodies, at touching between men and women, wanders through the house wearing only her white silk slip; prudish, but not a woman to bother with the nuisance and smells of underclothes. Since she hopes that any male she didn't know and care for since his birth will have the decency to stay outdoors, she turns quickly to leave when she sees my father, her mutters filling the doorway like a burst of black feathers. She heads toward her room to don a housecoat, her gray hair flying after her.

My father laughs. "*A que Nacha*, the house is asleep, and she's already mad."

"What is it? What's happening?" Aunt Chole's hands begin to tremble. Any commotion alarms this woman accustomed to the peace and pain of living alone.

"*Hay viene Nacha, bien enojada*," says my father.

"I'm not mad," Lobo frowns, buttons the highest button on her striped blue-and-white housecoat, averts her gaze from the large man sitting relaxed, chest hair visible, so unsightly to a lady.

My father winks at me, reveling in the presence of two women he can tease. The door opens again, and Mamande, patient maternal grandmother who died in 1962 enters also in a house coat, white hair in one long braid down her back. Now my father really grins.

"*Ándele, Amelita, más aprisa, más aprisa*," he says knowing his rushing irritates his mother-in-law.

"Don't start, Daddy. Go take your bath or do whatever you do, and I'll talk to you later, but stay out of trouble. Now just let me sit and listen."

He lifts his arms as if to spook the three older women sitting around the table, each so lost in her private morning reverie, fingers round a hot cup, that they don't even see him smile at me and leave singing, "*Yo soy la pa - lo - ma blan - ca . . .*" the shape-shifter then transforming himself into a white dove and flying off to the back of the house, probably to pester Mother who's sleeping as late as we'll allow.

How long can I watch these gray-haired women before they see me watching, one nearing the end of her dark life and two who slipped away from me? I offer to make toast for them, set knives, butter, and apricot jam out on the yellow cotton table-cloth, promise to brown Lobo's bread to a crisp the way she likes it.

"*Más nieve,*" Lobo says.

"How much snow is there?" asks Aunt Chole. "Listen, listen, can you hear my little birds out on the patio? How they miss me. I always fed them even in the snow. "*Los pajaritos, Amelia,*" she says to my grandmother. I watch two sparrows fly from the old cottonwood that grew here before this house was built. The sparrows peck below dormant rose bushes of the garden.

"These are the days of *las cabañuelas,*" says Lobo, "a system some use in México to predict the year's weather by studying its first twenty-four days. *Es muy interesante.* Start with the first as January, the second as February, all the way to the twelfth as December. Then on January thirteenth, count again, so the thirteenth is January, the fourteenth February, etc., and then average the two temperatures for January or April or November to fore-tell that month's weather for the year. That's what the old farm-ers did."

"Do you remember, Nacha," Aunt Chole says, "I am the last person you talk to before you die." I don't agree, but I say noth-ing, listen to my aunt's voice and to a cricket's lulling *crk, crk, crk.*

"I used to call you often," Aunt Chole says, then turns to me, "*Tan linda que era.* I said to her that last time that she didn't sound well. 'I'm sick,' she said. 'But don't tell anyone.' That was the end. *Era tan linda e instruida.*" Lobo sits tall at the praise, at someone calling her lovely and well-read; Lobo who savors books, even in her nineties while my children played, pulled out the *World Book* and studied maps.

"And I loved you too, Amelia," Aunt Chole says, seeing my quiet grandmother look down, iron the tablecloth slowly with her right hand. "I still pray for you both when I pray for the dead. Remember, Amelita, how you told me that every morning before I went to work, you wanted me to stop and visit you? She gave me an order," my aunt chuckles. "Your grandmother said that you'd all leave, and she didn't have anyone to talk to. Now, at this time in my life, I know how she felt."

I look out at the covered porch that borders the garden, that shades us when we sit in the wide, rawhide and wood chairs, *equipales*. On warm days, sparrows wade in the fountain whose quiet splash, *ps-slp-plop, ps-slp-plop*, lures us all into these adobe walls. In Nigeria, Morocco, Spain, Syria, fellow humans also find comfort from such mud-rounded protection. Rumors of my unending questions alter the pitch and rhythms of speech within these walls I know. All know: I'm after stories, brewed in the bone. It's the older voices and bodies who have the patience to talk and remember.

Watching white branches sway in the transformed garden, I recite John Greenleaf Whittier's "Snowbound" to myself, think of Sister Godfrey, her perfect posture and wild gray eyebrows, the acrid-smelling sheets of purple mimeographed lines she'd have us recite weekly in eighth grade. Where did they hide their doubts, those confident women in black folds? Maybe where they hid their round watches, in tiny, secret pockets near their hearts.

This is a "world that we can call our own," this family space through which generations move, each bringing its gifts, handing down languages and stories, recipes for living, gathering around the kitchen table to serve one another; in the walled garden, engaging in the slow conversation of families sitting to pass the time. Voices mingle with the voice of the fountain, parrot, broom, wind, *voces del jardín*.

The walled garden, a design indigenous to Mexico and also Iranian, then Islamic, brought to the Americas by the Spanish, is a tradition Moorish and Mexican. A garden can be enchanted, bewitched, bewitching. To enjoy the lush beauty throughout the year, Persians in the sixth century even created garden carpets patterned after the courtyard foliage and blooms. And gardens flourished on this continent. When the Spaniards entered Mexico in 1519, they found *chinampas*, which *los españoles* mistook for floating gardens, plots covered with dahlias, amaranth, chiles, corn, willows. Moctezuma, who had established an aqueduct to bring spring water from Chapultepec to the island city of Tenochtitlán, is credited with the construction of splendid, verdant spaces tended by experienced horticulturalists.

In the desert, a garden demands as love does everywhere, care, intentionality. Ignore the soil, food, light, and water needs of caladiums or cannas, and they will soon shrivel from neglect, vanish from this space both private and communal; a space of labor and frustration, also of meditation, solace, hope, and sensory delights.

Plants, humans' first medicines, through ritual and religion intertwine with our lives, become sources of food, shelter, warmth, weapons, clothing, dyes, cosmetics, wine. The world's flora nourish, inspire, intoxicate. Rich sources of mystery, magic, and mythology; they flavor our dishes, beautify our rooms, soothe our aches, scent our beds, decorate our bodies and altars, perfume our paths and poems; these green lifeforms that rise from the dark tangle of underground life, like our subconscious, fertile and full of promise.

In the evening, the family scatters throughout the house. Some work or pray in their rooms, some visit at the kitchen table. Lobo reads on the living room sofa, Mamande says her novena in her chair, and at the piano Mother plays Schubert and the adagio movement of Beethoven's "Pathetique," the notes of the treble sinking into us like falling stars. My father comes in, stands at the foot of the piano, conducts, eyes closed. After I water the houseplants, the ficus, bougainvillea, miniature orange, and snake plant, I sit on the sofa, read in the *Popul Vuh*, Quiché Maya book of creation, about the conversation between sky and sea gods, words that created this world, " . . . the earth rose because of them, it was simply their words that brought it forth."

Aunt Carmen, Mother's sister-in-law, hands me the new gardening catalogues, and I thumb through them, study ideas for the small wildflower garden behind the house, and for the small rock garden we started last year, a good excuse to buy assorted ice-plant and portulaca to tuck among the river-rolled stones that fit snugly in my palms, all the hard smoothness, embedded water sounds.

I show the catalogues to Uncle Lalo, Mother's brother and our favorite uncle, who says, "Reminds me. Tomorrow I've got to start cleaning, sharpening, and oiling my tools. New gardening year. Who knows what mischief your Aunt Carmen will have me up to out there."

I read of vespertine flowers, night bloomers like four o'clocks, opening like mouths in evening prayer. My devout relatives will like such bloomers near the grotto they built to San Francisco.

"*Planta flores con nombres religiosos como Varitas de San José*," says Mamá Cleta, my great-great grandmother exhorting me to plant flowers with religious names. She slid into my life this year, silent and transforming, like light shines through stained glass windows. She hopes for plants with the names of saints, hers a religious rather than scientific taxonomy. I know the hollyhocks she mentioned, the blooming staff associated with Saint Joseph, the name in English originally meaning holy mallow reflecting the belief that they had come to Europe directly from the Holy Land, but how many plants do I know that have religious connotations in their Spanish names? I make a note to look for *Manto de la Virgen*, Virgin's Bower, *Flor de San Juan*, Evening Primrose in English, and *Flor de Santa Rita*, Indian Paintbrush. "*Como siembras, segarás*," says Mamá Cleta, the gardener's wisdom, the link between sowing and harvest.

I also jot a note to buy crimson and white thyme this year for planting along the flagstone paths to scent the air when we walk through the garden with this small, erect relative, her gray hair always in a soft bun at the top of her head, her hands snapping off dead blooms, grooming the garden that holds the whispers of her long dresses. Even without the luxury of their scent, she and I enjoy the catalogue pages about roses, the flower of flowers, symbol of the beloved as well as the Virgin Mary. We read in a book on Persian gardens, about a hundred-petaled rose and the custom of sprinkling guests with rose water, of consuming the essence of the mesmerizing flower in rose preserves and sherbets. Mamá Cleta, never embarrassed by her synesthesia, sighs, "*¿La oyes?* Do you hear organ music when you look long at the yellow rose?"

The next morning, Aunt Chole shuffles into the kitchen wearing a purple velour jogging suit, two pairs of socks, sturdy shoes. "*Buenos días, buenos días.* Is that you, *reina?* What are you doing?"

I've been sitting at the table staring in wonder at the soundless movement of snow in the courtyard, at the bare honey locust branches, listening to the quiet of a new year. Such a hush, even when the wind blows through the trees sending snow flying from their limbs, the world seems dormant, pensive.

"Reading Lobo's missal, *Misal Diario San José.*" I take some liberties with the truth since I'd actually only opened my aunt's missal, sat and watched light slide on the gold edges of the pages like music on violin strings. Pictures and holy cards flutter out, prayers Lobo wanted to repeat, faces to be prayed for, pictures of my children when they were little. Out falls a holy card of the Good Shepherd, pale, sweet, brown-haired Jesus stroking a white lamb. The cold, black words on the back of the card given out at Lobo's rosary the night before her burial,

Jesús ten piedad del alma de Ygnacia R. Delgado,
November 16, 1983.

Someone tucked the card in her thick prayer book after her death.

She spills out to me from her missal, a photo dated November, 1966. She's standing by a bridge railing, brown skirt, black sweater, black scarf; with her sister, Dolores, Aunt Lola, who's frowning, probably giving firm directions to the son taking the photo.

"Read me the missal, *mi amor*," Aunt Chole says trying to suppress a cough. "You know I can't see to read." I ask her if she'd like tea with honey, urge her to eat more, my bent, fragile aunt.

"Did you put birdseed outside for *los pajaritos, corazón mío*? It's so cold outside, and my little birds will be waiting. *Ay, querida*, how I used to love to go out early in the morning to feed them."

My youngest daughter, Cissy, comes in wishing the snow would melt so that she could return to her jogging. "So what do you think of my idea of propping the Christmas tree in that corner as a bird feeder instead of just throwing it away? Pretty clever, huh? I'll put seeds and stuff on it.

"Aunt Chole," she says raising her voice, "I put food for the birds on a tree, *para los pajaritos*."

"*Ay, que mi querida tan chula*," her aunt says in a high, sweet octave. Cissy feeds the parrot more seeds, in the living room curls up with cat and book.

I savor each simple gesture in this kitchen, filling the tea kettle, lighting the stove, click of the cup in the saucer. They've all been here, are here, the family of women, nursing one another with teas—*de canela, hierbabuena, gordolobo*. Straight and erect in their good health or bent with age and arthritis, sacramental acts for another woman, or a husband, father, or child, steeping an old cure that began underground. "It is strange to be so many women," as Adrienne Rich says.

I watch Aunt Chole momentarily lost in the act of sipping the hot, sweet liquid, the comfort of memories, of repeated acts that stream us back to our small selves, the child bundled in the bodies of family, watch her freely since she can't see me watching.

"Smell this, Aunt Chole. It's a vanilla candle. I'm going to light it and put it here on the table while we talk." I love the privateness of this time with her. She rises in the dark, on Mexican time, she says.

"Vanilla?" she frowns. "*¿Vela de vainilla?*"

"Aromatherapy."

"*¿Qué?*" She looks confused.

"It's a new idea, Tía, or maybe an old idea using new technology."

"*¿Qué? ¿Vela de tecnología?*"

"Remember how you'd use rose petals and cinnamon sticks or cloves to make rooms smell good? Now they sell scented candles and oils and organic sprays, environmental fragrancing, herb and flower essences. They say the smells can relax you or give you energy," watching her face, I say the last words slowly, "or even make you romantic." Sure enough, her little laugh rises. "*Ee-ee,* romantic! Don't start asking me about that man today." She sips her tea.

"Are you eating, Tía?"

"*Querida,* you know how colds are. I'm not hungry these days, but I'm drinking that Assure." She sips. "Read me from the missal. I can't see, *mi reina.* You have to help me."

"It says the priest would wear white today, like the snow outside." I stare out again at the adobe walls of this refuge from the heat and cold of the desert and its denizens. Of course, walls, like doors and locks, can be confining, but a home can be liberating if I have the physical and emotional strength to enter and exit at will. In spite of the family tensions, like the tensions within myself or the structural tensions of any house, I retreat to this space to hear myself, and to hear those often silent when they left these walls, reticent to reveal themselves.

I read the liturgical calendar in Lobo's missal, the cycles of Advent, Christmas, Epiphany, Ordinary Time, Lent, Easter, Pentecost, the annual repetition of the events in Christ's life or in ecclesiastical language, "the re-enactment of the mysteries of salvation;" the religious repetitions—litanies and rosaries, rhythmic as the seasons. I read to Aunt Chole about the feast of the Holy Name.

"The missal says, 'Let every knee bend at the sound of His name.' " She begins to coo about her "*Diosito,*" how much He helps her.

"*Ya, ya, ya,*" teases my father entering the dark kitchen in his pajamas as always looking for something to eat. "*Uds. platicando y yo muerto de hambre.* And why are you sitting in the dark? *¡Ándenle, ándenle. A trabajar!*"

"*¡Ándenle, ándenle. A trabajar!*" the *guacamaya* echoes, urging us to get to work, another phrase the bird hears often.

We hear the *sw, sw, sw* of Lobo's broom, and sip in silence, listen to the song of the winter wind, its deep song, its *canto hondo*.

Enero friolero / Chilly January

DO YOU WANT ME to tell you again about the family?" Lobo asks when I refill her cup. "It seems we're the descendants of Spaniards since the last name, Delgado, comes from the coasts of Spain, from Santander, Barcelona, Oveido." The familiar Spanish litany begins.

"Those Delgados come to México, settle in different parts. We know that my grandfather is the son of Don Nepomuceno Delgado who marries Doña Anacleta Manquero, their children Jesús, Cruz, Francisco, Antonio, Beatriz, my grandfather, and Emeteria, whom we called Mamá Tela since she raises us when my mother dies.

"I am born in 1889, on January twenty-second, in Cusihuiriachic, in the Benito Juárez district, a very rich mineral district, in the state of Chihuahua. When I'm little, maybe two years old, my parents take me to a May fair or fiesta at the Church of Santa Rita in Chihuahua. At the roulette wheel, I win two *pesos*, imagine. It is late afternoon so we go home and celebrate my good fortune, such luck at that young age.

"Maybe that's why I like to buy lottery tickets. I always told you, *mis lobitos*, that if I win, I'll buy back our house, 704 Mesita, the house we lost, that we all hated to leave." I think she longed to dwell in the house my siblings and I grew up in all the days of her life, and in some ways, the four of us still dwell in our childhood home, carry it with us, like turtles carry their homes, only

14

ours is embedded, "inscribed . . . engraved within us," writes
Bachelard.

"I grow up in Cusi which at the time has many silver mines."
Lobo returns to the high mountain ranges, the mines, the nar-
row-gauge train that takes the minerals to Chihuahua or prob-
ably to El Paso, huge amounts of silver. "The mines in Cusi are
incredibly rich and the owner of one, called La Reina, becomes
so wealthy that he asks the government for permission to put
silver *vigas* in his home, a house with silver beams, *imagínate*.

"My father is a lawyer and a miner. My grandfather also lives
there, Ignacio Delgado y Manquero a miner too, *allí del pueblo*.
At night, Papá wakes us to see the silver flow. How beautiful it
is! Two clay jars, a special kind, not jars really, flatter, like huge
platters are the receptacles. When the flames are blazing, out
pours silver onto one platter and mercury onto the other. *¡Tan
precioso!*

"Small hills of what looked like black ash, carbon, are left
from the ovens, *grasa* we call it, like the hills in Smelter Town.
Remember how sometimes at night in El Paso we'd go out back
and see the blazing slag poured in the distance? In Cusi, when it
rained, my younger sister, Elodia, would say, 'Listen, *lluvia*, let's
go see the little witches.' Sparks would dance on the ash piles,
'*¡Brujitas! ¡Brujitas!*'

"Let me tell you about my father's family," Lobo says as I re-
start the teapot. Mother enters and rolls her eyes at words she
has heard often, but at this time in my life I understand Pablo
Neruda's longing in his *Book of Questions*, the sweetness of old
names, "*¿Dónde están los nombres aquellos dulces como tortas de an-
taño?*"

Eduardo Luis Delgado, Lobo and Mother's father whom we
call Papande, short for *papá grande*, is more of a name and face
than a person to us since he dies before our parents marry. He is
born on October 13, 1864 in Cusihuiriachic, Chihuahua, that
place rich in silver mines, the mining town of ghost Victorian
houses I visit as a child, the doors and narrow wooden window
shutters closed, the main street lined by their long, locked faces.

"Father's father, Papá Nacho, is a miner and very religious, ¿verdad, Lobo?" Mother says.

"He isn't that fond of the church, but he is very devoted to Saint Joseph. Every morning winter or summer, he rises at five and sings *una alabanza a San José*.

> Can - te - mos al al - ba,
> Ya vie - ne el dí - a,
> Da - re - mos gra - cias
> A - ve Ma - rí - a.

After this song of praise, my grandfather gets into a small pool."

"Up at five and in water outside in the winter? How can he be a relative of mine?" Mother asks shivering at the thought.

"On the feast of San José, even though he's not that wealthy, my grandfather has a fiesta for the entire pueblo. Papá Nacho taught me this prayer in Spanish: '*Señor San José, cuya protección es tan necesaria, delante de Dios, vengo con mis intereses.*' You saw the novena in English I taped in that notebook I wrote about the family, no? That one, that one." Lobo points to the spiral notebook with the blue flower on the cover, begins looking through it and finds the novena. "See. It says to be very sure you really want what you request. That's the power of prayer. It works miracles. 'Oh, Saint Joseph, whose protection is so needed, before God, I present my prayers.'"

Prayers and faith weave through our relatives' words like floral scents weave through the garden.

"Papá Nacho also has a great sense of humor like Uncle Lalo," Mother says. "When he is up in years, he stands in front of his house early in the morning and calls out to his neighbors as they walk by, '¡*Mira no más! ¡Hasta más feos!*' I can't believe it! You're even uglier than you were yesterday. They laugh and call back, '¡*Ay Don Ignacio!*'"

"¡*Mira no más! ¡Hasta más feos!*" says the *guacamaya* twisting its neck to peer at us.

"María Ignacia Barragán, my grandmother, Papa Nacho's first wife," Lobo continues, "is a very cultured lady. She has a gift, *el don de la palabra*, and speaks eloquently at any time, like your mother. She inherited Mamá Nacha's talent. She is invited to speak on many occasions which is amazing since in those days young women do not receive much formal education. She is short, with blue eyes, *azules, azules, azules*. The story is that when she'd go out in the morning to recite poetry in a nearby wheat field, her head was so blonde that her parents couldn't find her, lost in the golden spikes."

Lobo continues the names, the names. Mamá Dominguita, Tío Mariano Yrigoyen, Tía Josefita, Don Mauricio Heineman, Elena, Jesús, Herlinda, Baudelio, Antonio, Francisco, Ladislada, Beatriz, Damiana, Marina, Carlota, Enrique, Carolina, Luz, Guillermo, Margarita.

"Lots of begetting and begatting it seems to me." Uncle Lalo winks at me.

"*¿Qué, Lalito?*" Lobo smiles at her brother, happy he has joined us.

"*No, no,* it's interesting. Go on with the story, Nacha. My father was the nicest man I've ever known. I've heard that he played a beautiful guitar," Uncle Lalo says. "Of course, after he has his stroke, it hurts him to manipulate his fingers. I'd pick the guitar up, just bangin' on it and singin' cowboy songs, Westerns, you know, U.S. cowboy songs."

"Wait here, Patty," Uncle Lalo says. "Let me show you some of your grandfather's old documents." He returns with a stack of papers and begins to read the formal Spanish. "Look, in April, 1888, your grandfather is named a judge in Cusi, maybe just starting out since it says, '*del primero menor,*' whatever that means. And here, in 1896, for the whoppin' salary of 600 *pesos*, he is named Secretary of the Political District of Guerrero, and a telegram dated August 14, 1901 names him a judge in Cusi."

"Look at the time! I'll tell you more tomorrow." Lobo goes off to clean her room again, to buff the floor on her knees, and then to begin, *sw, sw, sw,* sweeping the halls and kitchen, daily tasks.

January sixth, the Epiphany, snow deeper now, silence also, the light outside my bedroom window shining white as a host.

In this land, light descends from above but also rises from the land, *la tierra madre*, reflecting its old bones. When the sun rises over the mountain to the East and pours its light on our heads, a daily grace, the braiding of light from land and sky pours into us, filling us, raising us to greet the day. When I leave this landscape, this light, I feel slighter, diminished.

Snow nestles into clay pots, onto dried red chile wreaths and rounded walls. Inside, I roam, explore the chambers of my heart, this wish house, oriented long ago to catch the breeze and long afternoon shadows. I wander its dimensions, try to understand its design and structure, revel in its red tile or wood floors, thick rugs, white walls with deep, recessed windows, wood shutters, the *vigas* and *latillas*—carefully crafted wood ceiling beams, the wall candle sconces and candle *arañas* hanging from the ceiling, the fireplaces warming each room.

At my desk, I listen, hear the rhythm of my heart, of the clock, the broom, the kitchen stirrings, the prayers, *clck, clck* of rosary beads, savor the inner voices. Opening a choir book, I press my fingers on the desk the way I used to press piano keys, in the majestic style of organ music. I'll always be nostalgic for the old church, the Latin church, the invisible choir, the priest's back rather than his face, the intoxication of incense and flickering candles.

Knowing the pleasure of communal voices rising and uniting, I recently looked forward to singing at one of those modern English Masses with the choir, guitar, and tambourines in front. I was about to say I don't come from a singing family, but that's not true—my father and, "Old Man Ri - ver, he don't plant cot - ton," my youngest sister, Stella, and, "We're off to see the wi - zard," Lobo and, "A - ve Ma - rí - a, gra - cia ple - na." I hear their voices, but we never sang together. My surprise a recent Sunday morning was that my throat literally felt rusty, like the Tin Man, Stella would say. It was as if I didn't know where my voice was, had forgotten how to raise it and release it, couldn't hear it even when I thought I was singing. The experience saddened me, so I resolved to oil the old voice with practice. Dangerous not to be able to raise the voice in song. Seamus Heaney says, "When I came here first you were always singing, . . . Raise it again. . . . We still believe what we hear."

This morning I open the red hymnal, look through the *As* for songs to sing alone in the snow. I long for Sister Eugene Marie's pitch pipe, my pale, blue-eyed sixth-grade teacher. Maybe they were all pale, except Sister Ermalinda who was more in the sourpuss category. Had any of my Sisters of Loretto been Mexican, I doubt they would have said it. All had escaped into the gleaming white collars, the black folds. I begin with songs I know well.

"Ama - zing grace! How sweet the sound," then a shaky transition into "An - gels from the realms of glo - ry," and then with full solitary bravado, the advantage of being in a thick-walled room alone, "An - gels we have heard on high." Caught up in the "Glo - - - - - - - - - - - - - - - ri - a." I'm startled by Lobo's high, faltering voice joining mine. She smiles, her gray eyes scooping me into them.

I point to her prayer book, *La Epifanía del Señor*. Like all the family, she doesn't ask why after all these years I've returned to these books. She just accepts me. Taking her arm and walking with her toward the kitchen for her morning coffee, I ask, "Did you ever put grass or hay in your shoes for the camels of the Three Kings the way I've read they do in Spain for this feast day? I've read that children with balconies leave small mounds of hay so the camels can nibble as they go by, and the Kings leave gifts for good children." Lobo stirs spoonfuls of sugar into her black coffee, settles down to remember the names of *Los Reyes Magos*.

"*Melchor, Gaspar, y Baltazar.* I read them in the paper this morning. Now more of us want to know the old traditions."

"*Bien hecho.* Is that why you made the *rosca de reyes?*" She eyes the round bread wreath topped with red cherries.

"We can't cut it till everyone's up. I hid the *Niño* inside and want someone to find it in their slice and have to give the party on February second, the feast of *la Candelaria*, when Christ is first taken to the temple to be blessed. It's Candlemas day in English."

"*¿Cómo?*"

"Candlemas day." Lobo still loves to learn, a relief to think learning continues beyond the body. "We never did this, and it would be fun, but also the series of celebrations kept families knitted together more closely. That's what I want, Lobo, not to lose any of you, to lure you, the living and the dead, into this un-locked house, as flowers lure us into the garden."

"*Una vez,*" Lobo the irrepressible storyteller begins, her words sweet and smooth as *flan* on her tongue still transporting me with her to the past, to the stories she told us over and over, wrote in spiral K-Mart notebooks near the end of her embod-ied life. On this cold winter morning, her voice and the voice of the fire in the small kitchen *chimenea* braid, warm me like the navy-blue shawl she once gave me. Neither large nor imposing, our aunt deceivingly looks like a gentle, elderly Mexican woman, but we know her potential, what she would have done to any men lurking outside our home. We know about the boil-ing oil.

"Papá had to go on an estate case to Jesús María Ocampo, Ocampo the name of the district, in Chihuahua. We have to go by mule, so they teach Mamá how to ride so that she can ac-company my father. My brother, Eduardo, is only two months old, and Papá would be troubled to leave us.

"We join a group led by Don Joaquín Chávez who goes back and forth regularly taking silver from the mountains and has soldiers and muleteers for the dangerous road since bandits can appear at any time. I'm about six years old, but I remember the road well, how my sister and I are placed on either side of the mule in *angarillas*, like huge baskets lined with pillows and quilts. My little brother is carried by an Indian on foot."

I know the story well, have heard it so often that I see myself there with her, begin the journey up the mountains to that room, that scream.

When they arrive in late afternoon at a place called El Du-razno, they look up at the tall pine trees, trees so tall Nachita, the child Lobo, can't see the sky. She and her sister, run up a small hill in their long blue and white dresses, long, black braids.

"*Cuidado, muchachas, cuidado,*" their mother calls, finds a secluded spot where she can nurse her son, listens to bird squawks high above her head as she unbuttons herself, offers her nipple to the the small, hungry mouth. She leans back on a tree trunk enjoying the sound of her daughters' laughter and the feel of her son tugging on her breast, his brown eyes staring up at her, his soft universe.

The girls, who shiver at the thought of sleeping under the stars, watch the muleteers build small canvas cabins and put little cots in them. Hand-in-hand, the sisters go stand near their short father, the grandfather I never knew, the judge who stands straight, walks slowly, never shouting even here, among the trees. They watch the men build bonfires, smell smoke twirling through the branches, shriek when the men joke about cooking snake for their dinner.

"*Ándenle, muchachas, les vamos hacer unas víboras pero deliciosas.*"

"*¡Ay no, no!*" they squeal running to tell their mother as the men light torches for the dinner hour. Later, the girls' mother says, "*A la cama, hijitas.*"

Nachita doubts that she can sleep even a second under a sky so alive with stars, no walls to keep away dark shapes moving through the trees. Long before Nachita, ancient Mexicans with their more fluid view of the world, believed that stars with their light arrows protect us from form-changers prowling the dark, that stars prevent rocks from becoming jaguars, their eyes reflecting light, two mirrors moving through the jungle night.

Nachita whispers to her sister in the cot next to hers, "*¿Elodia, puedes dormir?*"

"*No.*"

"*¿Mamá?*"

"*Ya, Nachita,*" she hears her father say in his quiet but firm voice. "*Ya, ya, a dormir.*"

"That evening," Lobo says stirring spoonfuls of sugar into her second cup of black coffee, "Mamá exclaims, 'Look who's here.'

It is Luis Delgado, a cousin who likes my father very much and who follows us everywhere. Luis eventually marries María Dioses, very pretty, María Delgado's mother who married the dentist Avelino de la Torre and mother to Corina who marries Adolfo Cuilty whose brother Gabino marries my sister Lola."

I don't even try to unravel the web, the names this family chronicler remembers, preserves in notebooks so we will know where we come from.

Nachita sleeps in those Mexican pines, dreams an immense butterfly descends toward her, its wings, the pale blue of the wildflowers she collected. Rather than running from the wings that rise and fall, she lies down on the grass to watch them as they come closer and closer the butterfly's soft wings gently covering her with blue light.

"Such beauty the next morning." Lobo says, "When we wake in those tall pines, red and green feathers dart through the boughs, calling out to one another, *guacamayas* of a thousand colors. Wildflowers frost the ground and nearby hills, and *arrollitos* of crystalline water scurry everywhere since it is summer.

"My aunt and uncle are waiting for us to arrive and have secured a place for us at this *pueblo muy feo con casas rete feas*, an ugly town, where many English, Americans, and Spaniards live because of the rich mines. The mountains rise so high I feel as if the town is buried way down there beneath them.

"My Tía Chonita lives there with her husband, Don Miguel Prado, who has the store for the miners. Mamá doesn't know these relatives well, but she has to make the best of the situation, *hacer como se dice de tripas, corazón*. She knows she must resign herself, adapt." The generational pattern for women and the dark-skinned and the poor.

"The *jefe político*, Don Leonardo Siqueiros, whom Papá likes immediately, comes to greet us. 'Pasen, pasen. Let us show you your new home,' my aunt and uncle say. Mamá looks at the town and its ugly, wood houses."

Holding her baby, Nachita's mother, María Dolores, struggles to conceal a frown as she lifts her gray dress a bit to step into the small house, careful not to brush against any dusty surface. She chose a dress she likes for today with a high neck and long, tight sleeves trimmed in white. Eduardo once brushed her cheek with his mustache, whispered that this dress brought out the gray in her grayish blue eyes, Eduardo so measured in his words.

After he lets all enter the small house before him, his wife hands him their baby, pats the bun of brown hair on the back of her head and touches the bangs above her thin eyebrows and oval face. Lobo's mother longs for a hot bath, washing away dirt from the trip, washing her face, looking at herself in the mirror. Though she may not be beautiful, she knows her fine nose, thin lips, and pale skin are ladylike, *una dama linda*, her grandmother who raised her, Mamá Dominguita, is fond of saying, patting her granddaughter's hand.

Telling herself to smile in spite of the darkness and smallness of the house, the plain, rustic furniture; María Dolores takes a deep breath. She runs a finger across the edge of a table when no one is watching, glances down at the greasy dust staining her fingertip. Feigning cheerfulness, and trying secretly to rub the dust away, she walks into the first bedroom.

"¡Ay!" she screams unable to contain her shudder. "¡Ay, qué horror!" she gasps and begins to cry, raises her skirt and runs out of the room, out of the house, crying, gasping for composure. Lobo's father follows his wife, pats her shoulder trying to comfort her. "Ay, *una víbora, una víbora*," she gasps.

There, on the middle of a bed intended for her family, Lobo and her sister see a snake, a coiled snake asleep on a white bedspread. Holding hands, they run out of the room and out of the dark house.

'*Calma, calma*, now don't be scared," the locals soothe. "*Mira, aquí no hay gatos en este pueblo*. These animals are called *jumares*. They hunt rats but are no danger to humans." The young mother just shakes her head, draws her daughters close to her long dress.

Years after this trip to the mountains, Lobo's aunt expresses amazement at the details her niece remembers, asks her, "But you were such a little girl, Nacha. How do you guard the story in your memory?"

Why do certain events become central memories, part of the core life story we create about ourselves? I wonder why in her late eighties and again in her nineties, Lobo continues to choose this story to include in the brief family histories she writes that say so little about her own private life.

Lobo continues. "Señor Siquerios offers us another, better dwelling that includes two bedrooms, a living room, a kitchen, and an orchard with huge, lovely, fragrant orange trees in bloom, *azahar, un olor, pero precioso.* That's where Papá settles us while he goes on to Pinos Altos near the border of Sonora to tend to an inheritance case. Mamá is happier in her new lodgings, and relatives and all the important people in the town, handsomely dressed, come to call.

"Papá and his guide see horrible snake nests on their journey. At sunset, in some of the ravines, the snakes entwine themselves into a thick, writhing, knotted hiss which, even though the snakes are *horrorosas,* do shimmer with countless colors.

"Returning, my father is bitten by a fly called *baiburí* or *baiburín* that burrows painfully between the skin and flesh producing intermittent fevers. Well, Papá returns quite ill then from his mission. Eight months he's in bed, an invalid unable to move. Now Papá hears that because there are few if any valleys in those heights, the dead are taken by mule in their casket. One man, *el sepulturero,* with his shovel and pick alone accompanies *el cadáver* up the steep, treacherous road to the high flatlands where graves can be dug. Papá shudders at such an ending to his life on that hard mountain. The thought is so horrifying to him, that even in his delicate condition, everything is arranged, and we set out again by caravan."

When a man climbs onto the mule that's to carry the judge down the mountain, Lobo watches them lift her father.

"Carefully now," the man says, "you two men lift Juez Delgado up to me. *Cuidado. ¡Cuidado!* Now let's just get him settled here in front of me. Can you hold the reins, Don Eduardo? *¿No? No* *importa.* I'll hold the reins for him, poor man. That's it. Now hand me his hat. *¿Cómo se siente, Don Eduardo? Aquí tiene su sombrero. Vámonos."*

The descent begins, the short judge swaying on the mule, protected by a muleteer's firm arms. My grandfather places his hand on a rein, stares at it losing track of time. Slowly, as the land opens before him, he lifts that hand to his chest, lets it rest there from its journey, then lifts it to his face. For the first time in months, he feels the stubble of his face, strokes it for the pure pleasure of feeling his own flesh.

He lets the hand rest again, and then finally reaches and touches the brim of his hat with his fingertips and can't suppress a smile. Gradually, he lets his tired hand fall down to the rein again. He rests, dozes a bit in the arms of the muleteer. He wakes, again lifts his hand to his face, more quickly now, and on to the brim of his hat. He grasps the brim and barely lifts it.

"Muy bien, Don Eduardo. ¿Se siente mejor?"

Eduardo nods, rests, takes the brim of his hat and lifts the hat from his head. He rests. He puts the thick fingers of his left hand around the reins, and the muleteer removes one of his hands, lets Don Eduardo begin to guide the mule. He rests, eyes closed, and then again lifts the hat from his head and brings it down on his hair. He does this over and over, enjoying the private pleasure of removing his own hat.

"As soon as Papá arrives at lower altitudes," Lobo says, "at more open spaces where there are fewer mountains, he begins to improve. He removes and then puts his hat on again and again. Finally, my father rides alone. Those mountains had depressed him, and his nerves had been weakened in that high, mountainous region."

The power of geography, how the landscape imprints itself; and when we can't see the world that is home to us whether mountains, desert, or beaches, we yearn to see the shapes and vistas that live in our interior; after a rain to smell the plants and trees whose names or shapes we know; to hear bird whistles or wind thumps, rhythms that comfort us like a heartbeat comforts a child; a vague, preconscious memory.

"Days and nights we journey always trying to avoid being attacked by thieves or wild beasts. We arrive at La Cascada de Baseseachi: a narrow waterfall 300 meters high, a billowy flowing, clear as a bride's veil. Such a beautiful waterfall, a shame I don't have a picture to show you."

Cleaning out a closet later, I find a postcard I've taken with me from place to place because it's such a dramatic Mexican waterfall, and when I read the back, to my surprise I discover that it's the waterfall Lobo wanted to show me, a card sent to me by a friend. The description says that the Cascada de Baseseachi in the Sierra Tarahumara is 310 meters high, the ninth highest waterfall in the world. I stare at the hard canyon and feel water drops misting the face of the young Nachita as she looks up in wonder at the veil of water.

Lobo goes to first grade in Guerrero, and then her father is offered a better position back in Cusihuiriachic as judge for that region including the Sierra Tarahumara. Dolores, her youngest sister, is born there. A year later, their mother dies in childbirth at twenty-nine.

"We leave our house that had been my grandfather's home with gardens and orchards and move to our aunt's, Mamá Tela's, who insists that my father who is thirty-three also live with her, his sister. At first we are too sad even to play, of course. We say that at night my mother comes down and covers us."

As Lobo speaks, I remember that when my children were born, she begins mothering them as she mothered me and my sisters and brother. Lobo, who finds even the hint of any physical relationship between men and women disgusting, loves babies, creaming their legs and hands, putting slender spoons into their anxious lips, always arrives with candies for them, cookies, a book, a toy, when they're older willing to sit and play Old Maid over and over, always willing to lose.

Just as she did for the four of us, she makes teas when the

children are sick, beaming at all they do, all they are, sings them to sleep,

> *Tan, tan, tan, to - can la puer - ta,*
> *Tan, tan, tan, la voy a a - brir,*
> *Tan, tan, tan se - rá la tu - za,*
> *Tu - za dé - ja - me dor - mir.*

Ready to help, Lobo whistles, *wh-wh-wh*, when she folds clothes, dries dishes, turns down beds. For years, Fridays are her day at our house, protecting the little ones from their parents' wrath.

"I spilled the cream today," my three-year-old son says. "What?" I say. "When did you spill it?"

"Lobo cleaned it up when you were gone. She said not to tell you so you wouldn't get mad."

She's with us for holidays, at Easter hiding eggs out back in obvious places. Complimenting every dish I serve at Thanksgiving. Thrilled at any Christmas or birthday gift we give her, then promptly giving it to someone else.

"I told your cousin you sent her that bracelet. It made her happy."

"But Lobo, that bracelet was for you! I don't even know that cousin. I don't care about her. I don't know why we give you presents when all you do is give them away." Why couldn't I hear what she was teaching?

Did Lobo's mothering begin when her mother died, before Lobo's a teenager, Lobo, the mother who never marries?

"In time though," Lobo says, "we're climbing hills like little goats with cousins and friends, tasting *pitayas* which we pretend are chiles and drinking from the *arroyo* called El Chicle because its fresh water tastes like gum and is cold as iced water. I go to an elementary school run by Señorita Marina Terrazas. Papá wants to marry her, but the young men there are *liberales* and support Benito Juárez's notion of the separation of church and state. Marinita's mother, *muy Católica*, is not going to allow her daughter to marry someone not devout.

"In 1906, Don Enrique Creel asks my father, who is still a

widower, to come to Juárez to deal with those involved in con-
traband on a large scale."

I sneak a look at the clock. "Lobo, should we continue this
later? Maybe I should try to get Mother up."

"Yes, yes, just let me finish this part. It's very interesting. We
arrive in October, Papá and the four of us, are treated well by
people in society, *la crema y la nata de la sociedad*, invited to parties
and dances, beautiful dances. Let me tell you about the meeting
between Díaz and Taft in 1909. The two leaders met on the bor-
der. What an event, so pretty! The festivities actually begin a
week before since bands arrive and give concerts of beautiful
music in the plaza." She sways, hums Strauss waltzes, "*Hm, hm,
hm - hm. Hm, hm, hm - hm.* Streets are decorated with flags and
flowers. Why persons who have been to Paris say that's what
our Juárez looks like. Imagine! It looks like Paris."

"What looks like Paris?" asks Stella, my youngest sister,
named after Mother, placing her hands on Lobo's shoulder.

"Juárez," Lobo says proudly. "You should sit and listen to this
story. It's very historical."

"If Juárez looks like Paris in the story," Stella whispers, "we're
talkin' hysterical not historical. Either '*ya se le fue el pájaro,*' as
Lobo used to say, or she's been nippin' at the daiquiris again."
Stella and I grin at one another remembering the time in L.A.
when someone orders Lobo a strawberry daiquiri, and she sips
it down in no time unaware of its alcoholic content and is ready
for a second and even third delicious fruit drink.

"Don Porfirio Díaz arrives in Juárez in his presidential train,"
Lobo continues ignoring us, busy with her story, her eyes again
seeing the customs house, well decorated with flags, seeing
Don Porfirio, greeted by ranchers, schoolchildren, politicians.
"Everyone wants to see him and talk to him."

"Wants to talk to who?" my daughter, Libby, asks.

"To *whom,*" I counter.

"Everyone wants to see Porfirio Díaz, *querida,*" Lobo says.

Libby quickly looks at me. "Isn't he on the wrong side? Mr.
Represso? Don't, don't tell me my great-grandfather is a conser-
vative!"

"Easy on the conservatives there, Libby," Stella says.

Lobo looks momentarily confused but continues unaware of the liberal stance of most of those around her. "*El presidente Taft*," I say.

"*Ah sí, sí*, at eleven A.M. Taft is greeted with a twenty-one gun salute and many ovations. My father is part of the welcoming committee at the meeting of the two presidents. There is a champagne lunch in El Paso and that evening a beautiful banquet in Juárez complete with table service from Brussels. When Mr. Taft leaves the banquet, the band plays his national anthem. *¿Cómo es? Ah sí*, 'O - o say can you see - ee' her voice quavers, the voice that once floated confidently up and down the musical scale.

"Mr. Taft brings his national guard, and the Mexican cavalry, infantry, and national guard line the streets too. When Don Porfirio comes out, and the band plays *el himno nacional mexicano*, 'Me - xi - ca - nos al gri - to de gue - rra. . . .' You have no idea how beautiful and exciting it is.

"In 1910, the Mexican revolution begins. That Pancho Villa changes our lives, such a bloody time. The Porfiristas rent a house in El Paso that they call Hospital de Sangre for their wounded. Bullets come all the way to Paisano Street that is then la Calle Segunda. We stay for a time on the El Paso side. When we return, my father is named *Agente del Ministerio Público. La revolución* continues."

Her repeated stories are about the exterior world. I wonder about what she loved, what she feared. How she spent her days? Who were the men she noticed, hoped would ask her to dance, or hold her hand, or whisper in her ear? "But tell me about you, Lobo. I want to know about your life."

"*Te voy a decir*. I begin working on this side at a small store called El Globo on Overland Street because with *la revolución*, my father often can't support us. I'm paid only a dollar a day, six dollars a week, and sometimes that includes working until six P.M. on Saturdays. I begin to learn English. At night, my father comes for us. Once in 1912, we can't return to my sisters. Papá and I have to stay in El Paso worried, so worried about my three sisters, knowing they are hearing the gunfire. I say rosary after rosary, '*Padre nuestro que estás en los cielos.*' "

My eldest, Bill, comes to sit with us, takes Lobo's hand for a minute.

"Luckily, the next day some kind gentlemen brings my frightened sisters across the river, Bilito," Lobo continues. "When things calm down and we are able to return to our home, my father is offered a large office at the court which he accepts so as not to offend anyone. Soon, his companions realize that he is a Díaz supporter, a Porfirista, that we are all his supporters and don't approve of what is taking place."

My son turns to me and says softly, "Mom, have you noticed that whenever someone benefits from a situation, he isn't too critical of it?"

"*¿Qué, mi Bilito?*" Lobo asks.

"Nothing, Lobo, nothing. Keep telling Mom your story. It's really interesting. I'm going to take a walk, see if I can find any good fossils." His sister, Libby, comes to listen.

"We to return to El Paso in November 1913, when Villa attacks Juárez. Sunday, November twelfth, General Castro, who commands the military zone in Juárez and is married to our relative, is eating at our house when he receives a telegram from Chihuahua directing him to repel Villa's forces.

"She's anti-Villa!" Libby gasps.

"*¿Qué, mi Libita? ¿Qué dices?*"

"Lobo," my daughter says, unable to restrain herself. "Pancho Villa is a hero. He took from the rich."

"*¡Qué!*" Lobo says, her gray eyes widening. "That assassin a hero! He steals. He robs. He murders."

"Okay, Okay, Lobo," I say. "Lib, weren't you off to do something?"

Libby kisses Lobo on the top of her head. "Tell Mom the story, Lobo. She likes them." I sneak a look at my watch, think of the unanswered mail, the unfinished manuscripts.

"Well," my aunt says leaning toward me and warming even more to her story, "at that time we've been invited to a wedding and Papá, as always, accompanies us. It isn't cold at all, and the moon is full and beautiful. After the wedding, my father and three sisters walk out onto the street, but I look around, slip behind him. He's a judge and must have enemies. I guard his back.

"Back home, I hear gunfire from my room on the second floor. My father thinks Castro's batallion has arrived, but I say, 'No, Papá. The bursts look like they're from large cannons.' My father comes upstairs to look with me. '*De veras. Sí, está raro eso.*' Our house has many rooms, and Papá rents some of them to employees at the customs house. He calls out, '*Señores, señoras, perdón.* You may want to get up and gather any personal papers. Something is strange out there. Cannons are firing at the barracks, only God knows what awaits us.' Everyone rises quickly, and we all meet in the living room where my father says, 'Turn off all the lights and hide any weapons or documents.' In the dark, people hide their papers under the rug. Some hide a few guns in the kitchen oven. In a bit here comes a horde of ruffians—I can't say it any other way—that fill the street shouting, '*¿Quién vive?*' Then they boldly shout their answer, '*¡Pancho Villa!*'

" 'Something is very wrong here,' Papá says. 'I didn't expect this.' With the butts of their rifles, the crowd begins to break the store windows across the street. They grab what liquor they can and take off. Since the moon is so bright, we see the ruffians out back riding off with the horses for my father's carriages.

"Our servant, Francisca, a huge woman, *grandota*, says, 'No, *Juez Delgado*, you must go with these young women and anyone else who wants to cross. God knows what will happen here, no safety for us with the Villistas on top of us.'

"We wait a bit, all dressed in black coats, eight of us. About four in the morning, Francisca says, 'Leave, *Juez Delgado!* I know what I'm telling you. Here, put on my big apron over your coat and take your daughters and some of these others and go.' "

Lobo signals her half-brother, Uncle Lalo, who has been listening, to join us.

He chuckles. "My formal father wearing a huge apron over his coat? Impossible!"

Lobo continues, and again I know the story, know we're headed for the river, the crossing in the dark.

Papande and his daughters slip out of their home, all dressed in black. Elodia, Lobo's high-spirited sister, calls out to the crowd outside their house, "*Buenas noches, buenas noches.* We've been waiting for you."

"Be quiet!" her father says. "What do you think you're doing?"

"Just look," she continues in a raised voice, "isn't it wonderful that the Villistas have arrived? We're going to have fiestas for you. Don't think we're leaving. We're celebrating your arrival."

"This way they won't suspect us," she whispers to her frightened father. They walk quickly toward the river, cut across a field. Bullets begin to fly over them, and the terrified judge pulls his daughters together, shoves them down on the field. When the gunfire eases, they pull one another up, covered in mud from head to toe, but relieved, not wounded.

The judge looks at the water of the Río Bravo, the river called the Río Grande to the north, its waters very high. In the dark, my grandfather peers at a man he thinks he recognizes.

"Antonio, is that you?"

"*Sí, Juez Delgado,* is that you?"

"*Sí.*"

"Well, what are you doing out here?"

"Well, what are *you* doing out here?"

"I'm trying to figure out a way to get my young daughters across the river. I have no way to defend them," Judge Delgado says.

Antonio, who's also trying to protect his family, brings his old, dilapidated *guayín* and a horse. It's dark but almost dawn. Nervous, the group goes in shifts, the old carriage wheels trembling in the cold water. The Delgado sisters clutch one another's hands, can't cry out their fear as the carriage bobs. Since they can't swim, they'd normally be terrified hearing the small waves slap against the doors, fearing the carriage will sink or tip, and they'll be gasping their last breaths unable to save one another, but the gunfire propels them through their terror.

"*¿Qué pasa?*" the U.S. officials on the El Paso side call out.

"Villa has entered Juárez, and we're asking for your hospitality until this episode ends, and we can return to our home," says Juez Delgado relieved to feel land under his shoes.

"*Sí, pasen, pasen.*" The officials dismount and extend a hand to help them reach dry ground.

"The U.S. officials find humor in our condition," Lobo says, starts to sweep the kitchen, but continues her story. "We probably are quite a sight in our rickety carriage and mud-covered clothes. In those days, no passports or documents are needed. We cross the river in 1913, but I don't apply for a passport until 1929. Do you know where we crossed? It was called *la isla de Córdova* then, where the Córdova bridge is now. The sun is rising, and the other immigration agents come out asking, 'What happened? We heard bullets last night.'

"A very kind lady says, 'Heavens! Just look at you. You're covered with mud. Let's go to my house.' We clean up and that kind woman gives us a nice breakfast, but we have only what we're wearing. I do have our deeds to the mine since Papá had whispered, 'I hope we can escape with those documents since we won't have anything to live on.' We have no furniture, nothing, *nada, nada,* not even eating utensils. My father gets in touch with Francisca back at our home who says, 'Don't dare come back. They've already asked for you. Don't you come back or any of the girls. I'll try to take you what I can.'

"Friends and relatives begin to arrive. By the end of that week, there are forty-six of us in a house on Second Street. My father wants to return to Juárez to bring over a few of our belongings, but people say, 'Don't. Don't go. You'll regret it. Better sleep on the bare floor. Villa is committing atrocities.'

"Since Papá speaks no English and doesn't know how he is going to make a living, he is very worried when we come to this country, *pobrecito.* He goes downtown having nothing but the deed to the mine. At La Plaza de San Jacinto, he sits on a park bench in his wrinkled suit drumming his fingers on his knees when an acquaintance, a Mr. West maybe or Grays, who is with the Villistas, stops to chat."

"Judge Delgado, what are you doing?"

"*Nada*. I'm frantic here with no way to support my family."

"*Mira, Delgado*, you know that I could steal your mine, La Minerva, but I have too much respect for you. *Te voy a dar para que puedas empezar aquí*. I once offered you $40,000 for your mine. Now I could go to Villa right now and just tell him I want it. You could do nothing about that since if you cross, they'll kill you. You supported the wrong side, Delgado."

"Yes, they'd kill me."

"But I'm not a bad man, Delgado. I'm going to offer you $16,000, and then I'll give you a percentage of the profit for eight months."

"It's that or nothing for my poor father," Lobo sighs. "With that money, he buys furniture and our little house at 1314 Wyoming."

Eduardo also starts a small taxi or jitney service from downtown El Paso to Smelter Town, the area near the tall smokestacks of the American Smelting and Refining Company. Eventually calm returns to Juárez, and so do the Delgados, but most of the people they know have left. The judge and his four daughters live in El Paso from 1913 on. He works in his Juárez law office, daily crosses early in the morning and returns in the afternoon.

"For a time, when the poor cross from Juárez, the immigration officials make them bathe in gasoline before *la pobre gente humilde* are allowed to enter this country," says Lobo. "One large store is owned by a Mr. Calisher. He makes a big mistake, *ese hombre*. From the beginning, he assumes that every Mexican who comes to his store is a thief. If we have a package or basket with us, he won't let us enter without first depositing whatever we might be holding outside his store."

Lobo pauses, remembering.

"He loses everything. A fire, a policeman dies in the blaze. Maybe *el señor* Calisher saw the error of his ways because later he opens a store in another location. He calls his new store Everybody. But he goes bankrupt."

In 1915, the judge marries a second time, marries my grandmother, Sotero Amelia Landavazo, and they have three children, the eldest, my mother. Often I hear Mother's stories about Lobo's sweeping and house cleaning, weekly bringing in the hose to wash out the kitchen. *"Ay esa Nacha y su limpiadería."* What is she sweeping and scrubbing away with such fierceness? After her death, my brother wrote,

> A broom became a savage weapon in her hands.
> In a windstorm of sand & tumbleweeds & leaves,
> there she'd be, outside, passionately sweeping
> as if to complete a task
> nature and God combined could not master,
> as if to rid the yard of all corruption,
> furiously defying disorder, muttering, broom in
>   hand,
> white hair flying wildly,
> true to her namesake, she all but seemed to howl,
> like one desperately trying to trip the march of
>   time,
> or darken the sun through sheer will
> & yet, from my vantage point,
> there were days she seemed to win.

"I begin to work at a fine department store in downtown El Paso, the Popular Dry Goods Company, on May 2, 1917. Don Adolfo Schwartz founded it, a very strict, very energetic man. When we arrive at work in the morning, he says if we do our job well, we'll always have work there. They pay us nine dollars a week. Soon I'm earning eighteen dollars. But we face the Depression, and my father's strokes begin in 1929. Since many have no work, we consider ourselves lucky. Some commit suicide. One of my sisters and I are working, our small salaries a great help even when my salary drops to twelve dollars a week."

"So how many years did you work at the Popular, Lobo?"

"Forty-five years, until 1963. I am a saleslady in piece goods and bedding, selling cloth of all kinds, satin, silk, piqué, and blankets, bedspreads, sheets. I do eighty inventories, and my figures are always correct. Many of my clients are from México."

Lobo lives at Queen of Angels, the boarding house run by nuns at which my grandmother at times also lived, or Lobo lives with us, first sleeping in the room with my younger sister, Cecilia, and me, and later in the room with our siblings, Stella and Roy. Weekdays Lobo leaves on the bus wearing a black dress, smelling of perfume though never touching make-up, content rubbing glycerine and rose water on her hands. Though she worked all her life, Lobo never owned a house, a car or a piece of furniture since her money goes to others—her sisters and the four of us. She buys us shiny patent leather shoes for our birthdays and Christmas, takes us to the movies on Sunday and then out to dinner.

"We'd go see Doris Day or Jane Powell," my sister, Cecilia, says. "Sometimes we sit and watch the movies more than once, and since the second time I know what's going to happen, I scream out warning the characters, 'No! Don't do that!' "

We love the movies—*Seven Brides for Seven Brothers, Singing in the Rain, Tea for Two*, follow Rock Hudson from room to room, smiling to ourselves, as he pursues innocent, wide-eyed Doris Day.

"And what about Lobo and the kissing parts?" Cecilia asks, and we both begin to laugh.

"¿Qué?"

"Oh yes, Lobo," Cecilia says. "Didn't you always embarrass us by muttering outloud every time someone kisses on the screen?" Lobo frowns. "Look," teases Cecilia. "Her fussy face." How we cringe when Lobo in no whisper begins her, "*Válgame Dios. Qué cosa tan horrible,*" when any man on or off the screen touches the body of any woman.

"*Hombres horribles, hombres horribles,*" the macaw says the phrase he hears Lobo mutter often.

And yet we go back week after week to the movies, perhaps because there is a fascination for her in that physical life between women and men; certainly because Cecilia and I, and later our sister and brother, want to go. Early we learn that this aunt can't bear our frowns.

Were you ever in love, Lobo? I know you loved dances when you were young, that you'd hum Strauss waltzes and dance with me. Did you ever want your own home? Were you happy? You deserved to be so happy.

Those Sundays after the movies, we walk to the train depot or the Greyhound station in the late afternoon and watch the trains or buses leave, enjoy a hot roast beef sandwich and mashed potatoes. Lobo, the long-lived nutritional rebel who avoids fruits and vegetables, to the end enjoys ham, macaroni and cheese, coconut cream pie, coffee—black; tonight savors lemon meringue pie and coffee, urges us to drink the bubbles in our glass of milk because they signal money in our future. We walk back to the *placita* to look at the alligators in the middle of the park, to listen to the thumping of the Salvation Army, and to take the Mesita bus home. It's dark, but we're safe, always safe with our fierce wolf-mother.

She turns down our beds, because she's needed, whistles her *wh, wh, wh*. We hear Mr. Clanton, the elderly father banished to a trailer in the neighbor's backyard, begin his nightly cough that can startle the stars. In her slip, Lobo checks on us later, with her hands makes shadow figures on the wall, a rabbit, two little mouths talking and talking. She looks out the back window and recites a moon rhyme,

> *Hay está la luna, comiendo su tuna,*
> *tirando las cáscaras en la laguna.*

Cecilia and I read in bed, and then Lobo tucks us in. If we have any aches, Lobo has us lie on our stomachs, and with firm hands rubs our neck and back, *una frotada*, one of her firm back rubs. She presses on our backs saying, "*Soy buena sobadora.*"

She sits on the edge of one of our beds and begins a story about her father the stern judge and Davíd, the Indian guide who read the land for clues or about when she was little. *"Una vez, cuando estaba yo chiquita,* maybe about ten years old, my friend Chele and I decide to have a wedding for our beautiful dolls." My sister and I pull the covers up over our shoulders, nestle into the words.

"My Tía Lupe and Mamá Tela make a bride dress and groom's outfit, very nice, and we decide to hold the ceremony on a large table in our bedroom. Señor Enrique Martín del Campo agrees to play the role of priest and the adults in the family also take part in the wedding ceremony enjoying the *bizcochos y chocolate* made for the occasion. My aunts and my father play their guitars. Yes, my father plays very well. Now the agreement is that Chele and I will take turns having the wedding couple in our homes for a week at a time. All is fine the first few weeks. One week we take the bride and groom for an outing by the brook, and I am to take them home. It is my turn, but *esa Chele* refuses to share the dolls, and we start to have a grand fight right on the edge of the *arroyo*. We grab hold of each other's long braids. We pull and pull and won't let go. *Y pam*, we end up tumbling right into the water.

"A gentleman by the name of Benito Zacatecano who owns a candy store and to whom Chele and I always owe money happens by. *Muerto de risa*, he pulls us out and takes us home, laughing to our families that not even a good dunking cooled our anger. Did we get a sound scolding."

Eyes heavy, lulled by the music of the story, we see those girls and their tug-fight by the *arroyo*. Lobo raises her hand and makes a huge cross in the air over our bodies, full of sleep, "*La cruz más grande del mundo, sobre su cuerpo se extienda.*" We drift, curl into the sound and rhythm of her voice.

All year Lobo saves to take us on the Sunset Limited to spend a week or two at her sister's in California. In our new shoes and matching plaid dresses and hats, new clothes for the

coming school year, Cecilia and I wave a teary good-bye to our
parents from the train window. We eat in the dining car, fret
about jumping from one train car to the next, but Lobo's there,
holding our hands. Weak with homesickness, we write Mother
letters heavy with tears, although Lobo, who loves to eat out,
takes us to lunch at places like the Pig & Whistle where our
menu is a paper pig mask, then walking through department
stores where she liberally sprays her black dress with an aro-
matic sampling of perfumes.

She takes us to Catalina Island to eat squares of vanilla ice
cream at the bird park, to watch rainbows of fish beneath the
glass-bottom boats, to gasp at the flying fish skimming by our
cheeks in the dark, to buy salt-water taffy and everywhere hear
the song,

I found my love in A - va - lon, be - side the bay.

We board the red train to Long Beach to ride the giant merry-
go-round and swim in the Plunge, Lobo forced to rent a black
bathing suit since we can't get into the large, indoor salt-water
pool without her. How did our modest aunt ever agree to re-
move her clothes in a cramped dressing room and open the door
wearing only two terry cloth pieces, her pale flesh lowering itself
into the greenish water of the noisy pool, revealing so much of
herself to the two nieces who wanted to swim, who stood on her
knees and jumped into the water believing they were beautiful
and bold as Esther Williams in the movies. Afterwards, foot-
long hot dogs and the train ride back, rocked by the rails.

"She had superstitions about everything," Cecilia says, "oh
God, everything. Don't walk under ladders, don't let a black cat
cross your path, don't put a hat on the bed, don't open umbrel-
las in the house, don't let mirrors break, if you spill salt, throw
some quickly over your left shoulder.

"At home, she'd sit and read Nancy Drew to us, *The Secret of
the Old Clock*, *The Bungalow Mystery*. She probably reads us the
whole series, sitting in the aqua-winged chair in the living room
with one of us on either side."

"Roy and I were so mean to her," Stella says joining us. "To drive her crazy, we push our beds together and wait for her to walk in. A boy and girl sleeping next to each other! She scowls and shoves the beds apart, warns us angrily about the terrible illnesses likely from any touching. '*Tengan cuidado, ¿eh? Se van a enfermar si no se portan bien.*' Every night she has to arrive not only with candy, but with a new comic—Archie, Jughead, Veronica, Betty. How can we expect her to remember which she's brought? But we do and get furious at her if she makes a mistake. '*Ay, Lobo,* we already have this one!' I never thought of her own life, that she was little once, that she was young. I knew she worked all day then came home and took care of us. That was what mattered."

Roy wrote that when she knocked at the door saying, "*Es el Lobo,*" all was right with the world. "She'd sail us to sleep, work her nightly magic, securing our night voyage. Prayers were her passion, her fragrance, her melody. With the sweeps of her hand, she'd build crosses of air."

Perhaps the stories that make us laugh most now when we remember Lobo are the memories of being with her when my parents go out or go to work at their optical company in the evening.

"*Bueno,* I'm going to close all the curtains so that any bad men outside in the bushes can't see inside. Don't worry. If they try to get in, I'll pour boiling oil on them. *Vengan.* Let's just convince them that there are plenty of men inside so they'll leave us alone. Go bring me your father's hat. Good. I'll put it on and walk by all the windows so they'll see a man's shadow. We are very clever, aren't we, *mis lobitos?* You have to be careful in this world of murderers and thieves."

Sensing, though unable to understand, the dark, pulsing depths of her love, its wild abandon of the self, the pain she would inflict to protect us, we're both terrified and safe.

"Now, I'll call out some men's names just to fool *esos ladrones tontos.* Walk with me, all of you. *Oye, José, ven acá. Manuel, te necesito. Julio, acuéstate aquí cerca de esta ventana.* Let's go by every window and do that and then we can read our book. *Juan, ¿tienes la pistola?*"

"No wonder we're all a little crazy," Cecilia laughs at the memory of our aunt's antics. "Lobo was a character."

"Who's a little crazy?" Mother wonders what her daughters are laughing about.

"Your four children thanks to Lobo," says Cecilia.

"Oh that woman was crazy all right," Mother says. "What a thorn she was in your grandmother's life."

Not in mine. *No hay rosa sin espina.*

During the Johnson years, Lobo agrees to become an American citizen. "You're entitled to these benefits, Lobo," we say.

"*Bueno*, I will always be proud to be Mexican, but I remember that when we were in danger during *la revolución*, the American flag wrapped itself around us to protect us."

She studies her citizenship booklet, learns "We the people," the structure of Congress, the branches of government, the official, national history, the symbols—the flag, the Liberty Bell, the Statue and her torch of hope.

"Do you know all the judge asked me," Lobo chuckles. "He said, 'Miss Delgado, how long have you lived in the United States?'

" 'More than forty years,' I say proudly.

" 'And Miss Delgado, who is the president of this country?'

" 'President Lyndon Johnson, of course.'

" 'That will be all, Miss Delgado.'

" 'You don't want me to tell you about the Preamble and the Constitution?'

" 'No, Miss Delgado, that will be all. I'm sure you will be a fine citizen of these United States.' "

She places her right hand over her heart, repeats with the group, "I pledge allegiance to the flag of the United States of America."

Lobo, the frustrated, frenzied sweeper and cleaner, struggled to control the gritty desert and its wildness, but also to clear space for a more genteel life, a clean life, a pure life. I look long at my aunt who after years of our nagging cut her gray hair, began to wear blue and navy blue dresses—never pants, of course, but colors other than black, her long mourning at the death of her father.

"We're not going to buy you any more black dresses. If you want a new dress, you have to pick another color," I say when I take her shopping. In her nineties, she still sprays on various perfume samples, after examining twenty-five purses buys one and then begins to look for a slip, mutters at the service, not like the old days when she worked at the store. "*Señorita*, do you know how long we've been waiting? What's the matter with you new people? Don't you know how to take care of your customers? And don't you forget to give me my discount. I started working here in 1917."

As we walk away, she accuses the saleswomen of laziness, says, "*¡Mujeres flojas!*"

"*Sh, sh, Lobo.* They can hear you."

"*¿Y qué?*" But she's proud of the merchandise "her" store carries though after each such slow shopping trip she decides to return everything. "The slip is too expensive, and the purse is too small," she says on the phone the next day.

"*Ay, Lobo. Me vuelves loca. ¿Para qué te llevo?*"

At the ninetieth birthday surprise party we have for her, Lobo surprises us, sets her cane aside, and dances with her brother. Her last years, she mutters about the *viejitas*, the old women where she lives, their wrinkles, their complaints. As soon as we drive up to the boarding house, she begins.

"*Ay*, just look at them sitting there on the porch, gossiping, *viejas tontas.*"

"*Sh*, Lobo, they'll hear you."

"I don't even want to go by them. They're all so old."

"*Lobo, ya.* They're very nice to you."

"Watch, watch that one. She'll start her . . . ," Lobo raises the pitch of her voice to a high, simpering sweetness, "'*Ay, Nachita, ¿cómo está?*' She probably just wants to use my phone. Don't worry. I lock my door."

"Lobo!"

"*Viejas tontas*, spending their days complaining. Walk me to my room so I won't have to sit and talk to them, *y todas sus arrugas.*"

I hold her missal, look again at all the pictures she kept in it, always praying for each of us.

"You and those Missals," Stella says. "So what is today, honey bun?"

"*La fiesta de la sagrada familia*, the feast of the Holy Family. I think our family is a holy body too, crazy, but holy."

Years after Lobo slips into a coma from pneumonia at ninety-four, and after writing about her repeatedly in essays, poems, and children's books, she slips into my dreams one night; thinner, more petite than in this life, maybe small with age. She begins to speak in a clear voice, but the sentence doesn't quite make sense. I look at her and ask how she's feeling, wonder if she's had a stroke. When she speaks again, I'm even more sure she's ill and begin to fear she's dying. I know there's still so much I want and need to hear from her. We're in a kitchen, and she's in my arms almost as if we're dancing. We're clasping each other, her bones pushing into me. Her voice is fading, but she doesn't want to leave me. I'm grieving and yet happy that I'm holding her, light and thin in my arms. Holding on to her, I press her to me, into me, relieved that if she has to go, she's here, in my arms, sinking in.

In my dream house, as in my dreams, we are together, the family spirits, the soul of this adobe.

Lobo wrote about the Delgado family in two spiral notebooks. In one, she ends with the following words:

> I finish here though this is so poorly written without
> form and with such poor penmenship. I no longer have a
> firm pulse. I make countless mistakes no matter how
> hard I try. I only hope that you can understand. *Ojalá y lo*
> *puedan entender.*   —*Ignacia*

She ends the other notebook with a blessing:

> . . . and now being eighty-eight years old, like my grand-
> father, I pray to Sr. San José for a good death and I pray
> for all of us that the blessing of almighty God and that
> the Holy Family help, guide, and protect us. Amen.

Febrero loco / Crazy February

IAM Patricia Mora, born in El Paso, Texas, daughter of the
desert, of the border, of the Río Grande del Norte,
daughter of Estela Delgado, who is the great-
granddaughter of Anacleta Manquera and Nepomuceno Del-
gado, granddaughter of Ignacio Delgado y Manquera and
María Ignacia Barragán; daughter of the circuit judge, Eduardo
Luis Delgado of Cusihuirachic, México, husband of María Do-
lores Prieto Yrigoyen, father of Eduardo Octavo, who died
young, and of the fierce and loving Ignacia Raymunda, of
Adelina, Elodia Natalia Zenaida, and Dolores Ester Delgado,
all born in México, their father, the maternal grandfather I
never knew who below Revolutionary bullets and stars, floated
in a carriage with his grown daughters across the dark Río
Grande, a widower who married, the orphaned, red-haired
Sotero Amelia Landavazo, daughter of the widow Refugio
Rochín and the sea captain, Juan Domingo Landavazo of Bil-
bao, Spain; mother of Juan Domingo Delgado and Eduardo
Luis, called Lalo, born in El Paso, as was Amelia's daughter,
   my mother, the feisty, articulate, Estela, who married my fa-
ther, Raúl Antonio Mora, the optician born in Chihuahua, great-
grandson of Elena Meléndez and Damian Monárrez, mayor of
Boca de Avino, Durango; grandson of Simona Porras and Gre-
gorio Mora, grandson of the tiny Tomasa Monárrez and Brígido
Pérez; son of the teary Natividad Pérez of Boca de Avino, Du-
rango, and the tailor, Lázaro Mora of Jiménez, whose first three

44

sons, Lázaro, Manuel and Saúl, all died young, who brought
Raúl, brother of Soledad, Salvador Saúl, Concepción, Julieta, Au-
rora and Edermida Mora, at three years of age, brought Raúl
across the Río Grande to live in El Paso, father of Patricia Estella,
Cecilia Teresa, Stella Anne, and Roy Antonio Mora,

always the crossing of that brown river of sorrows to that city
of our births, mine, my mother's, my children's, William Roy,
Elizabeth Anne and Cecilia Anne Burnside.

El Paso. Skies wider than oceans, a bare mountain that talks
to itself; hard, sandy mesas; fossils who murmur the time of
great waters; hawks and snakes; yucca and agave; roots and
branches thorny for survival; the smell of fear, fear of dryness
and fangs, human fangs and coilings; the clashings carried on
currents of water and wind, of music and silence; music of old
women dancing to melodies that come from their own mouths;
silence of sunsets and moon risings; storms, whirlings and gust-
ings; the grace of children who spin with the wind, deaf to our
fears and forebodings,

el río, the river, the listening river, the whispering river, the
river of rumors, the river of tears, the river of hope, the river of
stories slipping by on a hot afternoon, and in the breeze, the
green, wet scent of herbs, *manzanilla* and *hierbabuena*, the gifts of
wrinkled hands, the blessings, strummings and strokings, the
gift of light, of sun, moon, stars, and the gift, the gift of naming.

Voices weave through bare branches. I write what I hear, my
inheritance a luxury, the generation with time to record the
musings of turtles, the poetics of cactus, the stoicism of stones,
the voices from the interior of this family house, *la casa de casas*.
The garden like the stark desert in which it hovers has its
moods, its storms, its seasons.

Yesterday, January 31. At breakfast thirty-three years ago, Jan-
uary 31, 1962, our maternal grandmother, Amelia Delgado, says,
"I saw *un negrito* in my room last night. He smiled at me and
motioned for me to follow him. I wasn't afraid, *imagínate*." That

morning she slips into a coma in her morning bath, a cerebral stroke. She slips away from us at the hospital quietly, as she lived.

I look through Lobo's missal for the prayers for the dead and February saints, see that priests wear green vestments these Sundays of Ordinary Time. February second, triple observance: the Purification of Mary, the Presentation of Christ in the Temple, and Candlemas day, the blessing of candles, "Light to enlighten. . . ." February third the feast of Saint Blaise, the Armenian saint who, legend says, saved a boy choking on a fish bone, the saint prayed for relief from diseases of the throat. I still smell the white wax of two crossed candles placed on our throats in elementary school when we kneel at the cold marble altar rail to have our throats blessed on this day.

In the kitchen, its counters done in blue, white, and yellow Mexican tiles, its white walls decorated with wooden spoons of all sizes and small clay mugs, Mother and I sit at the blue table, watch my maternal grandmother sitting in the afternoon shade of *el portal*, as always avoiding the sun. When we're little, Mamande, this grandparent we know best, sits outside with us, watches while we play in our backyard, ready to comfort us if we fall and hurt ourselves, gently rubbing our bruise with her healing rhyme,

> *Sana, sana colita de rana,*
> *si no sanas hoy, sanarás mañana.*

a black shawl on her shoulders if a cool breeze drifts through the trees. She wears her hair in a bun like Auntie Em's in *The Wizard of Oz*; at night, weaves the strands into one long, white braid down her back.

"Your grandmother always put a shawl on because when we bring her to live with us, we tell her she has pleurisy," Mother says. "After that she is very careful about chills, but really, we bring her to die at our house. I never used the word *cancer*. The word would kill her."

Born a *pelirroja*, Mamande spends her adolescent years washing her hair with different herbs to tone down the long, loud red that shines so in the sun. "*Ven, pronto, Amelia,*" her cousin Chele whispers to my teenage grandmother, "*usa estas hojas en ese cabello,*" handing her yet another bag of dried leaves sworn to alter hair color. With that hair, of course, comes skin that burns easily.

An orphan as a child, a red-haired Cinderella, Mother says, Mamande is born on January 7, 1881 in Guerrero to Refugio Rochín de Barroso, called Doña Cuca, about whom we know nothing but assume she is Mexican, and to a Spanish sea captain, Juan Domingo Landavazo, from Bilbao, Spain. Little is known about the couple. Perhaps Great-grandfather comes to Mexico's flourishing mining towns, as do so many Europeans, searching for mountains of glitter and wealth, for silver and gold. Mamande is baptized Sotero, a name she later abandons for Amelia; Sotero, a lonely sound; *soltero,* unmarried, *solitario,* solitary. Maybe the name frightens her.

Lobo comes into the kitchen and sees us looking at my grandmother, her step-mother. "Your great-grandfather, Don Juan Landavazo, comes on government business between México and Spain," Lobo says. "He is somehow involved with mines also, goes all the way to Urruachic, an area where the women are attractive, blonde with blue eyes, and he falls in love with the widow, Doña Cuca. They have a son, José if I remember correctly, and two daughters, one, your grandmother whom Don Juan names Sotero in memory of his sister."

Sotero's father sails on his merchant ship between Spain and México and brings his daughters beautiful dolls.

> *Rru - rru, que rru - rru, que tan, tan, tan,*

Sotero and her older sister, Aurelia, sing, rocking their babies in their arms,

> *Qué le - che y a - to - le pa - ra San Juan.*
> *Se - ño - ra San - ta Ana, ca - rita de lu - na,*
> *Duer - me a es - ta ni - ña, que ten - go en la cu - na.*

Often their mother lies in bed, ill. Sotero runs to the window and throws small stones that she's collected at passersby, then runs and hides under her mother's bed. "*Pero ¿qué hiciste, muchacha malcriada?*" her mother sighs. The white-haired, gentle woman I watch sitting in our covered porch, once a red-haired imp.

When Amelia is about three, her father dies at sea, Mother's story goes. His sister offers to pay the passage for Doña Cuca and her children to move to España. "*Vengan, vengan.*" Alone at her kitchen table, Mamá Cuca, our great-grandmother, weak and weary, thinks of the cold, dark waves, imagines dying on a ship, her thin, tired body slipping into the depths, her long hair rippling on the undulating ocean until she is swallowed by the watery mouth of the sea. She remains in México, and soon her body is lowered into the dry earth she knew. "*Pobrecitos,*" relatives and friends whisper of the three orphaned children who are taken in by different relatives.

"As *I* remember it," says Lobo, "Doña Cuca dies first. Since Don Juan has to return to Spain, he entrusts his children to his father-in-law, Don Rafael Rochín, with the understanding that Don Juan will return for them. Sadly, he also dies. Don Rafael then takes Sotero to his daughter, Doña Merceditas Revilla in Cusi, who welcomes the quiet companion for her only daughter, Chele. We eventually call your grandmother Señorita Amelia Revilla since she is raised by the Revilla family who formally adopt her. I remember her, very blonde, her hair reddish, *blanquísima.*"

"*Mi pobre madre* said she always felt out of place," Mother says, "because of her looks."

"Since the Landavazos' father dies," Lobo says, "the children remain in México, but I think an aunt leaves them each 14,000 *pesetas*. Rey Alfonso is still monarch, and he sends someone to look for the heirs. They find the brother since he hasn't changed his name, but can't find a Sotero Landavazo. Years later, my father has to do elaborate documentation."

Where did Amelia's brother and sister go? Her brother eventually becomes a Jefe Maderista, a leader of one of Francisco Madero's troops. A family photo shows him on horseback decked out with guns and bullets. "In his uniform," Uncle Lalo says, "he looks like something out of a Hollywood movie." We believe he dies in Kansas in the late thirties. Her sister, Aurelia, may have moved to San Antonio.

"*¡Amelia, pronto!*" the commanding tone of Amelia's cousin, Chele, the only daughter in the Revilla house with four brothers. "*¡Amelia! ¡Amelia!*" Chele's parents, Don Celso and Doña Merceditas, whom the little redhead calls Mamá Nina, smile at the playmate for their spirited daughter, the princess of the house. Mamá Nina—hair pulled back in a tight bun, long, dark dress with a high collar, ruffle on the bodice, long sleeves puffed at the shoulders—rules with quiet pinches.

"*Pronto, muchachas, pronto, el vino.*" December 31, 1899, the end of a century. Mamá Nina looks around her living room at her entire family, formally dressed, sleepy after the soup-to-dessert dinner, *sopa de verduras, pollo, arroz, camote, natillas y galletitas con café,* poised to welcome the new year. "*Gracias a Dios que nos da de comer sin merecer,*" her son, Roberto had said as he plunged his spoon into the steaming vegetable soup. With her fingertips, Mamá Nina taps the thick album of family portraits, those who go with her into the new century, who continue in her.

Laughing, everyone in the room and those of us present but unseen, raise our wine glasses gleaming like liquid rubies in the candlelight as we join in counting the final seconds, "*Tres, dos, UNO.*"

"*¡Feliz año nuevo, Mamá!*"

"*¡Feliz **siglo** nuevo!*" Mamá Nina laughs. "*Ven, Amelia, ven. Un abrazo.*"

Hugs and kisses for all, the nineteen-year-old Amelia closing her eyes, imagining his gentle lips pressing on hers. Amelia moves with the Revillas to Juárez and then across el Río Bravo to the border town of El Paso. Young men come to call, lured by Chele's flirting. "Forget about him, Amelia," Chele whispers watching her cousin's pensive face. "He has no money."

Neither do I, neither do I, thinks Amelia, *lo traigo entre ceja y ceja,* longing for what she called that dear face, *esa cara tan querida.* Years pass. No word from the young man whose face she carries between her eyebrows. She notices that a friend of the family, the judge and lawyer, Eduardo Luis Delgado, begins to stop often to visit the Revilla house.

"Amelia, look your best tomorrow. Eduardo is coming to see you," says Mamá Nina one Saturday afternoon. Chele quickly darts a look at Amelia, sees the shadow cross her face.

"Mamá Nina, aren't his daughters my age?" Amelia continues her sewing, pulls the white thread slowly through the white cotton cloth, not wanting to confront Mamá Nina face to face.

"Look your best." Mamá Nina sits straight as a church pillar. *"Es un hombre muy bueno, gente decente."* She leaves the room.

In the shade of our *portal,* I see a short, bald man pull a chair up next to my grandmother and take her hand. Our maternal grandparents gaze at sparrows sipping from the fountain, at robins pecking the red pyrocantha berries during their annual desert visit.

I pour Mother a cup of almond tea. "Smell this." I watch her enjoy the scent. "Have you ever heard of Nuestra Señora de Begoña?" I ask. "She's the patron saint of Bilbao, her statue found in an oak tree. I've read she sits holding a rose and the Christ Child. She and her Son wear crowns and are surrounded by oak branches."

"Bilbao," Mother says, "none of us has seen the land of my Basque grandfather."

"Tell me about your father,"

"Very intelligent. After all, he's a judge, hard-working, honest, stern, pragmatic. After he marries my mother, he goes to church every Sunday. Before that, he'd forbidden his daughters from his first marriage to go to confession. They have to attend Mass on the sly because he disapproves of priests in skirts, 'esos hombres en faldas.' But growing up, we, his second set of children, have to go to Mass every Sunday with our parents, no Mass, no show in the afternoon, *¿verdad, Nacha?"*

"Sí, Papá era muy recto." Lobo comes to sit with us, smooths the bright pink and indigo tablecloth with the palm of her

hand, the glint of pride in her eye whenever she speaks of her father.

In the living room, Mother plays a Chopin polonaise and Mozart sonatas, the melodies drifting through the rooms of the house like candle smoke. I open an envelope of family pictures, look at my grandparents' unsmiling wedding portrait. On November 25, 1915, Sotero Amelia Landavazo marries Eduardo Luis Delgado and his four grown daughters at Holy Family Church, the priest saying, "*Ego conjungo vos in matrimonium, in nomine Patris, et Filii, et Spiritus Sancti.*"

Eduardo, once the altar boy, then Porfirista and agnostic, now returns to the church, to confessional whispers, absolution, the priest, a shadow behind the grate raising his hand in blessing, "*Ego te absolvo, in nomine Patris, et Filii, et Spiritus Sancti.*"

Mamá Nina probably sees to that return to the sacraments. Amelia's in her early thirties, about 5´4", a slender woman with gold eyes. She wears a long white dress, her veil like a net bonnet around her serious face flows down her back and glides behind her. The groom, in his early fifties, about 5´3", is dressed in formal attire, a long, dark morning coat and white gloves, an erect gentleman with a full mustache and receding hairline. His daughters' frowns go with them on the honeymoon to Alamogordo, New Mexico, by train.

"My poor mother moves into a hornets' nest," Mother always says.

"Your grandmother is very devout, very pious," says Lobo about the stepmother with whom she fought those years. "She leads my father back to the church, and my sisters and I are finally able to receive the sacraments. We hadn't even made our first communions, and it is thanks to Amelia's good example and *gracias a Dios Nuestro Señor* that we become at least better Catholics." I see Lobo, the young woman, close her eyes as the priest approaches her, places a host on her waiting tongue, "*Corpus Dominii Nostri Jesu Christi.*"

Amelia moves into 1314 Wyoming, a one-story house full of

grown stepdaughters. Daily, Amelia bumps into the eldest's glares.

"She, your Lobo, is the thorn," Mother whispers.

"Amelia," Nacha says, "you just don't know how to take care of our house nor of my father. I spend my Sundays cleaning and cleaning that kitchen and that's after I work all week, while you, you . . . *¿Y tú qué haces?* Have you ever worked a day in your life? You don't really understand my father like I do. He didn't need to get married again. He has the four of us. He probably just felt sorry for you, a poor orphan."

Eduardo works in his Juárez law office, and fortunately the daughters still living at home also work, Nacha and Adelina at a department store, and Lola at the El Paso Chamber of Commerce. During those hours, Amelia's home is hers.

A letter from Spain arrives, from Bilbao. Word of an inheritance for Sotero Landavazo. Amelia keeps the letter near her, after all these years, a link to her father who died at sea. An attorney by the name of Zarandona writes of a will. Amelia's husband watches her stroke the envelope all evening. "*Le escribiré a Ladislado,*" Eduardo says removing his glasses, confident that his brother in Mexico City will better handle the matter. Weeks pass. Amelia keeps checking the mail. Months. Her husband watches her search. "*Le escribiré a Ladislado,*" he says again. Finally an envelope, a letter from Mexico City where Ladislado and his brother Davíd live into their nineties. Amelia hands the letter to her husband, sees his frown as he reads. Nothing received from Spain. She feels foolish, but Amelia cries not only because they need the money, but because she so longed to hold something her father sent her, saved for her, the father who's a shadow.

"*Escribiré a España, Amelia.*" Her husband pats her shoulder. Again, weeks pass. Amelia checks the mail. Months. And then a letter she hands to her husband. Again, a frown, deeper now. A sigh. "Zarandona says he sent the money to Mexico City. My brother says it never arrived." He walks slowly to the kitchen for a glass of water unable to believe his brother stole Amelia's money. Amelia has her doubts. They don't say much the rest of that evening. In their room, Amelia looks up at the large sepia photograph of the mother who left her, gazing steadily at her from deep-set eyes, dark hair parted down the middle into long, thick braids. "*¿Por qué me dejaste sola, Mamá?*"

As usual, Amelia's husband takes his small gun from his wooden secretary, a habit of many years, loads the weapon, and places it under his pillow before going to sleep. Amelia lies awake in the dark, hearing her husband's breathing, her step-daughter's grumbling, a car horn, a dog, the lonely sound of a train. Tonight she lets herself wonder how her life might have been different with her young love, the man who disappeared. She thinks, "*Amor viejo, ni te olvido, ni te dejo.*"

Nine months after her marriage, Amelia's first child, my mother, Estela Delgado, is born at Providence Hospital. "*Válgame Dios. Apenas cubrí la honra,*" Amelia would say blushing at having a child so quickly, living with her four stepdaughters as her stomach swells. She cannot look enough at Estela, her first baby. "*Pero que niña tan hermosa,*" she thinks to herself. Her step-daughters watch their father proudly carrying his new baby around the house. And the child's half-sisters, all old enough to be her mother, can't resist. They too like to hold Estelita, to bring gifts to the baby sister with hazel eyes who coos at them. "*Tilita, Tilita,*" they say, cover her when she sleeps, rock her when she cries,

> *Cu - cu - cu - cu, can - ta - ba la ra - na,*
> *Cu - cu - cu - cu, de - ba - jo del a - gua,*
> *Cu - cu - cu - cu, pa - só Es - te - li - ta,*
> *Cu - cu - cu - cu, con u - na fal - di - ta.*

When Estelita is old enough to sit alone, Amelia has her daughter's picture taken sitting on a lace doily by a pillow embroidered with a flower-basket. I stare at this picture I've glanced at casually through the years, and for the first time, see its secret, Mamande, hiding behind the pillow, her arm holding her daughter's dress. I imagine her smile into the soft fabric at the exquisite beauty of her first child's bare feet.

My grandmother and I delight in the body of the woman between us, Mother. Mamande, silent, behind the scenes, gently holds her daughter, and later us.

Amelia's son's are born, Eduardo Luis, called Lalo, and Juan Domingo. Her daughter's chatter fills the house with light.

"Mamá, puedo ponerme tus zapatos?"

"Compra un vestido rojo, Mamá! ¡Sí! ¡Sí! ¡Sí!"

Amelia, who smiles at her high-spirited daughter's urgings to dress in red, buys her little girl frilly dresses, patent shoes, bows and hats for her short brown hair; sailor suits for her sons. When her children lean on her, she runs her hands through their soft hair. Outside on the porch, she sits and watches her husband in his striped shirt and suspenders, resting his three young children on his *pancita* when he carries them.

"Un retrato, un retrato, Amelia," He has her pose again, her long red hair in a bun, holding Juan, adjusting his cap, opening her arm to Estelita and Lalo to sit close to her.

"¡Otro, Papacito, otro!" Her daughter fluffs her taffeta skirt and adjusts a small green shawl on her shoulders. In his straw hat, Amelia's husband smiles at his last daughter, watches her sit in a small chair in the shade of the garden, then sits her on his lap, pointing to a nearby rose. *"Fíjate, hija."* Notice.

Papande, an atheist for years, teaches his three young children a morning prayer,

> *En este nuevo día, gracias . . .*
> *Por Ti nacen las flores, reverdecen los campos,*
> *Las aves en las ramas cantan en Tu nombre santo.*
> *Dirige, Dios inmenso, y guía nuestros pasos*
> *Para que eternamente Tu santa ley sigamos.*

Amelia's stepdaughters, my aunts, begin to marry. Lola moves to Cuauhtemoc with her husband, Gabino Cuilty, raises a family and opens a business academy in her home. Doña Lola, the small mountain town calls this short, firm teacher of typing, shorthand, and English to hundreds of students through the years. Elodia and her laughter and rages remain in El Paso, live near the Delgado home. Her husband, though much bigger than his wife, comes unsuccessfully to complain to her father about the iron she threw at him.

"*Mira,*" says the judge unwilling to become involved in the matrimonial struggle, "*tus problemas con tu mujer son tuyos. No vengas aquí a chismear.*"

Often Amelia sits at Elodia's kitchen table, the bent knives, forks, and spoons propped in a glass, Amelia's three and Elodia's six playing together while the women sip their *café con leche.* Amelia shakes her head, both shocked and amused at Elodia's stories of throwing a set of plates at her husband the night before, this stepdaughter, a five-foot terror when angry.

Adelina nurses her headaches. And Nacha? Nacha terrifies the Delgado house with her scrubbings, arriving Saturday night after work with her grocery bag full of cleaning supplies, boxes of Gold Dust Twins and ammonia, after Sunday Mass tying her hair up and sweeping them all out with her mutterings, pulling the outside hose in to really clean the kitchen. What besides dirt does she seek to scrub away watched by the three children she loves and yet their flesh, proof of her proper father's separate, private life. When the family returns from their afternoon outing to the park or the zoo, Nacha and her glares await them. "*Parece bruja,*" the three children, Estela, Lalo, and Juan, whisper and laugh at the broom queen, *la reina de la escoba.*

Mother and I watch Lobo's face, but we don't see the same woman since sight, like language, is filtered by whom we are. I gaze at Lobo, the wrinkled face I love, that lures me to the elderly, makes me want to sit close to them hungry for some hint of her in them, a laugh, a turn of the head, the shape of a fingernail.

Mother whispers, "I hated her for the way she treated my mother. I know you four loved her, but you didn't know her when I did. What a terror, her hair all tied up to scrub the kitchen, with the outside hose, mind you, always fighting with

my mother. Nacha was wonderful to all of you, but I hated her
then."

The young Estela hears them arguing again, day after day, her
mother and stepsister. Estela has seen her patient father listen-
ing and watching. Throw her out, Papá, Estela thinks, and her
buckets and ammonia with her.

Why don't you move out, you old witch? Why don't you just
climb on that broom you like so much and fly away? Why can't
my mother and father and the three of us kids live here by our-
selves? You'll never get married. Who'd want you?

Estela hides behind her bedroom door when they think she's
outside playing.

"I don't know why my father married again," says Nacha. Es-
tela hears crying, and when she peeks out, sees her mother, face
in her hands. Nacha begins arguing with her stepmother again.
"Why don't you at least try to learn some English like I did to
help my poor father?"

Estela sees her father walking in his slow steps down the hall,
toward the women who don't see him coming. Through the
door crack, the girl sees the look in his eyes, and she holds her
breath, her palms sweaty, presses her back against the wall, prays
he won't see her spying.

Grabbing Nacha firmly by the shoulders, Amelia the red-
head flares. "Why don't you leave if you don't like the way I do
things here? Did you ever think you might be in the way?"

"In the way! In the way! Who moved in here where she wasn't
wanted or needed?"

Locked in their anger, they don't see the judge until he pulls
them apart, reaches up and slaps them both lightly on the cheek
to shock them back to their senses. Estela's mouth and eyes snap
wide open. Her father has never struck her mother. She
clenches both fists, thinks: I want to slap you, Papá.

Amelia's children live much of their life a language she will
not learn. "Son buenos hijos," she says to herself, the woman who,
like Lobo, never wears pants or make-up. As soon as the Del-
gado children are old enough to play outside, new sounds dart

through the house since most of their neighbors speak only English.

"Hurry, Lalo!"

"Wait for us, Stella!"

The children run through the house with their English trailing like a banner behind them—unless their father is at home. When they see him, they stop, knowing he considers it bad manners for them to speak the foreign language in front of their parents. "*Es una grosería hablar inglés en frente de sus padres,*" he frowns.

"My father just had a quiet look about him that made us mind," Mother says. "Only once did he hit any of us. When he saw my brothers fighting with one another, he removed his belt, saying, "*Hermano contra hermano, nunca.*" One look from Papacito is enough. No one runs in the house if he sits in his chair reading his law books or newspaper. No one dares push past him even if late for school when he walks with slow steps down the hall. And all speak Spanish in those rooms that he considers Mexican territory. "*Cuando pisan en esta casa, hijos, pisan México.*"

In private, in his careful, smooth handwriting, he writes careful letters in English and Spanish in a small, leather journal, struggles to learn the new language that will always elude him.

> *Son mis hijos.*
> These are my children.
> *Eso no es justo.*
> That is not just.

"My poor mother, living in that hornets' nest with those four stepdaughters," Mother sighs. "Every morning she'd walk me to school. One day the sidewalk is icy, and when John starts to fall, she tries to grab him, falls, breaks her nose in the snow, the three of us, little, looking down at all that blood. I'll bet she had a pretty nose, but there's no money to fix it. Do you realize how much older my father was?"

In the garage behind the Delgado house a cow moos, chickens cluck, and for a while peacocks strut and screech, *Aaayyyhhh, AAAYYYHHH.* Afternoons, Mamande takes her three children firmly by the hand to the home of her friend, Señora de la Torre, who dresses in a black tunic, like a nun. "*Pronto, pronto, vamos a la doctrina.*" In Spanish, Señora de la Torre's daughters teach my mother and her brothers their catechism and to beware of *los Protestantes.* "Never walk in front of a Protestant church. Cross the street." The Delgado children learn their prayers,

> *Santo ángel de mi guardia,*
> *Mi dulce compañía*
> *No me desampares*
> *Ni de noche, ni de día.*

Evenings Señora de la Torre comes looking for the children, "*Muchachos, muchachos, hora del rosario.*" They hide behind the oleander bushes to avoid going to pray the rosary. "*¡Muchachos! ¡Vengan o los voy a castigar!*"

Friends stop by, the adults sit on the front porch in nice weather and visit, children's shouts flying through the air. A neighbor's daughter who likes to recite is invited to *declamar.* She begins emotionally reciting, "*O mi heroica raza.*"

The Delgado children poke each other, suppress their laughter when their father looks at them.

On winter nights, the family sits in the kitchen near the pot-bellied stove. The children do homework; Eduardo reads the newspaper, sighs at all the misfortune in the world, says, "*Algunos nacen con estrella y otros estrellados.*" Amelia murmurs her rosary or prays her novenas; prays for Elodia, again the coat hanger, the blood.

At Christmas, Estela, Lalo, and Juan go with their mother to Señora de la Torre's house for *las posadas,* go room to room with their candles, knocking at a door as Joseph and Mary knocked at inns in Bethlehem, singing,

> *¿Qui - én les da po - sa - da,*
> *A es - tos pe - re - gri - nos?*

The guests receive cookies and on the last night, nuts and oranges.

"My father loves to learn, all his life," Uncle Lalo says bringing his father's law exams and diploma dated 1927. "See here? Now he'd been a judge for years, but maybe he just wanted to keep learning."

"You mean Papande takes his law exams in his sixties?" Libby, the exhausted law student asks.

"You know what they say about legal documents, honey," Uncle Lalo chuckles. "What the big type giveth, the small type taketh away."

Libby, too tired to laugh, has trouble sleeping at night, frets about papers, cases, meetings. The older family women drift in at the tea kettle's whistle, but frown at Libby's insomnia, the tension on her young face. Even after death, the women worry. Mamá Cleta plans to heat rose petals with mint at night for her great-great-great-granddaughter and press them into Libby's forehead to drift her to sleep. The experienced healer thinks she could soak the young girl's feet in an infusion of violets, bruise some of the petals she saves and apply them to Libby's furrowed forehead. Smelling the purple petals once used as a love potion, Mamá Cleta frowns. "And what has happened to the *violetas*? Their scent that once tasted like smooth circles has vanished."

"Tell them I don't have time for this stuff, Mom. I don't mean to be rude, but I've got to finish these papers and try to sleep. How do I say I'm sorry in Spanish? Oh to be five again. Those were the days."

"*Toma esto, mi hijita.*" Mamande's mother hands Libby a steaming cup of *azahar*, the scent of orange blossoms momentarily erasing her frown.

"Be glad you're getting a good education, dear," my mother tells her. "That's what I wanted for my children, the chance I didn't have. I remember 1929, that year of losses, the Great Depression and my father's first stroke."

The left side of Papande's face sags, his eyes still as stones at times. Amelia studies her husband's face when she thinks he's not watching her. Though he returns to his work, she sees and senses a permanent change. His family watches him try to remain independent, but he begins to ask his sons for help to move from one chair to another. His daughters, Nacha and

Adelina, pay the rent and all in the house know it, pinched by their resentment. But the money is not enough, and the Delgados finally lose their home, have to move to 712 Octavia Street, four adults and three children in the small two-bedroom home.

Ironically, Elodia and her family are moved by the National Relief Administration into the Delgado's old home, her old home. Because Elodia's husband finally walks out the door and never returns, she also qualifies for huge sacks of surplus food, generic cans marked PEAS and CORN.

"They gave away lots of salt pork," Uncle Lalo says. "We didn't even know what salt pork was. We'd just boil it and boil it." In the dark, Amelia sends her oldest son to their former home where he fills his little red wagon with sacks of flour and cans of beans, pulls his wagon to their smaller home on Octavia. "*No es desgracia ser pobre,*" my uncle says, "*pero es muy inconveniente.*"

In 1936, Papande has a series of strokes, eventually is not sure where he is, "*¡Amelia! ¡Amelia!*" She and her sons move the large bed into the parlor near the big window, lie her husband there to rest, to sleep at night. A few weeks before his death, Papande slips into a coma. How quiet the house becomes. Estela brings a dark-skinned young man in, a new friend she says, to turn the heavy, silent judge, to protect his stiff body from bed sores. Every day at noon and night he comes, this Raúl Mora.

Papande never meets my father which Mother says is just as well since her father never would have allowed her to marry such a dark-skinned man. Amelia doesn't approve initially either, not that she can stop her headstrong daughter. Amelia watches Raúl lift and turn her husband's body.

His family watches Eduardo's breath, take turns sitting in the parlor, cry, his wife and all his children, cry, day after day.

Estela cries too, but she listens and watches, looks at her family and thinks: this can't go on. They'll all die too.

"*¿Qué pasa, hijita?*" her mother asks wiping away her tears with a white handkerchief.

"*Nada, Mamá, nada.*" Slowly she walks to a neighbor's. "I call my father's doctor and good friend. '*Doctor Molinar, por favor, lo necesitamos.*'

"Soon he arrives asking, '*¿Cómo está mi compañero?*' The doctor looks at me. He looks at his old friend, my father, and takes an injection from his bag. He whispers into my father's ear, bids his friend farewell, '*Bueno, compañero, hasta luego. Feliz viaje.*' Then quickly he stabs near Papá's heart, injects something, removes the needle, shuts the black bag. '*Que pasen buenas tardes. Me hablan si me necesitan.*' When he walks by me he whispers, '*Quince minutos.*'

"I did things in my life because I had to. Who was going to do it? I had to decide all kinds of things for my brothers and myself when I was young. I am the oldest, and my parents don't speak English."

Eduardo is buried at Evergreen Cemetery. Amelia stands by the coffin with her husband's children, hears the priest's words, "*Requiem aeternam dona ei Domine,*" watches Lalo, as the oldest son, throw the first handful of dirt onto the coffin, approves the headstone for her husband the miner, judge, lawyer born in México and dying in the United States,

Eduardo Luis Delgado, October 13, 1864–
November 19, 1936.

Amelia and her children fold his cape and top hat, box them and his legal papers, ribbons from la Sociedad Mutualista, *Alianza Hispano-Americana*, a mutual aid society.

After the funeral, Amelia lives with her three children in a duplex at 1419 Wyoming. Marriages begin. Her stepdaughter, Adelina and her headaches decide to marry Andres, the frightened security guard. A blow to the head, and that man hides inside himself the rest of his life. "They're following me," he whispers.

"*¡Anda, Andrés, qué hombre tan tonto eres!*" his future wife snaps often. Prim and straight, Adelina looks in her long, white satin wedding dress with the high lace collar and long train. Her veil whispers as it slides down the aisle. *"Ego conjungo vos in matrimonium, in nomine Patris, et Filii, et Spiritus Sancti."*

Her maid-of-honor, stubborn Lobo, stands at the altar in a stylish brimmed hat and long dress. Black. At the photographer's, the daisies wilt in her arms. I study the thin nose and lips, eyes that look away from the camera, see only her father's casket, and men and women's disturbing habit of touching, arm in arm, hand in hand. Or worse. She prays for the virginity of her sister, the bride.

Adelina and Andres move to Los Angeles where she works in a corset shop, and he flees from shadows. *"¡Anda, Andrés, qué hombre tan tonto eres!"* She lavishes her love on her collie, canaries and finches. *"Canten, canten, mis amorcitos."*

When she's dying in her eighties having survived a radical mastectomy and a lifetime of chronic arthritis, and after scolding and berating her timid husband unendingly, she whispers to my mother, "Tell Nacha I never let him touch me."

Andres paces on tiptoe in the quiet room of the nursing home terrified that the voice he clung to in this world of dark corners will disappear. What will he do with all the silence? How will he know what to do each day without the safety of Adelina's impatient orders? He rubs his hands together over and over, begins to gasp quietly unable to breathe, drowning in his tears. He moves toward the bed, to the body that no longer sees or speaks, bends to the pale wrinkled cheek of the strong woman in whose anger and badgerings he hid, cups his trembling hands around his mouth and says loudly, *"Ya me voy, mi corazón."*

"He says good-bye to his heart there," my brother says.

In 1939, Amelia's daughter marries my father. During World War II, Lalo marries Carmen Veal who moves into the small duplex where I'd go as a child when my mother and aunt go what they call "window-shopping." I sit in Mamande's lap, such a safe place, and look around the room, say, *"Pienso en algo verde,"* and she guesses what green object I'm thinking of. Mamande peels grapes and places the glistening, soft globes on my tongue.

"Mamande was kindness itself," Mother says.

"Her scoldings were too gentle to be scoldings," Cecilia says.

We see her, Cecilia, at three years of age running around the kitchen. "*Cecilia*," Mamande says continuing to stir the *sopa de arroz* she's sautéing, "*ya para.*" My sister grins and keeps running. "*Pero Cecilia*, stop running or I'll have to punish you." The little girl with black hair and dark brown eyes brimming mischief grins and keeps running by the stove, sink, refrigerator. "*Ay, Cecilia*," her white-haired grandmother says taking my sister's hand and gently tapping it. "*Ves, ves.* See what you made me do. I told you I'd punish you if you didn't stop."

Lalo lives with the tensions of a wife and mother under one roof, the woman once the young wife now the mother-in-law. Eventually, Mamande moves to a boarding house, Queen of Angels, run by the Sisters of Jesus and Mary. Then the shock.

"Cancer," the doctor says. "I'm sorry, Stella. There's cancer in your mother somewhere, and it has now moved to the lung. We're not going in there to find it."

"How long?"

"Three months."

"We brought her to die at our house," Mother says. My parents move Mamande and her prayers into what had been our playroom in the addition to our home. Our grandmother, who's told that she has pleurisy and needs care, is taken to have the fluid tapped from her lung, a long needle inserted between her ribs.

Mornings she hovers in the kitchen ready to toast or butter our bread. Later she bathes then sits in her wide-armed wooden chair and combs her long, white hair. She smokes but never inhales.

"She'd let Roy and me hold smoke from her cigarette in our mouths and let the smoke come out our nose," Stella says, seeing herself and her younger brother both pursing their lips to let the smoke drift. "We think that's big time. I always remember her in the kitchen though she doesn't really cook much, but she's always helping, and every night she fixes us a treat. Lobo brings us a sandwich, and then Mamande brings milk and maybe cookies."

"No wonder we were a bit roundacious," I say vowing never to eat again.

"Mamande was a saint, *más dulce que la miel*. Remember how she prayed?" Mother asks.

On her bed each day Mamande lays out her prayer books, rosary, prayers, novenas, holy cards of El Sagrado Corazón and El Niño de Atocha, covers the bedspread with them. All morning she prays in that large, sunny back room with the green linoleum floor, sitting in her wide-armed chair, her knees moving rhythmically back and forth, back and forth. Sometimes, she lights a candle when she prays.

She looks up at her statue of Saint Raphael and the boy Tobias holding a fish and leaning on the angel, boy and angel both pale and blue-eyed, like most saints. What blows that saint will receive in his future life with our family. A holy card says to invoke him to receive his help. Mamande prays to this *"espíritu de alto grado de perfección,"*

> *Señor San Rafael mío, a vos llego con alegría y*
> *contenta para que remedies esta necesidad mía antes*
> *de los 21 días, y para que me acompañes como*
> *acompañaste y guiaste al joven Tobías.*

A statue of La Virgen de Guadalupe stands on the chest of drawers, the dark virgin with downcast eyes dressed in a pink garment, her green mantle sprinkled with stars. And Mamande prays to the dark-skinned, Peruvian saint, San Martín de Porres because he's *"un santito humilde que hacía la limpieza."*

> *En el nombre de la Santísima Trinidad,*
> *En el nombre de Jesucristo, el Hijo de Dios,*
> *En el nombre de María, Reina del Cielo,*
> *En el nombre de José, Patrón de la Iglesia Universal,*
> *San Martín ayúdame por el honor y gloria de Dios y*
> *la salvación de las almas. Amén.*

"*Anoche, vi a un negrito en mi cuarto.*" Mamande stirs chocolate powder into my brother's milk. Mother continues scrambling eggs, thinks, my poor mother is losing her mind, imagining a black man in her room last night, that room where we've brought her to spend the last three months of her life. "He told me not to be afraid. That I would get well. You know who it was, don't you? *San Martín.* I recognize him."

Mother appreciates Mamande's faith but thinks: Mamá if you only knew. It's cancer. Cancer. The three months pass, the diet of rice and prunes continues. Each time the doctors insert the long needle to remove the fluid from her lung, they draw out less which baffles them. More x-rays. The shadow disappears.

"A miracle?" Mother asks the doctor.

"I don't know about miracles, Stella. I know she had cancer, and there's no sign now. I know I didn't cure her. That's what I know."

The months and years pass, years of Mamande and Lobo watching over us, giving us what they can, their love for us braiding the stepdaughter and stepmother together. Each nurses us if we sigh or moan which we learn to do quite well. Lobo can be counted on to bring tea for a cough and usually a cookie when everyone else is asleep, to sit on the bed urging me to drink the liquid as hot as I can stand, whispering, "I'm going to tell your mother that you shouldn't go to school tomorrow. You're too sick."

When I'm finished, she pulls the covers over my shoulders and, much as I like school, I smile to myself in the dark thinking of a day with all my storybook dolls on my bed, cozily reading my favorite stories of long-ago carriages and ankle-length dresses in the *Childcraft*, listening to soap operas on the radio, to Ma Perkins and Stella Dallas.

The next day, Mamande brings me tomato soup and crackers in bed, sits and pats my hand, her fingers cool, the skin papery, like her prayer books. She goes to her room to bring me one of her special aspirins. She counts her Bayers, not the cheap things her daughter buys, but real aspirin, and counts her candies too, frowns that she has only six Big Hunks left. She sighs, hides the candies and aspirin in her top bureau drawer. She'll have to ask

Estela for ten Big Hunks and a new bottle of Bayer. Why does she have to keep asking? She'll mention this to Lalo, such a good son, when he comes for his Friday night visit. She'll tell him that Estela sometimes ignores what her mother needs.

If we have a stomachache, Mamande has us lie down while she warms a bottle of oil, then slowly rubs the oil into our abdomen, her hand gently massaging in a circle and then thumping with her finger, massaging again. It's more her hands than her voice that we remember.

"Mamande likes all windows closed when anyone is sick," Mother says. "When she gets one of her headaches, she rubs mentholatum on her temples and covers it with small pieces of tissue paper, *papel de China*. And she loves her Bayer aspirins, '*Bahyer*' she calls them. No others will do." For medicinal purposes, she always has *mezcal con gusano de agave* on hand, the worm we look at, fascinated. And she likes a little *copita* of Mogen David wine. Not a wine glass, smaller, maybe a liqueur glass."

"It's great having both Lobo and Mamande in the house to feel sorry for our every ache," I say.

"They spoiled the four of you," Mother says, "Lobo bringing you comics and candy, Mamande making you peanut butter and jelly sandwiches."

"And we looked it," says Stella, "except for Cecilia. The rest of us are little butterballs."

"Those last years, Mamande would always save some kind of dessert for Lobo, pudding or pie," Mother says, "so that there would be something waiting for her when she got home from work, always in the dark, bringing what you four expected."

I look out at my grandmother listening to the fountain in the shade. Not three months, but eight years after she moves into our house, she dies of a stroke in the bathtub. What a time Mother and Uncle Lalo have with Mamande's funeral.

"Our family had been buried at Evergreen Cemetery,"

Mother says. "Papande is buried there, and that's where Ma-
mande wanted to be, near her husband, but the church opened
a new cemetery, where they want all Catholics buried, Mount
Carmel, far out of town. To ensure compliance, the Bishop de-
crees that priests won't attend the rosary nor the burial of
Catholics who don't select Mount Carmel's blessed ground. So
Nacha and I say the rosary for your grandmother, *Padre nuestro
que estás en los cielos. . . .*"

Sometimes we meet in the loves we share.

Sotero Amelia Delgado, January 17, 1880–January 31, 1962

"I don't know how I did it," Mother says. "My own dear
mother lying there in that casket, but I did. Since I was little,
I've had to do things myself, had to."

I walk out to the garden enjoying the pleasure of a warm af-
ternoon after last week's cold, unpredictable February, *febrero
loco*. I walk by my maternal grandparents, Papande reading a law
book, Mamande praying a novena.

"Watch out for the crocuses, Lalo," Aunt Carmen calls wor-
ried about her husband's rake. "Did you see them, Pat? Come
and look. Yellow and purple crocus. And over there see the
daffodils and the iris? And look at the color of these pansies, the
little velvet faces. But honey, I'm so maaaad. All this warm
weather is going to ruin my fruit trees. Come on out back and
see how they're covered, covered with buds. But it's too early,
honey."

I look at the trees with my aunt, think of the origin of the
word "pansy," *pensée*, French for thought, the flowers once be-
lieved to make your love think of you, petal power, gardens of
multicolored, velvet musings. I wander back to the central gar-
den, go find the old book on the gardener's year I was reading
last night that says a gardener, "is a creature who digs himself
into the earth." We probably dig some of ourselves into all that
we pursue, but there's something eerie or maybe appealing—all
that Catholic dust-to-dust stuff—about digging ourselves into
earth, loosening the soil and burying some of our essence, our

breath, as we turn the earth, even while we're alive becoming part of the compost.

The February evening arrives on the desert mesas; clouds blush pink, then peach. At night, I sleep with the full Snow Moon. Sparrows and robins wake me early enough the next morning to see mauve clouds and to watch the alabaster moon set to the west as the sun rises over the mountains in the east, the white globes that light our world silently greeting one another.

Marzo airoso/Windy March

ASH WEDNESDAY, dust to dust, forty days of penance and purification, Lent; when we're little, the "I Won't" season: I Won't Eat Candy, I Won't Chew Gum, I Won't Drink Sodas, I Won't Eat Ice Cream, I Won't Taste Pleasure, I Won't, I Won't.

Wind and then snow last night, bare branches dusted white, the tulip leaves now green cups filled with snow. My paternal grandfather, the tailor Lázaro Mora, follows my son, Bill, through the house, tape-line in hand trying to measure him, wanting to give the great-grandson he never knew some gift, something for his graduation, for completing his Masters, though Lito is not sure what that is. Lito, we called this dark-skinned, handsome, white-haired grandfather, short for *abuelito*, born March 17, 1880 in Jiménez. The dead continue their earthly habits, in this case, giving.

"*Mi padre era un encanto.*" Aunt Chole and I sit listening to logs crackling in the kitchen fireplace. "He never, never raises his voice, never hits us. *Mi padre era un hombre hermoso, moreno con ojos grandes.* He would get dressed up *y parecía un príncipe.* He never complained, never said a bad word. *Era como un santo. Ay, mi padre, mi padre, querido.* He was so wonderful, and he adored me. My mother loves my sister who is loud and loves to dance, but my father loves me." She whimpers. "I didn't want him to suffer. Don't ask me more about this today. I am his first daughter. His sons before me had all died. Because I am thin he gives me tonics, so many I think I have teeth at two months, *ee-ee*.

"Do we know where his parents come from?"

"*Nooooo, esa gente, tu sabes, no tuvimos contacto*. I think Simona Porras and Gregorio Mora are from Jiménez. Gregorio had a ranch, *una hacienda*. Simona and Gregorio's children are Lázaro, Pedro, Luisa, Santiago, and Josefa.

"I've got a story for you, *m'ija*." says Aunt Bori, the youngest and tallest of my father's four sisters, bringing us a cup of *manzanilla*. "When your great-grandfather, Gregorio, is *un chiquito*, about five or six, he's out riding a horse. Down the road he sees a man who's waving and waving at him, very upset.

" '*¡Mi esposa! ¡Mi esposa! ¡Por favor, joven, trae al médico!*' His wife is about to have a baby. Gregorio gallops off and soon returns with the doctor, then stays outside, waiting. As soon he hears a baby cry, he goes off to tell his family. *Pues ese Gregorio*, stops by every once in a while and checks on that baby girl. And guess what, *m'ija*, years later he marries her," my aunt laughs.

"Yes," says Aunt Chole, "that is Simona, and she is French at that. Gregorio, *mi abuelo*, dies blind. He is very Catholic and spends those dark years praying for everyone, like I try to do, *reina. Traía a Jesús en la boca*, Jesus always in his mouth. *Fíjate, fíjate, no más fíjate*," she says using that fine Spanish imperative from the Latin *fixus*, meaning to fix the gaze, notice. "When Gregorio dies, they dress him *como un santito*, and everybody goes to look at the old man dressed as a saint."

Through the year, in this desert house where family generations dwell, Lito's father, Gregorio, sits in clouds of candle smoke, *clk, clk, clk* of rosary beads. He converted the small room off his bedroom since there's no small chapel nearby, placed a small crucifix near the window, the only furniture in the fragrant *oratorio*, a wood chair and a small rough table with rosaries, prayer books Great-grandfather likes to hold, and small containers of holy water and holy oil. On the tabletop, candles flicker, through the centuries scent the walls and the statues of the Sacred Heart and Our Lady of Guadalupe. All day the family women tiptoe in to murmur petitions and light votives, candle tongues appealing to the patient virgin who rides the moon. Sitting in this, his private holy place, Abuelo prays, repeating, "*Virgen Santísima de Guadalupe, Madre y Reina de nuestra Patria.*" Through smoke, gold at sunrise; lavender at sunset; Abuelo Gregorio sees shapes of angels rising.

"The smoke sounds like a choir," Mamá Cleta whispers, "voices ascending."

Vé - ni Cre - á - tor Spí - ri - tus.

Crocheting in a corner of the kitchen, Lita, our paternal grandmother, gray hair in a tight bun, weathered, brown face in a tight knot, frowns at her tall husband still following Bill through the house. Her maternal grandparents are Damian Monárrez, mayor of Boca de Avino, and Elena Meléndez, my great-great-grandmother, Abuela Elena. She enters the kitchen and begins to toast chiles, tomatoes, and green *tomatillos* for making her chile sauce, this side of the family magicians with food. She begins to chop onion, cuts herself with a knife, quickly washes the cut and begins checking the baseboards and corners.

"Did you lose something, Abuela Elena?" I ask.

"*No, no.* I'm looking for spiderwebs to put on my cut to stop the bleeding." In no time, she's back at the stove, toasting chiles. "Do you really like this modern kitchen? Frankly I miss *mi cocina en el rancho.* Yes, it was darker and smokier, but it smelled so good with the herbs, chiles, corn, and fruits drying from the rafters, and I had my wood stove, my own big pots and a good *comal y metates.*

"Things were worn smooth, rounded with use, not all these noisy metal machines. Can't you hear the difference between these motors and the familiar voice of a wooden rolling pin? Sounds seep into a body or a house. Be careful what you let within these walls. And where is the crucifix, I keep asking. Every good kitchen needs a small *altar,* candles we can light dedicating our work to the honor and glory of Our Lord."

Abuela Elena looks at Lita, her granddaughter who buried so many babies. "*¿Cómo estás, Natividad?*" she asks patting my grandmother's knee.

Lita sighs and touches her head. *"Ay, tengo dolor de cabeza, Abuela."*

Abuela Elena frets about how to ease the younger woman's pain, gestures that she'll be right back, returns holding the long rainbow she stitched once from all her cloth scraps. Handing me one end of the collage, she unfolds the red, brown, green, gold, blue, and purple patches, some smooth and shiny, some rough and practical. She takes her long cloth, drapes it on her granddaughter's aching head, strokes it hoping the cloth will somehow ease the headache. Lita begins to cry at the soothing kindness and soon word spreads through the house of this sight, a woman with a multicolored cloth on her head.

"Why is she wearing it?" children whisper at the doorway.

"She had a headache."

"Oh."

"Yo tengo dolor de cabeza."

"Y yo."

"Y yo."

"Abuela Elena, I have a headache. May I wear the cloth?"

"Me too."

"Me too."

And so it begins, children of different generations taking turns walking through the garden all year long proudly wearing the magic cloth of many colors stitched by the rough fingers of Abuela Elena.

"We knew many cures at the *rancho*," she says. "When I am little, if we cough at night, Papá moves slowly through the dark to find us. Once he decides which of us is coughing, he rubs our feet with his hands, then takes a bit of saliva and rubs it into our soles. We go to sleep and do not cough again. For coughs during the day, *mi mamá* grinds a white rock, *piedra lumbre* and making a straw, blows the white powder into our throats. For deep cuts, sugar; for earaches, a few drops of perfume; for head colds, a pan of steaming water and a towel to create a tent for our face.

"If Mamá's back aches in the winter, my grandmother brings a candle and a small glass or cup to my mother's room. She makes Mamá lie down and bare her back. From the doorway, we watch our *abuela* light the candle, then place the glass over it and rub my mother's back, to suck out the cold wind my grandmother says, Mamá sighing, 'Ay. Ay.'

"In the summer, if we get too much sun, *mi abuela* makes us bend over in the yard while she puts a glass of cold water on our heads, a towel on our shoulders. She lifts our head and shoulders up slowly holding the glass on our heads, sits us in the shade to let the cold water slowly stream down our face and neck.

"For gum trouble, people chew wild pieplant, *canaigre*. If our eyes are red, Mamá washes them carefully with *manzanilla*. And, of course, we drink the teas I make for you—*hierbabuena y gordo lobo, romero* for rheumatism. Plenty of honey and lemon for a cough.

"We know things—to cover mirrors during a storm so lightning won't strike." Warming to her story, she washes and dries her hands, comes to sit with us, this woman who died long before I was born. "Have I told you about my sister, *m'ijas?* She is very scared of storms, and when she sees dark clouds covering the sky, she slips outside and makes a Sign of the Cross at them so they'll disappear. If the storm passes and we receive no rain, Mamá frowns at her and asks accusingly, '*¿Cortaste las nubes con cruces, muchacha?*' We always need rain, so my sister won't tell the truth. *Es muy mentirosa.*

"If we are pregnant during an eclipse, we pin keys on our abdomen so the child will not be born missing a finger or toe. Natividad didn't do that, and you know what happened. Did you do that?" Aunt Chole who never married, never had children, looks away, folds into herself. I shake my head, no, and Abuela Elena clucks her tongue at my foolishness.

I look again at Lita, the grandmother we didn't know well. Natividad Pérez is born in Boca de Avino, Durango on September 8, 1883 to Tomasa Monárrez and Brígido Pérez whose other children are Brígido, Leonor and Eustorjio.

"Eustorjio?" I ask the aunt who with her one and only hand can wallpaper rooms, paint houses, fill her kitchen counters with her apple and pumpkin pies. "Do you know how to spell it?"

"I'm still trying, honey."

"Do we know anything about him?"

"Only that he shoots himself because he's in love," she sighs.

"Kills himself?"

"Yes, *m'ija*."

"Oh."

"Mi Abuelita Tomasa, my mother's mother, always lives with us," Aunt Chole says. "*Era hermosa*. Tiny, thin, and when she's going out, she wears long dresses, pretty sleeves. Her hair's white, but maybe it was blonde when she was young. She likes us to fix it, to play with her hair and try to put waves in it. Not an affectionate woman, no. *Era de carácter*." From the other Mora sisters, I learn that the tiny, blue-eyed Tomasa Monárrez, is born near Santa Bárbara to a family said to be Basque.

"Where do the Basques live?" asks Aunt Chole.

"Southern France and Northern Spain. They speak a language called Euskara."

"*Pero son españoles*. They speak Spanish, *mi reina*."

Basques, apparently part of both sides of my family, that stubborn, old, mysterious culture with the hubris to say, "Before God was God and boulders were boulders, Basques were already Basques."

I watch Tomasa, our great-grandmother, who is part of the Mora household in Chihuahua and comes with them to El Paso, the woman my father loved and who fondly calls him Chato. I want to ask her, What did your husband do? When did he die? What did you love? Her daughter, Lita, probably meets my grandfather in Parral where Lázaro is a tailor who teaches Lita's brother, Brígido, his trade.

Lazaro, a young man, hands Natividad the small, sepia photograph, an oval in which she sees this slender man, dark hair and eyes, mustache, a white flower on his suit lapel. Our grandmother turns the small picture over and reads the dedication he wrote professing his loyal friendship,

Recibe este recuerdo en prueba de gratitud y cariño que te profesa tu fiel amigo.

Lázaro Mora
17–1901

A year later, Natividad hands him her unsmiling photograph. He studies her hair piled above her head. Below her straight mouth, he sees a dress with high neck, puffed sleeves, a gathered, tight bodice. He thinks of the body under the dark dress. Turning the picture over, he reads her flowing penmanship, imagines her hand shaping each letter stating her affection,

Te dedico este insignificante recuerdo en prueba del sincero cariño que en verdad te profeso.

Natividad Perez
Marzo 16 de 02

Tomasa moves with her daughter and her young husband to Chihuahua, through the years lives with this family, with her grandchildren Lázaro, Manuel, Saúl, Soledad, Raúl, Concepción, Salvador, Julieta, Aurora, and Edermida.

"Maybe things were better for my parents in Chihuahua where I was born and where my father had his tailor shop before we came to El Paso," Aunt Chole says. "Our house is on one side and his shop on the other.

"No, *no*," my father says joining us. "The tailor shop is in front and we live in the back."

"Anyway," my aunt says dismissing my father's comment with a wave of the hand, "my father takes me and my dolls to play while he cuts and sews. *Mi padre me adoraba.* I play under a table. At first the *revolución* brings him business, more uniforms to make. The soldiers come saying, '*Mire, maestro.*' But then come the guns."

Tomasa, Lita, Lito, and their three children, Chole, Concha, and Raúl, my father, come to Juárez from Chihuahua by train, bringing only their clothes. They walk across the bridge to El Paso, walk the dusty streets under the weight of the desert sun since without money they can't even afford the lurching streetcar.

My grandmother's sister, Leonor, secures a room for them in the apartment building where she and her family live near Sacred Heart Church. Lita has to cook in her sister's kitchen, but my grandmother gets her small group settled into the room that is their first home in the United States, in el Segundo Barrio. Soon, the family moves to Deming, New Mexico, where Lita's brother, Brígido Pérez, has a tailor shop.

"My uncle is good at making pants," says Aunt Chole, "but he needs my father. Oh, my father is a perfectionist in making coats. ¡Qué sacos sabía hacer! I wish I still had that picture of my father to show you, mi reina, even though I can't see it. He looks so handsome, so well-dressed with his suit and hat, and he had los muchachos in their cashmere suits he'd made for them. They're all dressed up and look so nice.

"He's quite a dancer, mi papá, and he loves classical music, always singing waltzes when he works. He doesn't like the rancheras my mother likes to hear on the radio, 'A - llá en el ran - cho gran - de, a - llá. . . .'"

The family experiences all the pain of the Depression, unpaid bills, bare pantries. The Mora children begin to speak that other language, English, that none of my four grandparents ever speak. As soon as they can, the children begin to work. Lita, who suffers from asthma, is always busy in her home—washing, cleaning, cooking, crocheting, knitting. "Ooo, esa madre mía, es una chispa." my father says. "She works from five in the morning to eleven at night. I've never seen anyone who has the stamina she has, and the courage."

Often Lita makes her children's clothes, sits in the evening basting and softly singing her sadness to herself,

Ay, ay, ay, ay, ya, no hay pa - lo - mas, ni flo - res. . . .

No matter how hard she and her husband work, creditors come banging on their door.

And undertakers come. Her mother Tomasa dies in her nineties in 1939, Lito, on October 22, 1943.

"My father dies at seven one night of a stroke, *un ataque.* My mother always says it is because he'd eaten fish," says Aunt Chole. "*Ay. Mi padre querido era adorable. El hombre más lindo que ha 'vido en el mundo.* He never scolded me. I think there has never been a father in the world like my father, *tan querido.* He is a saint, and he adores you though you never really know him since he dies when you are little."

We dance together again, this white-haired grandfather, my hands up, his hands up, his fingers snapping far above me like brown castanets. Mamá Cleta comes to watch, always ready with her bits of wisdom. "*Este mundo es un fandango, y él que no baile, es un loco.*"

A widow until her death, Lita lives with her daughter Concha's family.

"My mother screams and cries about everything," says Aunt Chole, lowers her voice to a whisper. "One of our cousins would take my mother's hand and say, '*Tía,* let's sit down here and have a good cry together.'"

My siblings and I don't see Lita often, and when we do, she cries so much. Perhaps because she frightens me, I was never close to this grandmother. What to do with all her sighs and tears?

"*Oye, Patsy,*" Aunt Bori says on her way to paint the indigo trim on the side of the house, a color once used to keep away evil spirits. "Mama had another brother. I'm trying to find the name for you, a policeman. One day he was coming down the stairs, and his gun went off, shot off his parts. He died, *m'ija.* I'll try to get you his name."

She walks on, and I ponder her matter-of-fact tone, willing to help me find stories, even bloody ones.

"*AAAYYY!*" the parrot screeches startling me, probably my father watching me jump.

"*Ven,*" says Aunt Chole. "Let's go find my sisters so you can talk to them about my mother. It will make them happy to see you. You go in first so they'll think it was your idea. *Sí, sí, reinita adorada.*"

I look at my father's four sisters, the Mora women who've outlived their two brothers, the women whose hands like their mother's know kitchen secrets, the glue of food, how to hold families together with tortillas and coffee.

"I'm trying to collect family recipes. Do you have any of Lita's? Could you each give me a favorite?"

Why do I crave recipes, seek to know how people who are part of me measure and combine ingredients in this life, how they nourish themselves and those around them, how they define sustenance.

I ask Aunt Julie, "Were you scared of your mother?"

She sighs. "There is only one mother." Aunt Julie laughs, and her three sisters nod.

Aunt Bori, the youngest and tallest, almost six feet, now a grandmother, begins to whimper, even a reference to her mother triggers tears. "I was her baby." She fumbles in her pockets for a tissue.

"I argued with her all the time," Aunt Julie says.

"Did you ever win?"

"No."

"She'd cough and cough, my poor mother," Aunt Chole says. "Yesterday a friend told me she'd cured her asthma. I wish I'd known this when my mother was alive."

"What did your friend do?" Aunt Concha asks.

"The doctor's medicine didn't help, but she bought a Chihuahua, you know, those little dogs, *chihuahuenses*, and that cured her. We could have bought my mother one."

Her three sisters squirm in their chairs, roll their eyes and shake their heads at the proposed dog cure of the sister who for years paced her rooms alone, momentarily resist saying, "But you didn't care about her. You left her, left her, for that other woman."

Aunt Concha whispers, "Just look at my sisters. They need to be out doing more. That's their problem. I'm eighty-two, Patsy. I'm up at five on Saturdays to get to the beauty shop, then grocery shopping and afternoon Mass. Sure I still volunteer! I get awards, and they even put my picture in the paper. I don't see that well, but I do about a thousand volunteer hours a year, so I don't have much patience with all this crying and sighing and complaining. I'm the kind that has to keep busy!"

"*Se esponja como pavo real*," mutters Aunt Chole about the sister who puffs up like a peacock.

Occasionally, I'd spend the night at Aunt Concha's house where my grandmother lived, ache for my quiet home, watch Aunt Concha in her kitchen whipping cream for homemade banana ice cream, dicing fruit for jello salads, her hands flying from bowl to cutting board to electric mixer, these Mora sisters' hands like kitchen butterflies heaping tables with tamales and *buñuelos*.

I'd tiptoe into a bedroom, stare at the artificial arm and hand, the hard, long perfect fingers that could be attached to the aunt whose arm ends at the elbow.

To ease the homesickness in any house but mine, I'd comfort myself with my left thumb, secretly I thought. "*Pónganle ese dedo en jugo de chile jalapeño*," Lita snaps, "*y luego no lo chupa Patricia*." The thumb that fit so perfectly in my mouth shrivels a bit and turns a dusty white in that chile liquid. Thumb and ego bruised, hurt at my grandmother's voice stinging more than the chile, I long to slip out silently like light slips under a door, long for my parents to come and rescue me.

We'd take day trips with Aunt Concha's family to Coudcroft or Ruidoso, the New Mexico forests only two hours away, car trunks full of her fried chicken, potato salad. My sister, Cecilia, and I color in the backseat with our cousins, their cigar box bulging with crayolas.

"Pass me the magenta."

"You color better than I do. You never go out of the lines."

"No, I like yours better. Really."

The air feels cool as a stream when we finally pull ourselves out of the cars, and I return to the haven, my own family. My father, who works from early morning to late at night at his optical company, wraps himself in a blanket, stretches out on the pine needles, takes a deep breath of their green. "I'm going to sleep here like my Indian uncles," he grins as he drifts to sleep, the father who likes to rub his brown arms for my children, say, "Look at this skin, *como mis tíos, los indios.*"

Two cousins suggest we take a walk, and Cecilia and I, two cautious souls, go with them, our hands clenched together, close to one another in the trees, hearing heavy bear paws moving through the bushes and trees behind us. At our older cousin's words, "I think we're lost," I feel flushed, inwardly start to pray. "Please Saint Anthony, let Mother and Daddy find us. Don't let us get lost. Please. Please."

A cloud covers the sun; wind moans through the aspens and pines. I imagine us lost for hours, maybe days, our parents frantic as massive, furred creatures lumber toward us. "Dear God, help us to find our way. Please. Please. Please. Dear Saint Anthony, patron of lost things, please let them find us, help us get back to the cars." Such trips end when we get older.

On January 1, 1965, Lita dies in her eighties.

As the earth warms, tulips, originally called *dulband* by Persians and *tülibend* by the Turks because the blooms resemble turbans upside down, open their red mouths in the garden, gradually reveal themselves, their stems curving like elegant green sculptures.

"My father has a tailor shop right in the center of Chihuahua," my father says as we sit in the *portal*, enjoying the soft sun. "Go get me the papers I drew for you, honey."

"That's okay, Daddy. I'm taking notes."

"Honey, get me the papers."

My father, Raúl Antonio Mora, is born in the city of Chihuahua at one in the afternoon on March 4, 1912, to Natividad Pérez and Lázaro Mora. The official document of the Estados Unidos Méxicanos states that Raúl is born at home, at la calle Ojinaga número 819, his mother, Natividad Pérez, then thirty-two years of age, *"de raza mestiza,"* his father, Lázaro Mora, thirty-five. Their eighth child, the document further states which means that the names of some of the infants who died have been forgotten.

A tiny, baptismal booklet reveals that when the priest pours the purifying water on my father's forehead, *"Ego te baptizo in nomine Patris et Filii et Spiritus Sancti"* he pronounces the child's Christian name as Antonio Casimiro Raúl since March 4 is the feast of chaste San Casimiro. We don't discover the shiny, ecru booklet until after my father dies.

"Good. Now, see here?" my father says. "Here I wrote *Taylor Shop* so you'd know and then *cloth samples* and *English woolens*, three or four workers, three sewing machines. Study this, honey, so you'll understand. Turn the page. Okay, okay. Here is the three-story building where my friend the lonely lady lives, the one who gives me *piloncillo*. I go visit her, and she gives me the brown sugar to suck, probably to keep me quiet. I drew the park here and the Chinese grocers. Here I wrote, 'I could see the shadows at night. Villa's battle.'

"My father has two particular customers, handsome fellows, who come in to get nice clothes made, and I love it when they come because these men let me handle their guns, great big guns with chrome polish. And here—turn the page, honey— I wrote you that a Doctor Trillo would come to my father's tailor shop. See, here I wrote, 'a very heavy & Big man. All I remember of him was his cars great big cars.'

"Read the next page to me. I wrote this all down for you, for your book. I stapled these pieces of scratch paper together and wrote some things down when I had a little free time at work. Don't waste paper, honey. Always use the back."

I read my father's scribbled writing,

> You can imagine my anxiety I wanted
> to know everything that went on in the
> place but every thing was hush *hush*
>
> I was my grandmothers Love She
> always wanted to know how I was
> & what I was doing.

"That's Tomasa, tiny, so tiny *mi abuelita*. We know *la revolución* is getting worse and worse because Lito makes clothes for the military. They order uniforms and then get my father what we needed, meat, half a cow, anything. When Mother and I go to Mass during the revolution, we have to cross a park, dead bodies all over. Every once in a while, I see someone come by and collect the swollen bodies, *pobrecitos*, and throw them into a cart. Those days you don't know if it's Villa or the others who are in town, see? If you're a pacifist, you say that, "*Soy pacífico*," and they won't do anything to you. They ask you, '*¿Quién vive?*' They just ask at random, bunch of soldiers, half-starved.

"In front of our house are some grocery stores owned by some Chinese. One night somebody knocks at our door.

"*¿Quién vive?*"
"*Pacíficos.*"
"Do you have a shovel or an ax so we can break those doors down across the street?"
"*No, no*," Natividad Mora says pushing her small son, Raúl, into another room. "We don't have any weapons, but if you want my sewing scissors, they're on the table."
"*No, no, esas no sirven pa' nada*,' the men say and leave empty-handed.

"Now Mother knows I have a little ax," my father laughs, "and that I'd probably give it to them so she catches me and takes me into another room."
"Do you think it was a hard decision for your parents to leave Mexico?" I ask.
"It is no decision," my father says firmly hitting the small table with his open hand. "It is the law. My mother is the law. When my mother says 'we're leaving,' there's no if's or but's, so my father just does the best he can. He has a lot of woolens, but he just has to leave them. We leave everything and bring only what we're wearing. The whole shebang of us comes to Juárez by train in about 1916 when I'm four. My grandmother, Tomasa Moná-

rrez, comes with us since she lives with us. I am her love," he
laughs. "The sun sets on me, yea, yea.

"Just keep reading, honey. Read it all. I like hearing what I
wrote. Read it, and then I'll tell you more."

> All I remember was that my mother she
> sounded like a General giving orders
> and she went and told my father
> Vasta nos vamos and with in a few hours
> he sold or gave away his belongings
> and we were on our way out
> of Chihuahua.
> Here we come like hungarians
> every one carring somethin on
> our way to the Station
>
> I remember dad getting some
> help & we are on our way to the US.
> Everything was *Pase Pase*
> and get your self moving but
> one way or another we were here
> It was a 70Ø Block of S. Mesa St
> Room # 5 they were 2 rooms My mother
> stardeted to get organized & dad
> to get his equipment ready to go
> to work.
> Before he knew it he had some
> business & this was the begining
> & end off our journey.

"We cross the bridge and get a few rooms on South Mesa,
not that far from the river. It's no problem to cross then."

"Is there fear associated with coming?"

"Fear? Fear? Honey, when Villa asks you questions, it's after
you're dead. If he asks a question and you don't answer fast
enough, he just shoots your ear off. If he doesn't like your an-
swer, he shoots your hand off. He's merciless. Of course, at that
age, I don't know fear, but Mother knows it. At night we see

those poor Chinese across the street leaving their stores, trying to hide because if Villa gets them, he'll kill them. He doesn't like foreigners."

My father smiles, *"Mi abuelita, Tomasa,* gives my father a gold piece to help with the move. Years later if she hears him fret about money she says, *'¿Y luego todo el dinero que te di yo?'* I guess she thought that money would last him forever."

At first Lito uses the corner of one of their rooms for his shop, doing mending and repairs. The Mora family lives next to a small Protestant church on Sixth and Stanton, and my grandfather arranges with the principal of its small school, who is anglo but speaks Spanish, to allow Raúl to attend and learn English in exchange for tailoring. Although the classes are conducted in Spanish, English is also used which helps prepare Raúl for public school in a predominantly Mexican neighborhood. He was just beginning to learn to read in Spanish, and now in El Paso faces a class of about forty and a teacher who says, "Raúl, you read."

"I just start sort of stuttering, and then I turn a few pages at once," he laughs. "The teacher probably knows the whole thing by heart, but she doesn't say anything. I hadn't thought about it until now. I ask myself, well what language am I speaking when I start public school? I guess I've learned enough English by then to be able to use it." He attends Alamo School, Bowie, San Jacinto.

"No, my parents never learn English. 'How are you, Lázaro?' people say, but my father just rocks his hand like this to say so-so. All of us kids begin to speak English, and my mother—*esa mujer*—knows what we're saying, but you can't get her to say a word. If we speak any Spanish at school, we'll get punished, but I don't know if I'm discriminated against. All they have to do is look at me, and they know I'm a Mexican."

Aunt Chole listening from her room comes to join us in the *portal* where we talk and watch the butterflies in the garden. Moving slowly, especially after her fall yesterday, she walks with a hand out to feel for a chair. My father guides her and begins his teasing, saying this is his story, and she's not to interrupt with her lies. "*¿Cómo estás, Chole? Este es mi cuento, ¿eh? No empieces con tus mentiras.*"

She tells me about a school official who hit my father, and how she hated the man; but my father recounts his triumphs, how he started selling newspapers at seven making twenty-one cents his first day, "big money," he says proudly. By nine or ten years old, he has the best corners in El Paso, on the weekend sells both the *Times* and the *Herald*. His grandmother, Tomasa, rises at dawn and helps dress him, but his jobs leave little time for study.

"Now about fighting," my father says, the father often too busy or tired to talk when we're young, who now savors his stories. Mother looks out the door, rolls her eyes and asks, "Does he ever stop?"

"Anyway, anyway," my father says, looks at Mother, "Don't you have something to do, *mujer*? Where was I, honey? Oh yes, the fights."

My father would read the sports page when the paper came out each day and begins seeing references to boxing matches at Fort Bliss. He takes the bus there and notices that men who say, "Press," enter free. A gutsy ten-year-old, he begins to say, "Press," when he enters holding up a handful of newspapers, chuckles now at himself, sitting on those papers to watch his gloved heroes, wondering what the ticket takers thought of the boy he was, is. He didn't like to hit anyone, but he likes watching a good fight.

"It's an art, honey, boxing," he says. "Touch this." He extends his hand. "This is the hand that shook the hand of Jack Dempsey. I probably don't want to wash it that night. I also work for a dairy, *El Vergel*."

"*Vergel*, what does that mean?"

"*Estela*," my father calls out, "*¿Qué quiere decir vergel?*"

"Garden, I think," says our translator, "but I've got my nice big dictionary here, let me check." Aunt Chole smiles her approval at Mother's ease with books. My father cocks his head toward her indicating he gets a kick out of her careful checking, this man who usually likes quick answers.

A milkman who delivers with a wagon and horse offers Raúl a job for all the milk the boy can drink, free hot cakes in the morning and Hershey's in the afternoon. While the man visits his female friend, Raúl drives the wagon himself, guides the horse as he delivers the milk.

At the restaurant where the boy and the amorous delivery-man have breakfast, a Syrian likes to run his hand up Raúl's forearm and tempt him into a fight.

"*Ah*, you're strong," the man says watching the boy's eyes. "*Fuerte, aahh, muy fuerte.*" Every day the man has a new opponent for Raúl, tempts him with, "*¿Le tienes miedo, eh, eh eh?* Afraid? *Está bueno este, ¿eh, eh? ¿Le tienes miedo, eh, eh?*"

"*No, no le tengo miedo.*" Not me, the boy thinks. I'm not afraid of any of 'em.

"*Eh, eh, ¿le tienes miedo, eh? ¿eh?* Scared? *¿Lo quieres pelear, eh, eh?*"

Raúl fights outside with his opponents, not angry, he says, just fighting because he wants to prove he can win. Then one day, the challenger is a bigger boy, heavier than Raúl.

"*Aaahhh, este sí te va a ganar,*" says the Syrian rubbing Raúl's arm, stroking the developing muscles. "*Este muy grandote. ¿Le tienes miedo?*"

"*No, no tengo miedo.*"

"*Aaaaahhhhhh, aaaaahhhhh.*"

Just when Raúl thinks he can't win this match, and his opponent prepares to come down on Raúl with full force and weight, Raúl slips to the right. The other boy hits a wall, and his arm gets limp. Raúl decides to stop his daily fights.

Whatever money the boy manages to make at his various jobs, he takes home to his mother. "I never know not to have money in my pocket," my father says, "and still don't. I give Mother my money, and she gives me some back. Do you do that, honey? You should make your children give you, even if it's just a penny, from their paycheck."

At about twelve years of age, the year that he begins to drive a 1923 Dodge truck to deliver the milk, he wins a 1923 black Ford touring car in a raffle. "I've always been lucky, honey," says my father who lives the adage that we're about as happy in this life as we've decided to be. Proudly, the boy climbs behind the wheel, starts the engine and takes his family out for a ride.

"Ay, Raúl," Aunt Chole chuckles at her brother the trickster, "Always, *puro jugetón*, your father, *mi hermanito querido*. Do you know what he does when we we're young? Whenever someone dies, he puts on a sheet at night knowing I am scared of ghosts. 'Oooooo,' he wails and walks into my room, 'oooooo.' And then I yell, '¡Aaaaaaaaaaaaay!' He loves to scare me to death."

My father and aunt talk about their grandmother Tomasa who when elderly falls in love with voices on the radio, men who brazenly sing her their passion.

"*Qué mi abuelita*," my father says.

I watch my father at eighty remembering his grandmother at ninety, how she sneaks food to put behind the radio for her romantic singers, how she scolds them, "*Sh, sh, ¿qué no ves que te van a oir?*" shushing her ardent, secret loves.

"One time when I'm a teenager," my father says, "*mi abuelita* Tomasa, gets sick, really sick. She can't even sleep so finally we call the doctor to come and see her. He says there is no hope. I hate that guy for those words."

When the doctor leaves, Lita wipes her eyes with her hands, the tears bathing her neck. She tells Raúl and her other children to leave the room and let their grandmother rest. The boy Raúl looks down at his grandmother lying in her bed, her eyes half shut, her small body jerking in exhaustion under the white sheet. I can't let her die, the boy thinks. What am I going to do? I can't let my *abuela* die. She moans.

"*¿Qué quiere, Abuela?*"

"*Estoy tan cansada, Chato*," she whispers, reaching for his hand, says she needs to sleep and can't.

How can she get well if she doesn't sleep? the boy thinks, I'm going to get her up.

"*Abuela, Abuela*," he whispers hoping no one will come into the room and catch him, tell his mother who'd hit him hard for this, but how can he do nothing?

"Ay, ay, *Chato*," she moans, her voice like a wind tired from its

long journey. He places his arms under her armpits and gently
sits her up, his hands supporting her back. Steadying her, a
hand holding her shoulder, her bones, he lifts the sheet away
and begins to swing her thin legs over the mattress but feels
how cold they are.

"Ay, ay, Chato."

"Yo sé, Abuela, yo sé, but we have to do this. You can't die,
Abuela. I won't let you. You have to sleep so you can rest. I have
an idea, sh, sh."

He reaches down with one hand for her slippers, blue chil-
dren's slippers, and puts them on her feet, realizes he has them
on backwards, thinks: who cares? It's not important. He swings
her legs then over the side of the mattress.

"Ay, aaay," each moan that sounds like it comes from some
place far away.

Raúl takes a deep breath not because she'll be heavy to
hold, but because he has to win, and he needs all his energy
for this.

"Ándele, Abuela, se tiene que cansar." Holding on to her elbows,
he stands her, holds her trembling body on her backwards slip-
pers. She's shaking, her eyes half closed, but he won't let go. He
thinks: I'll just hold her up, hold her with all my strength until
I wear her out.

"No se puede morir, Abuela. No."

"Aaahhh, ah," her body trembles, but the boy holds on. "Ah
ah a...." Finally her body goes limp, and he sits her on the
bed, holds the back of her head while he lies her head on the
pillow, her mouth open, her breath heavy, "A   a   a."

He puts her legs back up, pulls off the slippers. He thinks:
she's too close to the edge. If she rolls over, she'll fall off, so the
boy pulls the sheet off again, lifts his grandmother in his
arms, the woman light, like a pillow. He covers her, brings a
chair and puts it next to the bed so she won't fall out, his tiny
abuela.

He looks down, watches her. But is she breathing?

He studies her chest and her mouth.

"¿Qué 'stás haciendo?" his mother asks making him jump.

"Didn't I tell you to leave your poor grandmother alone? Don't you understand how sick she is? Now get to bed."

"The next morning," my father says, "I go to check on her, and Tomasa's bed is empty. I get so scared. I think: she died, *mi abuelita* who loved me so much is gone, and they've taken her body. I feel awful.

"Then I hear pans in the kitchen. I walk in there, and there's *mi abuela* cooking eggs and *chorizo*. She lives another five years." He grins.

He begins to win circulation prizes from the newspaper, sweaters, knives. While other employees fear going to the South side, Raúl who has lived there begins adding new delivery routes in the Mexican area, notices the tricks of those around him who have more schooling, always trying to learn. During the Depression, the teenager handles circulation for *El Continental*, the Spanish newspaper, and makes a hundred dollars a week with his commission.

"I'm a rich man, honey. That's a lot of money then."

Always teasing with the women in the office, he begins to hear from them that Anglos are coming to take over the newspaper. No one says anything officially, but his friends tell him that there's talk about starting a newspaper in English. Raúl, who starts seeing some new men in the building, doesn't like the way they look at him.

One day when he stretches out a newspaper on a bench for a quick nap during his lunch hour, one of the new men comes by and kicks Raúl's knee.

"You know me, honey. That's it. I don't let anyone look down on me, so I just quit. They can't believe it."

With the money he's saved, two or three hundred dollars which he equates with two or three thousand today, he attends Gardner's Business College, studies typing, shorthand, and commercial business. A teacher who takes an interest in Raúl wants him to erase his frown, to smile and show people his personality.

"Why are you so mad?" the teacher asks.

"I'm not mad," the young man responds. "That's just the way I am."

"Then why are you frowning, smiiile."

When Raúl can no longer afford the business college, he learns typesetting at the local vocational school, works fixing car batteries. Since the acid eats holes in his pants and he can't afford a new pair, he waits until it's dark outside to start home.

Aunt Chole, who takes pride in guiding people, as she approaches ninety is still anxious to give the young her *consejos*, to help her relatives with what she's learned the hard way, says she secured the first job that began my father's optical career through a friend. My father's story, however, is that one day while washing his car wondering what work he'll find after leaving the newspaper, a man walks by and asks Raúl if he wants to learn the optical business.

Through the years, my father learns about vision and the movement of light, about how light passes into us forming reverse images of all we see, the world upside down in our eyes. He learns about blurred sight and focus, about reflective surfaces—the eye and glass, about refraction, the bending of light, about the power of the lens.

He works at Riggs Optical, a subsidiary of Bausch & Lomb, for over ten years, during which time he marries my mother in 1939, and becomes an American citizen in 1941. The naturalization certificate describes him as: age-29, sex-male, color-white, complexion-dark, eyes-dk. brown, hair-black, height-5´10˝, weight-168.

World War II begins, and the children. My father isn't drafted since his optical work for the army base in town is considered part of the war effort. In 1949, he opens his own company, the United Optical. Like his mother, my father works long hours the years he owns his optical business on Myrtle and later on Texas Street. He leaves on the bus when we we're in elementary school so my mother can have the car to chauffeur us around. He calls when he can come home for dinner, and often he returns to work again in the evening.

"Work, work, work, that was Daddy's life," Cecilia says. Days he grinds lenses, hand-cuts the pattern, drills the holes, checks the thickness with calipers, checks the prescription with the vertometer, heats the temples in white salt to adjust them, pushes himself and his employees, many of them his relatives who cringe when he starts yelling to get the work done, to get the jobs out faster.

"Where are the jobs for Schuster? What do you mean they're not finished yet. ¡*Tito!* ¡*Tito!* ¿*Qué voy hacer con este muchacho?* ¡*TITO!*"

He yells, always competing with the newer, slicker, larger opticals, until in the early sixties, after years of supporting our family, he has to declare bankruptcy. A man with four children, the eldest in college, has to begin again.

"It was the second time I saw Daddy cry," Cecilia says. "The first time is at the cemetery at his mother's burial. The second is when he has to close United Optical. From the window in our room, I see him carrying boxes down into the basement, and tears are sliding down his face. I don't know what to do."

The privateness of grief.

My father's embodied life is probably lengthened when he begins dispensing for an ophthalmologist in Santa Monica, then finally opens his own dispensing business.

He knew how to savor life's small pleasures, my father. He'd stand at the small apartment kitchen window and look out. I thought I knew what he was seeing—what I saw—two Italian cypresses, palm trees, an average street, a few cars driving by, a few owners walking their dogs, nothing special. Way in the distance, hardly visible, the Pacific Ocean ebbs and flows. "Just look out this window, honey," he says. "Where else can you get a view like that? This is the best breeze in the world."

In the mid-eighties, a cancerous kidney is removed that seems to cause no permanent damage, only an indented place in his side reveals the scar. "My fat saved me, really honey. It just surrounded that cancer and didn't let it spread."

January 2, 1988, he sends me a note he scribbles at work, something he did only once.

El indio viejo no pelea pero hace flechas.

—*Confucius Mora*

I don't know if my father read this or if he composed it, the image of the old Indian who no longer fights but still helps by making arrows.

In time the four of us say to one another, "Daddy's rent is more than what he's bringing in. He likes his routine, walking to the office, a few patients, puttering with the frames, a cup of tea with an office neighbor, a walk home to lunch with Mother, a little rest, back to the office, home at five. What will he do all day at the apartment? He and Mother will drive each other crazy."

"You can rest now, Daddy," we say. "You've worked all your life."

"He sounds tired, worried, not quite himself," we say to one another. "If he visits a strange house, he gets lost in it."

"We'll move his desk and equipment to the apartment, set up his office there."

Reluctantly my father closes Mora Optical in 1991. Stella and her husband try to create an office in my parents' spare bedroom, put up what her father had on the office walls, pictures of his children and grandchildren, his certificates from the California Society of Ophthalmic Dispensers. Mother looks around at the disorder in every room, feels annoyance at her disrupted quiet and space, but also says, "*pobrecito, pobrecito.*"

"You can rest now, Daddy. You've worked all your life."

I look up and see Aunt Chole rubbing her bruises from yesterday. "No, no, I'm all right, *corazón querido.* You know how I like to water early."

"Aunt Chole, I thought you didn't go out alone anymore."

"*Sh,* don't tell. I have to do everything *a escondidas.* Anyway, *reina,* I didn't see that hole. My clothes get all wet, and I can't pull myself out. Finally, I crawl until I can hold something and pull myself up. No one is around, *ee-ee.* When I touch my head, I feel all these lumps.

"When was I happy?" She repeats my question. "Totally happy? Probably never. My sister has been happy. *Ay, los detalles de la vida*, life's details. You want to hear about that man? I was happy then. He was an orator. Have you ever heard *declamación?* It's poetic recitation, but with feeling, real feeling. I just call him that day to say thank you, that's all, with esteem. I've been so sad for so long. He doesn't know. How can he, *reinita?* He brings me so much happiness, even though it's just mentally. He doesn't know I'm not educated. I can't say it without crying. I never finished school. How could I? I feel I'm the dumbest in the house." She starts to whimper.

"Want a cup of tea before you go to bed, Tía," I ask when I see her touching the kitchen counters.

"*Sí, mi amor*, that would be so nice. Listen to that wind. I hope we're not going to have one of our dust storms, *marzo airoso.*" I imagine the dust devils spinning across the desert.

"Smell these, Aunt Chole. I'm starting them now for the herb garden—mint, oregano, thyme, lavender." I pinch a leaf from each between my fingers, bruise the leaves to release the volatile oils, the source of their green fragrance.

"*Mmmmm*," my aunt says savoring each scent. "Let me touch each herb, *mi reinita*, see if I can feel the difference. *Ay*, so many people have been nice to me in my life, thank God. Once when I was a young girl, my cousin feels sorry for me, the one who has 'heimers now like your uncle had when he hits your aunt not knowing what he's doing.

"My cousin notices that my shoes are worn out, sad shoes. So what do you think she does? We wear the same size so she gives me this pair of red shoes, high heels. Now how can I use those to work, *reina?* I try to dye them black, but the material won't take the dye. Imagine, red shoes. What to do with them? They're for night, but she's trying to be nice, *corazón.*

"I'm going to bed now," Aunt Chole says finishing her tea. "I have to get up early. They're taking me out tomorrow, my sisters."

I hear her talking to herself in her room, planning every move so as to take care of herself, so as not to embarrass herself, so as not to be a burden. Her sisters are taking her out to lunch, away from the space she hardly ever leaves. She rises early, pulls on her hose, pants, buttons her blouse, ties her shoes, everything takes so long. She plans what to order—fish, rules out meat since she can't see to cut it, no appetite for a long time. She misses it like you miss a neighbor you've had for years, but she just wants to be able to walk, to take care of herself, her voice, sad now.

"I've been fine," she says in the evening. "I didn't make any mistakes so I must be better. But I can't see anybody anymore. I can't see anything clearly, nothing, nothing.

"The other day I saw a shape outside. He must have a red hat. I call out, 'Excuse me, sir, are you a policeman?' He says he works with the city, that they are fixing some walls. They work hard, *reinita*, so I tell him I'll have ice-cold water ready for them. They come and tell me when they finish, very late. I think they clean and rake everything, so nice. *Ay*, God is good to me, *mi amor*."

March, month of the vernal equinox, the Awakening Moon, days gradually lengthening again, warm afternoons for repotting houseplants, the spathyphilium, hearts and flowers. Green feasts of Saint Patrick and Saint Joseph, in the month that hints of re-birth, *varitas de San José*, hollyhocks will bloom soon again near gold mud walls, infused with light.

March twenty-first, spring, and the earth behaves accordingly—forsythia splashes adobe courtyards yellow, daffodils nod when I walk by, narcissus scent the air, gray chamisa and bare trees unfurl their green dreams; velvet pansies, in Lenten purple, once called heart's ease, *pensamientos* in Spanish, ponder deep purple thoughts. Tulips blare, daffodils lift their round faces to the sun, apricot trees—unable to contain their joy— swing their white-veiled arms, and the river out back rushes, swirls into spring, spring.

"How old are you this month, Daddy?" He's reading the

newspaper in the garden, relaxing on the wrought-iron bench under the cottonwood. He chuckles. "How old would you be?" I ask.

"I don't have to count that way any more. I can be any age and any shape I want. Watch." My transparent father stretches and widens into a giant cottonwood, deeply furrowed trunk; wide, bending branches, but I see his eyes, brimming mischief, winking at me as birds leave the chattering fountain and fly into his arms. I've thought of him as a tree since his death, those green songs of praise, an *álamo* or, of course, a *mora*; trees—life's largest living creature, in the fullest sense, a tree of life. When one falls, a crashing sound and then an emptiness against the sky. And yet, life continues in them; matter transformed into energy, burned to light. Trees, sacred in ancient Egypt and prized in any arid landscape, house life as my teasing father now holds chirps and whistles in his leafy hands.

"Come back here," I say, and he—the tree—takes a slow step toward me, birds bursting startled from the branches. "It's Lent. Behave, Daddy!" Reluctantly, the shape-shifter returns to his human form, sits next to me.

March twenty-fifth, the feast of the Annunciation, "*Dios te salve, María, llena eres de gracia, El Señor es contigo,*" the "Hail Mary" repeated and repeated by our grandmothers and great-grandmothers sitting and sewing on this gray day by an altar covered with flickering candles, smoke and their prayers ascending, "*O Dios, que quisiste que tu Verbo tomase carne en el vientre de la Bienaventurada Virgen María.*"

"What are they saying?" my sister, Stella, asks.

"Literally they're saying, 'Oh God, who desired that your Verb become flesh in the womb of the blesséd Virgin Mary,' but listen to the use of the word *verb*, that Christ is to *be*, animate, and in Spanish *encarnación* reverberates because of the *carne* embedded in the word, flesh, meat."

"English majors!" she says waving good-bye.

Sw, sw, sw, sweeping the *portal,* Lobo softly sings "*La Zan-*

dunga," her high voice trembling, breaking like crystal water cascading gently in the mild sun, "*laaaaaa - la - la - la.*"

My niece, Niki, when she was little, walks in measured, regal steps down each of the four garden paths and circles the fountain wearing Abuela Elena's long cloth on her head. I watch Abuela Elena guide my father to a chair in the sun.

"*¿Qué quiere, Abuela Elena?*" He notices the bowl his great-grandmother is carrying. "It smells like onion," he says.

She smiles. "*Sí, jugo de cebolla, m'ijo.* Sit here in the sun. I'll rub this on your bald head and soon you'll have hair again."

"*Nooo,*" he says pulling away, pulling away from this short woman, but she is firm; in a matter of seconds has her great-grandson seated, his eyes closed while she rubs the pale liquid into the brown skin at the top of his head.

I walk out back, over the *acequia,* watch a roadrunner dart through the vegetable patch. I continue down toward the river, a moving mirror, see Lito teaching my three children when they were little to make small adobe bricks, the word, *adobe,* one of the many words in Spanish of Arabic origin, from *at-tōba* meaning "the brick." Growing up, I was unaware of this influence on Spain, that even *mora* can mean Moorish woman, unaware that cultural purity is a myth.

"What are you kids doing?" I ask watching their pleasure in pressing the earth mixed with water and straw into the small wood molds made by their great-great-grandfather, tape measure protruding from his pant pocket. They proudly show me their six muddy hands saying, "Don't tell Dad."

"Lito says we need to let the bricks dry, and then we can make a little adobe play house," Libby says.

"And when we're too big for it, my cats can live in it. I'm going to have about a hundred," says Cissy.

"Yea, sure Cis," her older brother says.

"I am. Just you wait."

I stare out at the mesas to the west, at the familiar river sliding by us. So much of comfort in life is the familiar, the muck from which we've built this adobe house from the old river of deep memories, the fertile unconscious, memories of a purple tree scent on a warm afternoon, the sound of a prayer or a sonata, the coolness of old fingers, the taste of a warm *bizcocho*, my father's voice.

I walk back and sit under the garden cottonwood with my aunts, the Mora sisters, feeling the tensions between them, the different lives they chose, the bodies fate gave them. They talk about their mother, her hands always busy, crocheting or cooking, about her crying, the grandmother who seasons her food with tears, *recetas de lágrimas*. I ask again for any stories, cures, prayers, recipes.

"There nothing Mama can't do in the kitchen, *m'ija*," her daughters say.

"Abuela Tomasa had a *metatito*," says Aunt Chole, "and she and my mother grind pumpkin seeds to make *pipián*, make *galletitas y gorditas y sopaipillas y menudo y tamales y champurrado*."

"Where's the *champurrado?*" my father asks conveniently appearing at talk of food, savoring the thought of the warm, thick drink, the mixture of *masa harina*, *piloncillo*, and Mexican chocolate.

"*No empieces*," the quartet of his sisters warns. "We're talking to Patsy."

"*Pero panza llena, corazón contento*," my father says. His sisters ignore his words, wave him away.

"Mama makes great *mole*, Aunt Julie says. "It's not like that *mole* you buy in jars. We peel the almonds because she makes everything from scratch. She gets out the onions and starts frying them and adds sesame seeds and chocolate and tomato, two kinds of red chile, and toasted tortillas to give the *mole* body."

"*Nunca, nunca, comí mole como el de mi madre*," Aunt Chole says wistfully. "And her tortillas, not like the store kind. She presses them with one of those old black irons until they're toasted, *doraditas, doraditas*." Lita's daughters drift to their childhood kitchen, the taste of food seasoned by their mother's hands and tears.

"That's how Lita shows her love for us too," my sister, Cecilia, says sitting with us, "through food, like the tamales she makes for Christmas."

"Do any of you have her cookie recipe?" I ask. "Can you look through your recipe boxes and see if maybe one of you jotted it down? I remember her cookies," think to myself, you would. Little, I watch Lita at our kitchen table cutting the dough, her hair and face each a tight knot, dark hands handling the dough with ease.

"Oh, her animal cookies," Aunt Chole says. "I tried to get the recipe, *corazón santo*, but *mi mamá* would just say that she added a little bit of this and a little bit of that."

Abril lluvioso / Rainy April

THE DAYS warm this month, the last days of Lent, then Palm Sunday, the return to the Passion of Christ, to shrouded statues, Peter and the crowing cock, Judas and the dry kiss, Pilate and his compulsive hand-washing, the Stations of the Cross, the beating, the blood streaming from the head crowned with thorns, the Seven Last Words, "I thirst," and the wrenching, *"Eli, Eli, lama sabachtani?"* the despair of the forsaken Christ.

The month everything changed.

My father wakes slowly, and the tears spill out. He feels he's dissolving, bones and muscle melting into the two small rivers born in his eyes. He dries his face with the flowered sheet, careful not to wake his wife who frowns at mornings. He walks barefoot to the living room, sags onto the sofa, the two rivers flowing slowly down his cheeks, down his chins. He doesn't know the time, doesn't care.

Mother wakes, wonders what she's hearing from the living room. What is that sound?

H-h-h-h-h.

"Raúl? Raúl?"

No answer but the sighing sound continues, like a wind that has lost its way. The sound abruptly brings her to full consciousness. She pulls the covers back, gets out of the large bed and walks her knock-kneed walk slowly across the bedroom and down the short hall to the living room. She sees her sev-enty-nine-year-old husband on the sofa. Crying.

"What's the matter, Raúl? Did somebody call? Are the kids okay? What's the matter? Tell me." Her stubborn husband shakes his head. Mother sees his body drooping like a tree that has forgotten the taste of water. The sight softens her. "Come on now, Daddy," she sits next to him and pats his hand, "tell me what's the matter."

"I'm going crazy," he says and wipes his wet face, "crazy, and I don't want to be a burden to my family."

"Now, Daddy, why do you say that? Did you have a night-mare? Is that it? You're fine. Let's make some coffee." He shakes his head and continues crying. "You'll see your patients here. Is that it? Are you worried about closing your optical?"

Something has changed. She goes to the phone and calls the daughter who lives nearby. "Stella, you better come over. There's something wrong with your father."

Since Mother calls often, Stella isn't worried at first and says, "But Mom, can it wait a little? I'm in the middle of some work."

"No, I think you better come now."

Stella rushes over, walks up the white steps she's known since she arrived in Santa Monica as a teenager. Her father sits on the orange sofa in his gray and blue pajamas, no teeth, no toupee, a sagging man, not the teasing man, not the impatient man, not the careful man who always dressed up in a nice coat and tie for his children. Her father is crying like a baby.

"Dad, what's the matter?"

The rivers flow and flow, the release bathing his face. "Don't take me to a hospital. Don't put me in a hospital. Don't put me away."

"Dad, let's get you dressed," my sister, the nurse, says, her face and voice calm. "Come on. Let's get out of this apart-ment and go for a ride." What happened she asks herself? They dress him, put him in the front seat of the car, can tell he's disoriented, not completely sure where he is. Stella thinks: he's had a little stroke, thinks: I've got to get him to his doctor.

My brother, Roy now Anthony, arrives, the whispered conversations begin. My father eats, part of my father eats, part presses inside against walls we can't see. Medications and more medications. Mother's phone calls. "I don't know what I'm going to do with him." Doctor visits. The words "acute depression" written on his chart.

"I'd call you, Daddy, when you got sick," I say later, when he's better.

"I know, honey, I know," he says patting my hand. "I know what you are."

Good days he teases again, "Why's everybody worried about me? Just look at these muscles." I serve him coffee and sweet rolls. "We're so lucky," he says. "There are people starving, *y unos son güeritos, pobrecitos.*"

But he begins to see things, "Look, over there in those flowers, honey. Don't you see the matador?" Objects lose their meaning, visual agnosia. He holds a can of shaving cream, finally asks, "What's this for?" We hide anything that might confuse or hurt him, razors, scissors. He sees small crawling things. "See them, see those roaches?"

"No, Raúl, where?"

"*No seas tonta, mira, mira.* Look at all those roaches."

At night Mother hears him. "This is going to kill me!" she mutters dragging herself again out of her warm bed to see where he is, what he's up to. "Raúl! It's two-o'clock in the morning! What are you doing?"

He holds a can of bug spray. Points to a corner, whispers, "The roaches."

Her phone conversations become interrupted by calling out to him whenever he's out of her sight. "Raúl, what are you doing in the kitchen? Tell me, Raúl."

"Just a minute, honey," she says into the phone receiver, "I'd better go see what your father is doing."

"No, Raúl. Don't be turning the burners on. I know you want to help with lunch, but I'm not going to cook now. Come over here and talk to Patsy on the phone. It's Patsy, Patsy."

Later Mother walks into the bathroom finds towels all over

the floor. "Raúl! What is this? Why did you throw towels all over the floor?"

"The water," he says. "It's spilling out from the bathtub. We've got to stop it, soak it up."

Mother goes to her room, stares in the mirror and opens her mouth into a silent yell. She picks up the phone and calls my sister, my brother. We worry about her, ache at the adjustment she's having to make, losing the quiet and tidiness of her apartment, slowly losing her husband, watching him disappear. He's in there, locked in that familiar body, but language must find its way through a labyrinth. We wonder if he knows.

At first he can still remember the past though communicating is more difficult. "What's that game the British play?" he asks motioning with his hands as if aiming to ring a small iron post.

"Horseshoes?"

"Yes."

"And what about the one like golf but with a bigger ball."

"Croquet, Daddy?"

He smiles, pleased at our accomplishment, says, "Between the two of us we can make out the language. I give you a hint, and you get it right and give me a hint."

Mother calls, alarmed, saying my father doesn't recognize her, that he's sure his wife is in New York and he's going to the airport.

"Raúl, it's me. It's me, Estela."

"I've got to go find my wife."

"Come quick, Stella," Mother calls my sister, "your father is out in the middle of the street. I can't get him to come in."

Stella calls my brother and races over, praying at each stoplight, "Don't let him get hurt, don't let him get hurt." She turns the corner and sees her father. He stands alone in the middle of the street in a T-shirt and pajamas, the one long strand of hair to cover his bald spot sticks out wildly from his head.

"Daddy, what are you doing out here?" Dressed in suit and heels, she takes her father firmly by the arm and guides him toward the apartment. "Let's go inside."

"There are smugglers in there, honey. Don't go in there. It's dangerous."

"Daddy, I was just in there. There's no one in there. Come on. Let's go together."

"I know something, but I can't tell you," he whispers. "Ever. It's a secret of the Knights of Columbus. I can't tell. I promised."

"He needs to go to the hospital," the doctors say.

"You don't know him," Stella says. "He'll fight you. You'll have to strap him down. It happened when they removed his kidney, a reaction to a medication. He was convinced that when we'd leave some Japanese workers would come in and build furniture in his room. I'm afraid hospitalizing will make things worse."

"He needs to be hospitalized. We've put him on so many medications. We want to try taking him off of them, detoxing and then doing more tests."

Stella, Anthony, and mother take him to the hospital. They chat to distract him, the man alone in the middle of his family.

"Hi, Mr. Mora. How are you?" A doctor says.

"Fine, fine."

"Mr. Mora, who's the president of the United States?"

"They've already asked me these questions."

The doctor laughs. "That's right, Mr. Mora. I bet we have asked you these questions. Where did you go to school, Mr. Mora?"

"The school of hard knocks."

Everyone laughs. "Pretty good, Daddy," Stella says patting his shoulder. "Pretty good."

He looks around and smiles at all of them, the doctors who keep asking him to take his clothes off, at his wife, his daughter, his son, glad to have done something right.

The faces around him change. "How are you feeling today, Mr. Mora?"

"Fine, fine. They're waiting for me out there, my patients, nice ladies."

"Your father thinks the other patients in this psych unit are his optical patients. At first he wouldn't attend the current events class we have in the morning. Now he started coming. We always ask them the date, and your father glances at the newspaper so that he can give us the right answer."

"*Ooooooo*, was I popular there with the ladies, honey," he tells me later, when he's better. "They'd have us walk around the place. I guess for exercise. There aren't many men so women are always holding my hand on the walks. As soon as one lets go, another walks up and takes my hand. That's okay. I figure it makes them happy, *pobrecitas*."

"We want to do an MRI on your father tomorrow morning," the doctors tell my sister, "see if we can find any physical cause for the massive trauma he has experieneced."
"It won't hurt, Daddy. You can just take a little nap when they slide you into a big machine."
When he comes out of the room he's grinning. "Honey! Honey! I did it! I'm the first Mexican to go into outer space! *¡VIVA MÉXICO!*"

"When you leave," he says, "they stick me in an icebox at night."
My sister finds a nurse. "I think my father's cold at night. He thinks you put him in an icebox."

"We tried to do a sleep disorder test on your father, but he rips the electrodes off."

At the end of their daily visit, Stella and Mother smooth his hair, straighten his pajamas. "Remember, family is the most important thing," he says. My sister digs her nails into her palms to keep from crying. "If you don't have family, you don't have anything," her father says. "Remember that. Sometimes one falls down and needs help, and you have to give them a hand and help them up." Silence. "I can't help anybody up anymore," he says, and the rivers flow again down his sagging cheeks. "I just want the family to stay together."

"It's like a faulty radio signal," Stella says. "Sometimes the signal is clear, and then he's fine and we're all sure he's on the mend, and then the signal fades, and he hears only static, I think, and then he's not himself anymore. Books say dementia is like a roller coaster ride for the caregiver. There are real plateaus, people stabilize."

He seems better, talking about improving after his illness. "Before when I was sick, I was doing what I thought was right," he says probably referring to running out in the street in his pajamas away from the smugglers. "I'd been doing what I thought was right for seventy-five years." Maybe his body and mind are healing, we tell ourselves.

He's teasing my nephew again, his youngest grandson, Christopher, swatting him lightly on the bottom when he walks by or pulling his hair, "the baby."

"Stop it, Papa," Christopher says. "I mean it. Stop it."

"*Ándele, ándele, qué muchacho este.*"

"How are you doing, honey," he asks when I visit, fighting tears every minute I'm with him. "When I get better, I'm going to read your poems."

"I'm working on my writing," I say wondering if my parents were disappointed when I left a safe university title and salary, decided to write and speak full-time.

"We all know our medium," my father says. "What we do best. It's like baseball. One throws this way and one throws that." With totally open hands, my parents gave me my life.

He disappears, walks out of the apartment one day. My sister calls the police, hospitals, calls me long distance. "We can't find Daddy."

"What do you mean you can't find Daddy. Where is he?"

"He must have walked out. I'll call you as soon as we know anything." I watch the clock, frantic. People go in and out of the apartment looking for him, and then someone happens to glance up the stairs to the next landing. There he stands, has been standing, while people ran in and out looking for him. He has been watching but doesn't know how to move his feet, how to walk down the white steps to his door.

When I visit, I sense he wants to diminish clutter in his life, nervous around too many people, too much food. "No, honey, I told you I wasn't very hungry. Don't give me that much. What am I supposed to do with all that food?"

My father, who has always liked reading the newspaper, picks up the paper and stares at the front page. "I need to go to work, honey. What's today?"

"Saturday, Daddy," I lie. "You don't work on Saturdays anymore, remember?"

"*Ooooooo*, it's always Saturday or Sunday, honey. When's Monday?" He looks at the newspaper. I watch his eyes, wonder if the letters still form into words for him.

> saturdays and sundays wont stop
>   they knock me
> down like i knock
>   men down nights in
>   just a jab of my   dreams
>   wheres monday

"Rest, it's Sunday.
You've been sick."

> where did i put
> the clean walk to the shirt and tie, *dónde*
>   where did i
>   put unlocking the week,
>   thumbing through monday and

drawers   opening   papers looking for
                    checking around lenses   dreams and frames
        for   where did i
              put it   wheres monday

"Rest, it's Sunday.
You've been sick."

                  what was i talking about
              oh yes, about that kid, just let any punks try
        look at these muscles   this kids always been a fighter

              last time i hit someone
                                    maybe fifteen
              where did i put that kid
                                          almost eighty
        but   ready   to knock anyones block
        off   for her   she says i throw punches
              nights in my   just jabs   dreams
                  where is it   where did i put monday

"Rest, it's Sunday.
You've been sick."

                  this newspaper says
              where have i been   where
        i am its always   saturday or   sunday
              where did i put that monday kid

              i ll sit read the paper
        what whats his name is doing
                    in the white house   the
              headline

              who set this type   i did   back then
        set   just a jab of my   did i tell you my
                  what was i talking about

dreams   letter by letter
dónde   wheres monday

"Rest, it's Sunday.
You've been sick."

this is my favorite chair
this is my newspaper
but the letters
where did i put   what was i
all mixed up
where was   i
when   they   moved

April 1993, his eyes seldom dance now, most of the mischief
gone, much of the time he stares forward, eyes stiff.

"He worked all his life so we have to keep him busy," Mother
says. "It's so sad. Your sister has good ideas. First she brings him
coins to sort for her. Now we give him a deck of cards, and he
just moves them on the table, or he keeps busy cutting the
newspaper, and we give him paper and chalk. The other night I
woke up to find him shining a flashlight in my face. The day be-
fore I found him in front of the mirror cutting a piece of his
hair. Today he wouldn't go to the bathroom. I called your sister.
She's so good with him, talks him into doing what he should."

I dream I'm at a desk and Cissy, my youngest, is a little girl
playing with a tiny, silver screw that holds temples onto eye-
frames, the kind of screw that can fit under your fingernail, that
my father would sit at his optical lab and turn with quick preci-
sion. I begin to cry, that tiny silver object bringing my father
back to me, the father I'm losing. In the dream, my daughter
sees my face, begins to cry because I'm sad. "No, no," I say. "I'm
fine, honey, see? Mom's not crying anymore."

I fly to California again, feel that for years I've been taking the
last flight to see my father, blinking back tears, know my parents

and I will sit and visit at their dining room table, the trio of my infancy.

My siblings and I console ourselves and one another saying, "But he's not suffering; he's not in pain. He doesn't know, does he? I can't stand it if he knows in there." We look for hope in his every sentence, try to believe he has been spared a clear sense of loss. Mother and I rent Disney movies for him, and every few minutes she mutes the sound to explain what the dogs in the movie are doing. "Aren't they cute, Daddy? *Mira al perrito.*" She tells me that her wish has been granted, that he will go first because he couldn't have handled her bossy children who would have ordered him around.

"Your mother read me your new book, honey," he looks over at me and says. "What I feel is more than I can express."

He comes toward me with money shoved into the waistband of his pajamas, still slips me a hundred dollars when no one's looking because he thinks I need it. We get him dressed up to go to a nice restaurant. "Thank you," he says, "thank you, honey," when we button his shirt, zip his pants, buckle his belt. "Thank you, thank you, honey." He looks down at us as we tie his shoes, and I think, how can this have happened to you? Don't be embarrassed, please. Don't be embarrassed. This isn't your fault.

"Look at these flowers, honey," he says as we drive along. At the table, he looks around and there are brief moments when he smiles. "Isn't this nice, honey?"

We cut his food trying not to embarrass him, notice that he has forgotten what to do with the piece of broccoli in his mouth. He struggles to remember what is on his tongue and how it got there, how to get rid of it. Stella calmly takes a napkin and removes the green object from his mouth. "That's okay, Daddy. Did you see the boats out the window?"

When my father can still go out, but the world has changed for him, like a movie when the projector fails, the sound and movement garbled, distorted; he paces back and forth in the apartment hours before it's time to leave.

"When are we going?"

"This afternoon, Daddy. We'll get you ready."

"When are we going?"

"Later, Daddy, later."

"When are we going?"

"When . . . ? When . . . ? When . . . ? Well, you'd better rush your mother. You know how she is. '¡Estela! ¡Estela! Ya nos vamos.'" He sticks his tongue out and winks at me, knowing he's needling her.

"Now don't you start on me, Raúl." Frowning, she ambles down the hall as she says her father did,   one   step at   a   time. "I haven't even brushed my teeth yet, and I'm going to have my coffee."

So he'll be less agitated, we wait until it's almost time to leave before we help my father dress, button his shirt, tie his shoes.

He's pacing again in the apartment, faster and faster from the living-room sofa to the cabinet at the end of the hall, sofa to cabinet, cabinet to sofa, until he's almost running, his body tipped forward, his thin legs barely able to hold him up now. Nurses begin to come to bathe him.

"Where are you going?" he asks his wife.

"Just to get my hair done and to get some groceries. I'll be back soon. Someone's always here with you, Daddy."

"It's the pharmacist. You've fallen in love with the pharmacist."

"Raúl, don't be ridiculous. I take a lot of medicine so I go to the drug store." He looks down, and she begins to go out less and less. "He gets scared if he can't see me. Such a good man. This is driving me crazy. We're both going crazy."

Mother calls. "Pat, your dad won't get out of bed."

"Let me talk to him, Mom. Hold the phone to his ear. Daddy, this is Pat. I want you to do me a favor. Will you do that, Daddy? I want you to do me a favor. I want you to get up. Will you do that, Daddy? Get up and have some breakfast, then if you want you can go back to bed, okay?

"Mom, Mom, now go put a Neil Diamond record on." Neil Diamond makes my father happy. When he closes his eyes and won't get up, Neil's music lures him out of his dark place.

Sweet Car - o - line, good times . . . .

Gradually my father opens his eyes, agrees to get up, to go to the dining-room table, agrees to drink a little coffee, chew some toast. The music seeps in

We're com - in' to A - mer - i - ca . . . .

He begins to snap his fingers,

What a beau - ti - ful noise . . .

taps Mother on the shoulder, his eyes beginning to dance again. He grins, toothlessly. On good days the music lifts his body, and he begins to dance again, dances in his pajamas to

Song sung bl - ue . . . .

I look for my father in every man over eighty. In an art museum, I study the eyes of an old man in a Chinese painting, eyes heavy, slack, closing. I imagine my father's life moving across his closing eyelids—the boy born in Chihuahua later selling newspapers on a downtown corner of a border town, the young circulation manager at a Spanish-language newspaper, the man falling in love with my short, feisty mother while he learns about optics, the father of four who opens his own optical company and years later goes bankrupt, leaves town to send money to his rock home, moves to California where he takes deep breaths saying, "Isn't this beautiful, honey? Just look at the view from this kitchen window. These cypress trees are like the ones we had back in El Paso, remember? The ocean's out there. Imagine." That man. My father.

The walks stop. He gets thinner and thinner. Every morning my mother listens before she opens her eyes to hear if her husband still breathes next to her.

"Maybe you should sleep in another bed, Mother."
"I can't, honey. It would hurt his feelings."

A priest comes to administer what used to be the sacrament
of Extreme Unction, now the Anointing of the Sick, a healing
rite. He stands over my father's body that lies all day in his bed,
anoints his hands with holy oil, "May the Lord forgive you by
this holy anointing and His most loving mercy whatever sins
you have committed . . ."

Days, my father sits, naps. At night he falls asleep in the re-
clining chair while Mother watches the news in English and
then in Spanish. She looks over at this man with whom she's
fought for over fifty years, who drives her crazy now with his
questions, who's dying.

"Come on, Daddy," she says after the late-night news. "Time
for bed." It's hard for her to pull his big frame from the chair.
She tugs singing, "One, two, three a - lery, four, five, six a - lery,"
to coax him up, their nightly ritual, a game.

Once she has him upright, she puts his hands on the back of
her shoulders to guide him to their room. "Time for our train,
Daddy. Hold on tight now. Ready?" My short mother begins to
sing again as she moves slowly across the living room with my
disappearing father's hands on her shoulders, the two move
down the hall to their room. "Here we go, 'Ví - bo - ra, ví - bo - ra,
de la mar.' " .

For two years, his mind and body slowly vanish. Near his
death at eighty-one, he whispers to his wife, "Remember the
first time?"

"I saw your mother last night, Estela," her husband says. "She's
fine."
"Your father is beginning to see the dead."

"I saw her last night," he says to his son.
"Who?"

"Her." He motions with his head toward the large, framed picture of Our Lady of Guadalupe that like the pale crucifix has been in our parents' bedroom for years.

"Is she beautiful?" Anthony asks trying to make casual conversation with his dying father about seeing the Virgin Mary.

"Not really," his father says. Each of his four children grieve privately, the four of us who had the same parents, the four of us who also had different parents.

A priest comes again, stands over our father's body that lies all day in his bed. The priest anoints the open hands with holy oil, "May the Lord forgive you by this holy anointing and His most loving mercy whatever sins you have committed. . . ."

My father can no longer chew. Ensure, baby food, puréed food are spooned into his disinterested lips. He gets thinner. "I feel a burning. My stomach is on fire."

Stella, his daughter/nurse, becomes his midwife, eases the father she loves out of this life with puddings she works down his throat, ice chips she places on his tongue, glycerine swabs she smooths on his silent lips to keep them from cracking.

Her six-year-old son says, "Mom, it's time for Papa to die." The boy comes and leans on his grandfather's body. "Papa, I came to say good-bye. Take care of yourself. Say hi to Baby Jesus for me. Look down and take care of me. I'll see you in heaven." My father squeezes his grandson's hand.

The day before his body dies, his lips move with difficulty, but he whispers to his youngest daughter, Stella, "Take care of yourself, honey."

At the mortuary, we select In Loving Memory Of cards with the Prayer of Saint Francis of Assisi on them, a prayer we all like,

> Lord, make me an instrument of your peace,
> Where there is hatred, let me sow love . . . .

We bury our father under a pepper tree. Years before, my parents had decided to be cremated and buried in this small garden. Generations change. In my grandparents' day in Mexico, men let their beard grow in mourning, maybe their hair watered by their tears. Anthony shaves for his father, arrives without a beard at the grave site, his gesture to the father who always wanted to see all of our faces, found each of the four of us so beautiful.

"*Mira qué bonita se ve así esta muchacha sin esas greñas en la cara,*" I'd hear him say to Mother. To me, "You look so nice that way, honey, with your hair up. I can see your face. Did you see how handsome your brother looks without his beard? He's so handsome. Why does he grow that beard? Remind me to show him my electric razors. Feel my face, honey. Feel it, feel it. I just love to sit here with a razor in each hand, get my face all smooth. Feel it, feel it."

After a priest has blessed the ground, a man from the funeral company moves toward us carrying a small box as if it holds explosives. The man's voice pours out of his lips thick, like oil. "Here is your father."

Our father? Our father, the unending tease, must enjoy the humor that eases the unbearable grief. Such a small, dull box could never contain my father.

Raúl Antonio Mora, March 4, 1912–August 28, 1993

After the brief burial ceremony, his wife, four children and spouses, go eat the *mole* Daddy loved at his favorite restaurant. We laugh to avoid the tears that we fear would never stop. Anthony lifts his glass of *sangría*, "To my father and his huge heart."

Four days after he dies in 1993, he takes a walk with me. We had last walked together three months before. He had only been able to circle one block by then, his legs so weak after the steady fading away for two years of his body and mind, his slow vanishing.

On that last arm-in-arm walk, we stopped often to admire the flowers that flourish so effortlessly in California, luxurious hibiscus, imperious birds-of-paradise; blooms that required green-house care in El Paso, desert city once our home. A special favorite was always bougainvillea. "It grows even in alleys here," he said in years past. "*Ven*, come and see."

So we stopped that day to admire the orange, red, gold, and watermelon pink blooms festooning a modest white fence. "*Mira no más*. Just look at that," he said, but his old delight was disappearing, weariness detaching him from his body.

Four days after he dies, I slip out alone for a walk. At least, I think I'm alone. I set off to see the ocean hoping that the sight of that centuries old repetition of waves, their *sh-sh-sh*, will comfort me. En route, I discover a weekly produce market, urban-style.

As I approach the vendors calling out their morning greetings to one another, I think of the baskets of multicolored potatoes in Peru, of the gleaming candied fruits and vegetables in Mexico—green figs stuffed with coconut, rich brown sweet potatoes, oranges crusty with dried syrup. And I begin to hear my father's voice enjoying this meandering from stall to stall with me.

"*¡Mira todos los chinitos!*" he says, as he studies the faces of Asian merchants busy bringing out their white, green and purple vegetables. Like many Mexicans, my father is fond of the diminutive, *-ito*, an ending he uses when observing any ethnic group including Whites. "*Pobres güeritos*," he might say, "poor Anglos, they're doing the best they can," watching some awkward attempts to dance *salsa* or unwillingness to display emotions. His use of the diminutive conveyed his general affection for most humans, his compassion at their/our antics, his awareness that every group has its difficulties, his belief that people are basically trying, the guy who pumps gas, the woman at the cleaners.

"What are those?" I ask a vendor, pen in hand wanting to hear the names of the Chinese produce, to find comfort in specificity, even if my father might be lost admiring the shapes or lines of leafy and gleaming vegetables.

"Chinese okra, white squash, bitter melon."

Bitter, indeed, to contemplate life without the huge physical presence that was my father, his six-foot, two-hundred-and-

ten-pound incarnation on this earth that had vanished before
our eyes; the mind that had been able to make sense of the
country of his birth and the country of his life, that in the end
lost its way in some internal labyrinth where we could not fol-
low. The concreteness, physicality, of the market flowers and
produce provides a link to pleasures my father and I share. I
hear the personal pride he takes in California's abundance.

"*Mira no más*, honey," he says. "Just look at the size of those
strawberries!" I roll limes, lemons, grapefruits, and oranges in my
hands. We smell the syrupy peaches, marvel at the flower stalls
and chuckle at the wealthy yuppies carrying home huge bouquets
to their color-coordinated, earth-tone apartments. He smiles and
shakes his head as I press for the names of things, tell him, "They
say the little orange suns are straw flowers; the trumpets, foxglove;
those are caspia, stargazers, phlox, bells of Ireland."

We stop at the snapdragons remembering the scrawny ver-
sions we watered in our backyard in Texas. My father had
bought the piece of land that became our home instead of tak-
ing Mother on a honeymoon, a decision that made her frown.
How often each of their four children stand holding a hose
through the years trying to tempt roses or larkspur or snap-
dragons to survive in that hard dirt below the glaring sun. My
father remembers only successes. Perhaps, he's too busy work-
ing, grinding lenses day and night at his optical company, to
consider just how difficult life is in that border town. Little
flourishes with ease, whether a plant or a business, particularly
a business owned by a Mexican or Mexican American.

"When I'd take doctors out for lunch," my father says to me
late in his life, momentarily admitting the prejudice he'd en-
countered, "the waiters would always make a big fuss over the
Anglo doctors, then hand them the bill. They don't think a guy
who looks like me can pay, even when the waiters are Mexicans."

"Why?"

"Honey! I have a map of Mexico on my face."

We linger at the honeys—wildflower, orange blossom, sage,
melon, star thistle, eucalyptus. "Let's get a bottle," he says.

"Sometimes your mother gets a cough. Remember, just put a bit on the tip of your tongue, that or glycerine. You'll stop coughing." In the room in which he died, there it was, a bottle of glycerine by his bed.

We leave the market for a bit and walk down to the ocean, another sight we both love. Gone is the casual stroll along the palisades. Street people sleep on benches and under shrubs, reach out their smudged hands. The white statue of Santa Monica, hands folded, eyes closed, reminds me of my father's body, also still, before the frame we knew was zipped into a shroud, black, then wrapped in white.

We walk to the market again in the bright sun. More browsers arrive, women with shopping bags looking for bargains. I fumble in my purse for another pen. When my father dies, every pen I use runs out of ink. I want to write down the names, always the names, of the fresh herbs, names sweet on the tongue, lemon basil, baby dill, the green scents a counter to the cement streets and sidewalks in which I live. He studies the cartons of sprouts and sunflower greens.

"*Para los conejos.*" He laughs at humans buying rabbit food, then says, "What did I tell you?" and walks toward a sign, JOJOBA. My father always had what he called "million dollar ideas." He reads an article in a newspaper or magazine and decides how he, or we, can make a fortune. Another of his favorite phrases is "very scientific," and articles about jojoba through the years combine scientific and financial possibilities for him. He tells any of us who'll sit and listen about the growing of jojoba, the oil that can be extracted, the money to be made. And now here it is, proof, a stand with jojoba seeds, products, brochures, and a woman ready also to talk endlessly about this marvelous plant. I listen briefly to humor my father, relieved that the saleswoman is oblivious of his enthusiasm.

"*Mira todos los mexicanitos,*" he says noticing the faces that resemble his own, the sound of Spanish.

"*Buenos días,*" a woman calls out to us.

"*Buenos días,*" I answer for us both. "*¿Cómo está, señora?*"

"*Trabajando para mantener esta familiota grande que tengo. Esto nunca se acaba*," she says stating what my father understood so well, the constant need to work to support a large family.

"*You* did it, Daddy, support the four of us, Mother, Mamande and Lobo."

"No big deal. I like it." He begins examining the multicolored chiles, orange, green, yellow, red; the *jalapeño, torito, serrano*. He wants to buy some knowing his purchases always drive my mother crazy. He laughs at his ability "to get her goat" after fifty-four years. "I'll tell her that I'll show her how to cook." We laugh at Mother's predictable flaring at that phrase.

Our walk is sweet sorrow. I miss the body of this big man, buffer between the world and me, the gentle man with the booming voice who never lifts a hand except to help a person up, and yet who always talks of being ready to knock out any threat or intruder.

"Just let me at them," he says of invisible muggers or thieves, and many a time my mother has to shake him awake since he's swinging punches in his dreams. A bull of a man, a gentle bull.

We hear Spanish at another stand, and my father follows me to eavesdrop. A couple in their late sixties, who could be his relatives from their facial features, chat with a couple from Spain, comparing growing seasons, harvests. The California grower boasts, "*Cinco cosechas al año*." We smile to hear the global aspect of his work with the soil. "*Semillas de Amsterdam*," he says with pride, the secret of the delicate carrots he sells, five harvests with seeds from Amsterdam.

We walk toward the apartment where Daddy and Mother lived for the last thirty years. Music from a sax swirls through the air. "*Fíjate, fíjate en el pie*," my father urges me to notice the steady tapping of the Black man's foot as he plays. My father loves music, dancing, rhythm. We both hear the unsung phrase, "Don't come a - round much any - more," which says it all—my fear that his voice, my father's voice inside me, will also fade, that I will cease to hear his sound, his words, his faith in me and his admonishings, his insistent, *"fí-jate, fíjate."*

Last year on Good Friday I saw pilgrims going to Chimayó, the small New Mexico church now the largest pilgrimage site in the States, prayers mixed with laughter and joking, low riders cruising by the faithful, including a tall, blind man and his dog. Was the man led into the small candle-lit room of hope near the altar? Its walls are covered with pictures and statues—Saint Teresa, the Infant of Prague, Our Lady of Perpetual Help, and of course, San Martín, el Sagrado Corazón, Nuestra Señora de Guadalupe, and the most venerated image here, El Santo Niño de Atocha, the Christ Child who wears out his shoes on his nightly errands of mercy. Brought to Mexico from Spain was the devotion to the Child, Son of Nuestra Señora de Atocha, the boy who tended imprisoned Spaniards during the Moorish occupation, arriving in pilgrim clothes and hat carrying a basket and a gourd on a staff.

Did someone bend to the holy place in the cramped room, the dry well, *El Posito*, and scoop the sacred dirt, rub it gently on the blind man's lids in this season of miracles?

"Did I tell you about seeing Jesus Christ here, in the living room?" Aunt Chole asks. "He is on the Cross, dressed in white. The wood is dark and thick. An hour later, I see Him again. A few days later, I see Him again. Something white always covers His head."

We sit listening to the sound of Mother playing the piano, first the scales to warm her fingers, then chords, then études, sonatinas, sarabandes, minuets, practicing one measure over and over to the steady beat of the metronome, angry at her stubborn fingers.

"I have something to tell you, *reina*. You'd better sit down." I wonder if this will be about another vision, or about the man Aunt Chole hints about. Perhaps what she wants to share will be like my visit to her last spring when she still lived alone and by phone had intimated that what she had to discuss could only be done in person. I arrived with tablet and pen.

"Let's walk out back, *corazón*. I know you're writing about a garden so I have something to show you." There is an air of ceremony for Aunt Chole about this moment as she takes my arm, and we go out to her now bare yard. She points at what she can barely see. "Look, look. It bloomed after so many years. I thought it was important that you see it, for your book." In the middle of a flower bed, the dirt cracked from dryness, a large copper king gazania blooms. "I saw something orange, and I thought: I have to tell Patsy. Tell your husband to come out and take a picture of it. Is he comfortable reading in that room while we talk, *reina*? I opened the window so he'll have some fresh air, and I put some cookies and coffee by his chair. *Es tan lindo*. Tell him to come and take a picture of this flower."

What will my aunt share with me today?

"Sit down, sit down, *corazón mío*." I take out my pen. "Did I tell you what happened last Good Friday? This would be good for your book. Sometimes when I knew my sister was coming, I'd wait by the window. I can't see the car, of course, but I hear it come. What I'm going to tell you happens on Good Friday, *fíjate, reinita, en viernes santo*. I'm sitting by the window, and I see a car go by. At first, I don't even notice that I've seen it. Then I think: but I can't see, how could I see a car go by? *Me quedé pensativa*.

"I go to the living room and think, I'm seeing the curtains. I'm seeing. I'm seeing! I don't see perfectly, of course, *corazón*, but I can distinguish things again. I had only been able to see to the side, *tu sabes*, and had to tip my head to see anything. I put on the television, and I can distinguish him again, Paco Stanley. I haven't seen him in years. I call a friend and ask her to take me to the church, yes, to San Patricio, to give thanks. I put on a black blouse one of my sisters gave me ten years ago. So that it won't look so bad, I add a pink tie.

"The church is dark. Remember I lost my sight in '79, sixteen years ago. I send my friend to pay for a Mass to be said in Thanksgiving. *Tal vez mi Diosito me dio este premio*. I see a white spot on my blouse and start rubbing it. Later, my sisters tell me that it isn't a stain, *ee-ee*. The blouse has white flowers. The priest comes out and says a prayer. Yes, *reina*, in Spanish. The cleaning woman and a few others who are there praying in the dark church get close and hug me when they hear my sight is better. When we get to the house, the mailman is there, 'Richie! Richie! My eyes are better!'

" 'Miss Mora, I'm so happy!' He comes over and gives me a big hug, and then the yard man comes and hugs me, and then my sweet neighbor who helps me. So I give thanks, *reina*. Life isn't so hard then."

Silence at church on Holy Saturday and then the vigil of Easter, the blessing of the Paschal candle and of the baptismal water, "*Alleluia. Alleluia.* You are new."

This month of miracles, of the full Sprouting Grass Moon, of annual resurrection, rebirth, songs of hope rising.

April twenty-fifth, the Celebration of Litanies, prayers asking God to bless the crops and preserve us from calamities. Early the voices begin, before the broom begins its daily *sw-sw*, the calling on all the saints: pray for us, *ora pro nobis*, sleepy voices joining the responses, Abuelo Gregorio in his tiny room hearing the family prayers rising like the smoke from his candles.

> *Señor ten piedad.*
> *Cristo, óyenos.*
> *Santa María.*
> > *Ruega por nosotros.*
> *San Rafael.*
> > *Ruega por nosotros.*
> *San Martín.*
> > *Ruega por nosotros.*
> *Santa Cecilia.*
> > *Ruega por nosotros.*
> *De todo mal.*
> > *Líbranos Señor.*
> *De la muerte perpetua.*
> > *Líbranos Señor.*

Mayo / May

Enero friolero, febrero loco, marzo airoso, abril
lluvioso, sacan a mayo, floreado y hermoso.

Chilly January, crazy February, windy March,
rainy April bring on the beauty of
flowering May.

IN THE ADOBE SKIN of this house in which the living
and dead dwell, as our dead dwell, move, and speak inside
the layers of our human skin; my father and I enjoy the
petaled breeze drifting through the garden's mimosas and
honey locusts. I lug out house plants: the ficus tree, miniature
orange, crown of thorns, red hibiscus, bougainvillea; spray the
winter dust off with the hose, water them well, imagine their
pleasure, like mine, at being out again in the company of doves,
damsel flies, katydids. Spring-green leaves of honeysuckle,
morning glory, and Carolina jasmine begin their annual climb-
ing, up walls, trellises, posts. Taking a deep breath, I think of the
old Provençal chanson, "It must have been May morning when
the world was made."

Great-great-grandmother, Mamá Cleta, rustles out in a pale
blue cotton dress, carrying a bird cage. "*Qué día tan lindo,*" she
says. "Our canaries will enjoy this fresh air." Soon an aunt brings
out her cage of orange-beaked finches. "So all the *pajaritos* can
visit on this nice day," she says.

"*¿Y yo?* And me?" the bilingual *guacamaya* squawks in the
kitchen. Cissy helps me bring out the demanding bird and his cage.

"I'll fix them their treat," my daughter says, stirs a package
of thawed mixed vegetables with fresh carrots and oranges she
dices, adds seeds, spoons the mixture into the food bowls.

She wishes she could release the parrot into the Tambopata National Park in Peru, let the bird join the thousand other parrots in the lush rain forest. Because the birds eat seeds with high chemical concentrations that could be toxic, they gather in the morning sun at a mud bank to eat clay that detoxifies the tanins and alkaloids in the seeds, but also nourishes them. How do their bodies know to crave the clay? Very scientific, her grandfather said when she showed him an article on the park. How this opinionated parrot would enjoy the noisy morning congregations, she's sure, and the freedom to sail through the green noise of the jungle canopy.

"*¡Ay, que pájaros tan tontos!*" the raucous macaw squawks looking around at the other birds. I wonder if my father is up to his mischief. Did he teach the parrot to insult the other birds or has he slipped into those green and red feathers?

Later, leaning back in a chair under the cottonwood, eyes closed, my father rocks and softly sings, "*La don - na mo - bi - le la - la - la lalala*" soothed by the sun.

May, Mary's month, month of the full Flower Moon. At church, the priest wears white these weeks after Easter, season of poems and processions to the Virgin, Mother of God. In elementary school, we annually memorize,

> Lovely Lady, dressed in blue,
> Teach me how to pray.

We'd cut roses and larkspur in the backyard, put them in vases in front of statues in the house. Mother wraps the cut flowers in damp paper to keep them fresh, wraps the paper in foil so the thorns won't prick us. At school, we hand the pink and purple blooms, our offerings, to the nuns who put them on their orderly desks or before classroom statues.

The pink spring scent takes me back to Lobo and the processions of girls in white dresses at Holy Family Church, the church she once told me was built before I was born to get the Mexicans out of Saint Patrick's Cathedral. Each girl carries flowers to the Virgin, our voices rising to church ceil-

ings on wisps scented by sweet peas, candle smoke and in-
cense.

> *O Ma - ría, Mad - re Mí - a, o consuelo del mortal,*
> *Ampararme y guiarme a la patria celestial.*

Women thumb their rosaries, "*Dios te salve, María, llena eres de*
gracia."

At school, guided by Sister Eugene Marie's pitch pipe and
the arcs of her arms, we practice for the day we'll enter the high-
ceiled cathedral in straight lines, genuflect before entering our
pew, then watch a nervous child carry the silk pillow and crown
of flowers to the altar, watch a lucky girl step up to place the
moist crown on the head of the demure statue as we sing,

> Hail! ho - ly Queen en - thron - ed above,
>   O Ma - ri - a.
> Sal - ve, Sal - ve, Sal - ve Re - gi - na!

Nuns' eyes patrol each class, mentally recording gum chewers
and rib-pokers, watch us say in unison,

> Remember, O Most Gracious Virgin Mary,
> that never was it known, that anyone
> who fled to thy protection, implored thy help
> or sought thy intercession was left unaided.

Entering the vestibule of Saint Patrick's Cathedral in El Paso
is entering a sacred cave I know well. Dark and inviting it felt on
a hot day to leave the desert's glare and dip my fingers into the
marble font trimmed in green and red marble as are the altar
and communion rail; bless myself with cool holy water, enter
the body of the church. Long, stained-glass windows line both
sides, filtering the light. I would look up to white Saint Patrick
in his bishop's miter holding a staff high above the altar, the pa-
tron saint who has since been brought down to earth. Although
I can see the details of the statue more clearly now at a side altar
when we're eye to eye—his three fingers raised to remind me of
shamrocks and the Trinity, snakes slithering away from his
feet—he's far less imposing, smaller than I ever imagined him, a

sober man but not a prophet, reality in this space where once I knew awe.

I'd look up at the windows when I said the Stations of the Cross, study holiness, pale haloed figures with long, slender faces, aquiline noses. On one window, another snake. Mary floats white in a starry sky surrounded by angel faces and tumbling roses, sails on gold, a half-moon, her bare feet crushing the bright, green viper.

> I will put enmities between thee and the woman.
> She shall crush thy head,

the words from Genesis below the image. I'd look at glass images of Christ kneeling in the Garden of Gethsemene, at the Good Shepherd, the Sacred Heart, Mary ascending into heaven, and Mary Magdalene drying Christ's feet with her thick, chestnut hair. "Many sins are forgiven her because she hath loved much."

The votive candles that scented and transformed this space have disappeared. We'd light their flickering tongues to accompany and perfume the prayers we whispered to the patient, attentive statues. The glowing tongues vanished. Silenced, the danger of fire.

San Isidro Labrador, a May saint, the patron of farmers, was so devout that God sent an angel down to plow Isidro's fields while he prayed, his statue venerated all over New Mexico, carried into the fields for the blessing of the earth.

> *San Isidro, barbas de oro,*
> *Ruega a Dios*
> *Que llueva a chorros.*

When I ask my father if he's heard of San Isidro, he barely shakes his head no, so drowsy is he in the spring air, but he chuckles at the humorous prayer for rain.

I sit next to him enjoying both the sound of a mockingbird playing with sounds and the thought of its accurate Latin name, *mimus polyglottos*, many-tongued mimic. I read about how to attract hummingbirds and butterflies to the garden, wondering if we should try penstemons, maybe the bluish purple and the scarlet bugler. Who wouldn't want a bugler with its scarlet sound? Accompanied by trumpet vine, yes, its orange blarings, symphonies of color. We'll buy a mix of scents and colors to lure the wings: wild hyssop, beebalm, purple coneflower, columbine, gaillardia, cosmos, zinnias, and Mexican sunflowers, *mirasoles*, and their craning necks.

They'll come, the whirring black-chinned hummingbirds, *chuparrosas*, rainbowed reflections of light. Again, I'll watch my son when he's a young boy, green net in hand, chasing the monarchs, painted ladies, black swallowtails and great spangled fritillaries, luring him to dart under wisteria's lavender clusters, to leap over alyssum, irises, Indian hawthorn.

The next morning, I walk to the door that opens onto the front courtyard where the children play, hear birds whirring above me high in the *portal*. Although I try to watch the house finch that built her nest in the ivy, for days flew back and forth furnishing the nest with her feathered bursts of energy, she's skittish. Rarely will she rest on her eggs and stare at me, a fellow nest builder. Only if she thinks I'm gone, does she return, settle, philosophical in her task.

Outside the gate, I find a small, paper basket left by a friend, homemade surprise: orange cookies, blushing apple blossoms, sprigs of lilacs, sprinkling of violets. I take the basket to Aunt Chole, happy to find myself alone with her. I tell her about the house finch and the old custom of May baskets, of bringing delight to friends.

"Smell these lilacs. This is the dark purple, this is the lavender, and this, this is the white."

"*Ummmmmmm.*"

"Were you eighty when it happened, the man on the radio?"

"Oh no, *reina*. I was seventy-nine. He was five years older. He recited poetry, *poesías preciosas, preciosas.*"

Aunt Chole insists on feeding me, on serving me, feeling her way with her fingers. "With these new orthopedic shoes, *reina*, I don't even need my cane anymore." It stands unused nearby, still decked with a red cloth so that she can find it in the shadows in which she lives, like the red cloth she ties to the front screen door to let the mailman know she needs to talk to him.

"*Corazoncito, siéntate aquí, chulita.* I have something to tell you, but I'll tell you after you eat. I have to take care of you." I chew the cold scrambled egg she fixed for me, the coffee and corn chips. "I thought you'd like these. I brushed the salt off each one. I thought you'd like them better this way.

"And I have water in the refrigerator. I don't drink it that way, but I have it for you. Just in case. *Ya tengo todo listo.* And cookies," she reaches up to her hiding place, brings the box down, bends her back bent by osteoporosis over the box, reading the cookies with her fingertips to find the ones she seeks. "Some of these have a good filling, *reinita adorada.* I want you to taste them."

I feel swollen with health sitting by this slender, gray-haired woman in her purple velour jogging suit. "You look great, Aunt Chole. *De veras*, you look really great."

She laughs her high-pitched, "*Ee-ee.* My sister gave me this outfit. She had two. I'm not a beauty parlor person, *reina*, so it takes me a long time to fix my hair.

Quietly, I slip out my pen. "Tell me about when you were little," I say to my father's eldest sister.

"*Voy a contarte mi historia porque mi historia es triste*," she says firmly. "My father always wants the best for me. First I go to a Catholic school in Chihuahua which is a mistake since all we do is pray and pray and pray. Then when we come here, my father sends me to some nuns in El Paso, *unas monjitas* over at San Ignacio. I think he is partial to me, *reina. Mi padre me adoraba. Te lo digo, me adoraba.* But all we do with the nuns is sing and pray, *rezi y rezi y rezi.*

"*No era tan tonta*, but they didn't teach us enough. My teacher, Madre Celenita, likes me very much. I think that every year they choose the best student, and the bishop gives them a gift. My teacher tells me to be present on Sunday and to go up to the bishop when my name is called. He gives me a small heart I keep for years that has a little pearl on it.

"When we go to Deming, I go to a public school. Think what a good tailor my father must be that my Tío Brigido sends for him. You know, in New Mexico, to help him in his tailor shop. I don't learn English until that move. I'm very good at arithmetic, at calculating in my head which is good since now I have to do everything without paper and pencil.

"What? I'm not sure exactly when we come to the United States. I'm about eight or nine, and my mother wants to get away from *la revolución*, too many guns. I'm born June 16, 1907 so you figure it out.

"Noooooo, *mi amor*, none of us are born in hospitals. How can we? We have no money. *Ay*, I never like my name. Think how sad it is. I am named for La Virgen de la Soledad, a lonely name," she whimpers.

Our Lady of Solitude, after her Son's crucifixion dressed in black and white, bereft of parents, husband, Son; woman alone, patron against loneliness, thought by some as the archetype of the crone, woman of earned wisdom, woman of power.

"Did you know that my grandmother's name is sad too?" I ask. "Her name was Sotero, but she changes her name to Amelia."

Aunt Chole's eyes open wide. She laughs, "Did she really? She changes her name? I wish I had brains like that. *Ay*. Anyway, *reina*, in Deming we have a nice green house, three wood rooms. My grandmother sleeps in the living rooms with the boys. Nearby there's an orchard with big trees that bloom and a vegetable garden where we go pick tomatoes and peppers."

She laughs at herself. "I was so silly, but you know *corazón*, we don't have much. I save things, boxes and milk cans, and then I make designs with them, like little houses. I like to cook so my parents give me a small iron stove and guess what I do? *Ee-ee*, I try to cook beans on my stove. Well, you know how long they take, so my father and mother laugh at the hard beans I serve.

"No, *corazón mío*, how can my mother garden? In those days there isn't time. We have a few roses and geraniums in metal cans, but I learn when I buy my own home because *mi Diosito* helps me. I go buy food for my roses and ice plant, my crape myrtle just covered with bouquets. I'd feed them at night and on weekends. *Umm,* one year I grow coleus, the leaves of different colors like dark velvet, three or four feet high.

"We come back to El Paso when I'm still little and live on Ochoa Street and then on Virginia and on North Florence. Our house on Virginia is a nice place with a pretty porch and a big bench. I still remember the address, 405 South Virginia.

"Yes, I spoke English, but it isn't like now when everyone speaks English at home. At San Jacinto School, I have a teacher named Mrs. Boone, so pretty, so tidy. She wears blouses with high collars and narrow, nice ties. And guess what? *Adivinaba la suerte.* I never knew another teacher who told fortunes. She is very kind to me, but she tells me that I'll always carry something on my shoulders. How does she know? I think it's that I had to leave school to begin working." She sighs. "I only finish seventh grade, at Bowie. That summer, the doorbell rings, and I answer."

Chole, not yet a teenager, opens the door and looks up at a strange man big as the door.

"I'm here for the money. Is Lázaro Mora here?"

Chole doesn't know what to do. The man's eyes sting her skin.

"No, he's not here."

Angry, the man slams his hand on the door jamb. "You tell your father . . . Is Lázaro Mora your father?"

"Yes."

"You tell your father that I came for the money. He owes me money, and he knows it, damn him."

Chole shuts the door, her feet and hands cold, blue. The next day when she sees that man walking toward the house again, she runs and hides in the closet. She hears her mother's black, laced shoes going to the doorbell, and Chole bites her knuckle in the dark, scared of the man with eyes small and hard, like gun shot.

"Is Lázaro Mora here?"

"*No.*"

"You speak English?"

"*No.*"

The man raises his voice. "¡*Dinero!* Understand? You tell your husband I want my *dinero.*"

In the closet, Chole bites her knuckle and cries. The man comes again and again. Other men come too, shouting about the money her father borrowed. The doorbell rings and rings. Chole hears men shouting, "Is Lázaro Mora here? We're here to collect the money. Damn Mexican!" She hides in the closet, but she hears men banging insults on the door, even when she covers her ears with both hands.

"I got very nervous, honey. I hide, but I hear them yelling at my mother, worse, yelling at my father because he's in debt. That's when I realize that my father is borrowing because he can't find work. He worked for a Mr. Morehead who owns Morehead Tailor Shop on the corner of Main and Oregon, but then comes that Depression. He borrows money and can't pay it back. He doesn't have work.

"So what am I to do when those men insult him? I have to quit school to help him. I didn't have a blessed youth worrying about money, money, money. I slip out of the house quietly one day. Now my mother goes to a place called Houchen Settlement for sewing classes. They're Baptists or something. I go to a lady there.

" 'Mrs. Queensberry, do you think you can help me find work? My father isn't making any money.'

" 'Let me think about it and see what I can do.' Soon Mrs. Queensberry or Brandyberry, some berry, calls me and says she's found me work at a clinic they have for poor people. Someone's going on vacation, and I can take her place. I work at the adult and children's clinic. I like the work, *reina*. We have so many little ones at the children's clinic that I work from eight in the morning to eight at night. I arrive at seven to clean the clinic, and then I begin to assist the nurse. One day she asks me, 'What size shoe do you use, Chole?' She's noticed my poor shoes and brings me a pair of Oxfords.

"I'm happy to be working, *feliz*, earning five dollars a week to pay the rent. The people at the clinic want to send me to St. Louis to study to be a nurse, imagine. I think I would have liked that, being a nurse, but they say I need to pay my room and board. *Ni modo.* There's no way I can do that. I have to find other work. Your aunt begins working at Kress after school and on Saturdays. I'm working, working, working. My brothers sell papers to buy food, and I pay the rent. I need things, though. My feet are delicate, and I can't wear just any shoes.

" 'Mamá, doesn't my sister give you money to help? I need a pair of shoes.'

" 'How can you ask me for money?' *Mi mamá* gets mad at me, always, so mad at me. 'Don't you know your sister likes to dance? She needs to buy dresses and shoes. You don't like to dance and go out. You don't need those things.'

"How can I go out if I don't have shoes, *reina?* So the *detalles* start. Is my grandmother, Tomasa, around? She would get mad at me because I get up at five to clean the kitchen, so it will look nice. We're *pobres, pobres.* My grandmother gets mad at me for being like that."

Chole works for a dentist in Juárez, but he touches her and she runs crying to a pharmacist who's a relative. She can't even take the streetcar home because of motion sickness, says to herself: my family doesn't understand the sacrifices I'm making. All they do is criticize me. No wonder I cry so much, wiping away the tears as she walks home in the dark, frightened, often frightened and alone.

"No matter what I say, my mother says the opposite. Finally, I have to leave. I can't stand living in that screaming house any more. *¡Aayy!*

"I move into a boarding house run by a Mrs. Bennett. Her husband was a consul, to Spain I think. I sleep in the attic with all his books, in a little bed. No bathroom up there, just a sink. I meet Isabel in that house and eventually begin to live with her. In some ways she's good since she keeps the house nice for me. *Siempre he sido muy arreglada,* but Isabel has a cruel side. *Ayyyy, querida,* what I've suffered, *los detalles de la vida.*"

I ask her about her parakeets, the creatures she'd talk to as if they were children. She begins her high laugh, *"Ee-ee,* Isabel and I have Baby who's very smart," and she's smiling again, feeling the feathered kisses of the creatures who rode on her shoulder.

"How does Baby know never to step on the furnace grate?" she asks. "Delicately she walks around it, and when the doorbell rings, she follows me to the door, like a person. *Oooo,* does she get mad when your sister comes on Sunday evenings to have dinner with me.

"Toni never says a word. We have a painting of birds, and he loves to kiss it, but our smartest, *¡AY!* is Peachito. I have his picture and even taped his voice once. Let me show you. Do you want it, *reina?* Yes, yes, anyway I can't see it anymore. I'd say to Peachito, '*Toni es muy tonto.*' And Peachito says, '*Toni es muy tonto,*' imagine. And he says, '*¡Cómo te quiere tu madre!*' and, '*Dame un besito.*' He knows thirty words, so he is no ordinary bird. Peachito only drinks water from a glass.

"We have the parakeets all the years I work at the store. I wanted to work some place nice, and a rich woman I know takes me to the White House Department Store. I start in 1938 and work there for forty years. Many of my clients are from México, *mujeres de dinero, damas,* like the wives of the presidents and wives of governors, *gente rica, tú sabes, fina.*

"How do they treat me? *Todas mis clientes eran adorables, adorables.* Well, in those days, I'm *algo pasadita,* and the owner, Mr. Miller, uses me as an example of a good employee. 'I want more like Miss Mora.' " She laughs, enjoying the pleasure of being valued. "I'm very happy there. Mr. Miller *es encantador, encantador.* Every morning on his way to his office he stops and gives me a pat on the back. He says, 'Hire Miss Mora's friends.' He encourages me to become an American citizen."

I see the two aunts, Aunt Chole and Aunt Carmen, Uncle Lalo's wife, standing at the top of the department store escalator when my sisters or friends and I, young girls, walk by them en route to the Ladies' Room, their backs straight, always in plain black, a rule on the fashion floor. They're sales ladies in those days, year after year standing, standing, smiling at their customers, "You look beautiful in that mink coat," or "*Pero se ve linda en ese vestido verde.*"

"Hi Aunt Carmen. Hi Aunt Chole."

"Hi, honey. What are you girls doing?"

"Going to a movie," we say and rush away.

Aunts and trees. Now I could spend weeks listening to my aunts, their voices like a balm, scented by an affection brewing for over fifty years. I lean into them as I lean into the purple scent that transports me to our childhood backyard, the tree from my youth, the old Chinaberry, *la lila*, I'd climb; in the spring, climb into the lavender aroma of its delicate flower clusters. Native to Northern India and China, its botanical name, *Melia Azedarach*, means noble tree in Persian. It's also known as Persian Lilac, Pride of India, Holy Tree, and Bead Tree because of its hard, yellow berries once strung as rosary beads.

Neither the details of my relatives' lives nor these botanical facts interested me back when I'd climb into the tree's arms, firm and outstretched like the perfumed arms of my aunts. Now I study the tree's bark and branches, stroke the warm smoothness of its trunk, hear the wind ruffling the delicate leaves, taste again the fragrance purple on the tongue, breathe in all I can hold of a time when love was offered to my young self again and again and again.

"Remember what I'd make you do, Aunt Chole, when I'd go have dinner at your house?" My sister, Stella, remembers running from our back yard, across the alley to Aunt Chole and Isabel's white house in the sixth grade. "I was so crazy," Stella says, "I sing in a loud voice on the way. 'You talk too much, you wor - ry me to death . . .' You were always so happy to see me, Aunt Chole. Isabel leaves to go play canasta, and I have you and your house to myself. I am a queen there."

Laughing, Aunt Chole says, "You'd say, 'Let's go clean your drawers.' You don't want to clean my drawers. You want to clean them out. 'Oh, I sure wish I had a bracelet like that,' you sigh slowly or 'That tiny perfume bottle is very pretty.'

" 'Anda, anda, take it,' I say, and she takes everything *esta muchacha*. We don't stop. She says, 'Now let's play cards. Now let's play with the bird.' " Stella sees her aunt then cooing to the bird on her shoulder, bringing him to her lips for kisses.

Stella would walk into that house with the dusty rose carpet and the pastel furniture, the doilies crocheted by Lita for the daughter who left her; the dancing prisms of small chandeliers, casting tiny rainbow fish on the walls; parakeets chirping, delicate figurines—girls with bouquets, pink poodles pulling carts of tiny flowers, the oval glass tray covered with slender bottles of perfume, deep blue Evening in Paris, Taboo with its image of passionate lovers. Aunt Chole, trim, back straight, her skin, smooth, her make-up—powder, rouge, eyebrow pencil, lipstick—applied with care, peers at Stella's face, hands, cuticles, urges her niece to use cream and take better care of her skin, hair, nails.

"I'd do homework," Stella says, "and you let me call my friends and talk as long as I want. Not like my house. And we have dinner on TV trays in your back sunroom and watch what we want, sherbet for dessert. Maybe the best part is that I make you turn on the radio, Aunt Chole, make you sit there, the two of us listening to KELP for hours until my favorite song comes on. We wait to hear, 'Oh, Ve - nus in blue jeans.'"

"*Aaayyy, queridas,* but those last years Isabel lives with me are horrible, horrible," Aunt Chole says. "She wakes me up at five to clean the garden, screams at me all day. I'm retired then. I'd be so angry, I go out back to the wash room. I hit the dryer with a damp cloth over and over, hitting, hitting, hitting, and cry. Isabel hits me on the face, *reina,* breaks my glasses once. She throws plates at me. I hear programs on the radio about abuse, and finally I get help. They take her to a nursing home.

"She takes my Peachito just to hurt me. A woman says to me, 'Isabel wants to give me that bird. Why would I want it?' ¡*Ayyy!* I sent her out of the house—I'd paid for it, worked for it all those years, and she wanted to throw me out, so she took him. *Ayyy,* how I screamed and cried. *Me solté llorando a gritos.* 'Don't, please don't take my baby!'

"She just glares at me, her eyes smelling of hate. I can see then, so I call someone to come and take my baby's picture for me the last day he's with me, my Peachito. I stroke him, cover him with kisses.

"Remember that woman who came to live with me and help me a few years ago? She took the tape I had of my baby talking. Imagine. She stole so many things, and I couldn't see. So I didn't want anyone living in my house. I was better off alone, *reina*. Life is heavy for me." She sighs.

Birds and Aunt Chole, both startled by loud noises. I think of her internal fluttering in her family home, radio and voices loud, until she finally leaves, her mother fainting at the news.

"How do you remember everything we tell you, Aunt Chole? You're eighty-eight, and you remember it all in your head."

"Maybe that's why, *corazón*. I work my memory. Who's with us now? I see a shadow, but I can't see the face. That's how I knew, that I was going blind. *Ay, son los detalles de la vida. Mi Diosito sabe lo que he sufrido.* One day I look in the mirror, and I can't see my face, imagine? I look and look, but I can't see me. I can see things from the edges of my eyes, but not my face. I don't know how I look, *mi reina*.

"It's not my sister, is it?" Aunt Chole looks at a shadow and makes the sign of the cross. "I'll bless myself just in case. *Ee-ee.* I have to laugh. Tell me if it's her because I'll stop talking. No matter what I say, she'll scold. She doesn't like me to have friends. I don't know why she hates me. *Problemitas. Me dice cositas.* You know how she is. My other sisters are scared of her too. She only stops when she's asleep, always with her volunteering and her exercising and her nagging. I pray for her and then I think, 'Why do you pray for someone who's so mean to you?' One day last week she was in a good mood. She even called me *honey*.

"*Mi Diosito* knows I'm good. I don't say bad things. Why do people treat me badly sometimes, I ask my sweet God. The truth is I'm ready," she reaches for a Kleenex. "I ask God to remember me, to take me now. It would be my rest. Sometimes I hear my heart, *poon, poon, poon. Pero Dios sabe lo que hace.*

"The Holy Spirit is so good to me. I complain to Him and He resolves things. When I lose things, He lets me look and then He says, 'And where were you looking?' Then He tells me where to look. He solves problems for me, *me ilumina.* The other day a light bulb burnt out, and I needed a light for when I get up at night. I found a little lamp I had, but it wouldn't fit in that niche in the hall, and then He said to me, 'Remove the lamp shade, and it will fit.' *Ves, me ilumina Él.*

"But some days I feel better mentally. I try. I don't do anything wrong. I guess our body changes. I still put on the radio. I don't enjoy the music like I used to, but it's one thing I understand."

Legally blind, my aunt says she sees with her hands, lives alone until she's almost ninety.

"I go blind in 1979. I have two friends who had often come to my house. I feed them or take them out to dinner even if they have more money than I do. I do it *con gusto, reina*. But after they hear I've lost my sight, I never hear from them again. Don't you think that's cruel?

"You know me. I'm afraid of everything, everything, everything. I have nightmares. My screams wake me in the dark, but my *Diosito* knows I take care of myself.

"I like to be independent. I keep busy. Mornings are hard, *cositas de la casa*. I've got to make my bed, have my breakfast, wash my dishes, straighten my room. I keep my mind busy. I have to remember where everything is because I can't see, honey. I can't see. When the seasons change, I spray my clothes with alcohol when I bring them out, so they'll be nice and fresh. Then I lay them on the bed so the sun will shine on them all morning.

"I make my mistakes, of course, and the Holy Spirit makes me struggle. I tell Him I'm sorry when I make a mistake like one time when I cooked a carrot salad thinking it was soup. Sometimes He gets mad at me, but He has His sight I tell Him, *ee-ee*. I have to do many things in secret. If my sisters know, they just scold me.

"In the afternoon, I take a little nap. I only let myself have one of those cookies you gave me a day. Don't worry. I keep them hidden. A few times a day, I walk for my circulation. Your uncle always reminded me of that, and he was an eye doctor so he knew. One brother an eye doctor and one an optician, and I go blind. My sister's going blind too. *Los detallitos de la vida.* And I pray. I pray for the children that don't have parents, and for my sick friends, for my poor friend that has Pakistan, you know, that disease. And I pray for the family. I like to be of use. I've had a sad life, *corazón, muchos trancazos en mi vida.* I don't want others to suffer the way I have, so I pray for them. I even pray for my sister to control her temper, *ee-ee.*

"Sometimes when my sisters scold me, I cry and cry. You know me. I tell them, 'I'm the oldest. You should respect me. Don't yell at me.' Sometimes they yell again, 'Why did you leave the house back then when you were a teenager? It hurt Mama.' I cry. I'm so dumb. *Soy muy mentecata.* Why do I cry for people who are so mean to me?

"*Ayyy, reina,* what I've suffered. What? Well, the doctor wanted to use electric shock once because of my condition. I was so nervous, and Isabel made me suffer so much and then she took *el pajarito.* She wanted to take my house, and I'd paid all the payments. She's dead now I think. She kept wanting me to add on to the house or to improve the house, and I'm paying, paying, paying. Occasionally I'd visit my cousins in California, but most of my life is work, work. I was very close to my cousins. We suffered together. My mother and their mother, both hard women.

"*Mi Tía Leonor era de un carácter muuuuuy duro. Mi Tía era más española que mi madre. Mi madre era más mexicana.* Every Saturday they have a list ready for us, and in those days bringing the groceries means carrying a heavy bag of flour. It takes us all day to do the errands.

"Is my grandmother close by? Why can't she let us visit by ourselves? Does she tell you I was a *llorona?* Ay, sure I cry, *reina,* but look at my life. *Mi historia es triste.* I can't see! I can't see!

"Both my brothers die at about the same time a few years ago. Well, they are together. Isn't that beautiful, honey? They die together. Well, they were together a lot when they were little.

"Have you seen either of them, Raúl or Salvador, Abuelita? Raúl always slept with you, and Salvador was at the foot of the bed. You get up and dress them at three o'clock in the morning so they can go deliver papers. If it's cold, you make them wear caps and jackets. The neighbor's black dog, Jack, is at the door waiting to go with them, a very nice dog that knows if they buy cookies or *pan dulce* or something, he'll always get some. Such good boys, my brothers, aren't they, Abuelita? Soon after they die, I see them standing in their nice suits at the foot of my bed.

"Who's that laughing at me? Who's the shadow? What does he mean, '*Jesu Cristo*'?"

"Stop picking on her, Daddy. You know she can't see you."

"Is it your father, *mi hermanito querido?* Why didn't you ever call me or come and see me like your brother did? I don't understand this talking with the dead. It's one of Patsy's ideas. It's okay. It's okay. If she wants to do this, it's okay with me.

"Are you hungry, Raúl? No, I can't make you a ham sandwich. I can't see to cook anymore. At my old house, I'd eat the same thing every day when I'd get up at four. It was really five. I go by Mexican time. I'm used to it. I'd have my egg, toast and coffee; at lunch some chicken I'd fix every few weeks and just warm up; at night, my cereal, banana and milk. Do you want a cookie? I thought so. *¿Quieres café?*

"That's okay, *mi reina querida.* He's not bothering me. I need to move around. Last year at my house, I'd go out in the morning about six before the sun got strong. I felt like the happiest person in the world. I had a railing put out front, and I'd hold on to it or to the back of a chair to water. Out back, I'd sit and water my grass and my garden. That made me so happy, just being outside and watering, feeling the wind on my face.

"You can visit with Patsy, Raúl. No, I can find everything, honey. I have everything memorized. I have to. And I do everything slowly. *Soy muy viva, no creas.*"

"Well, now I've lived many years alone," Aunt Chole sighs, a bird trapped in her house, she hit against her mother's and sister's frowns, later against the anger of the woman with whom she lives, the woman her family hates. The years without the turmoil from her mother or Isabel, perhaps the years alone have their tranquility, feeling her dark way but with no one yelling in her face.

"I've cried. Luckily, I can. *Lloro y descanso.* I wanted to tell you. You know how I wake up early? Well, yesterday morning, I fell back asleep for a while. When I wake up, I see a child, dressed in green. I scream, and he runs away. Do you think it was el Santo Niño de Atocha?

"But last night I had a bad night, *corazón santo*," she says. "You know that I'm devoted to *el Espíritu Santo*. My first church here, though, was Sacred Heart down on Oregon. When I woke up this morning, I have my eyes closed, but I see. I see *el Sagrado Corazón*, there at the corner of my bed. He looks as if He is made of four pieces, of plaster, and I think, 'Just look. I can see His heart.'

"Something is there. *Ay, reina adorada*, when I pray to the Holy Spirit, I remember everything. I remember that one day I dreamt the Sacred Heart. I felt so happy after I dreamt Him, like I felt today after I saw Him."

"What was the hardest thing in your life, Aunt Chole?"

"Leaving school. *Lo más duro fue teniendo que abandonar la escuela.* I've always felt so dumb, *corazón mío*, because I had to leave.

"*Ay, ya se me hace larga la vida.* I'm tired and tell *mi Diosito* that I'm ready to go. You know me and my troubles. If I go, I go with troubles. Well, I have to go to heaven if I can. *Ya, ya, ya, quiero descansar mentalmente.*"

Aunt Chole stands before me and begins to bless me saying, "I pray that the Holy Spirit will guide you, that he will put before you everything that you need as He does it for me. *Que te guíe en tu camino, mi chula.* Tell me again. You leave Friday, and you speak Saturday. *Te voy encaminando.* I'll pray for you that they'll listen to you. And I pray for *mi amor*, your husband, and for the children, for Libby at Stanford and her boyfriend, Roger, for Billy that he'll find a good job, and for the little one because she's the little one. A redhead, right? Imagine."

Aunt Chole and I sit in the covered porch with Mamá Cleta who listens to the secret life of spiders, to beetles burrowing, pods swaying in the trees. She touches the yellow columbine, hears its clear, soprano melody calling to butterflies and bumble bees. "*Ay, mayo, mayo*," she sighs in pleasure, hopes her grandchildren and great-grandchildren will remember what she's taught them about watching the moon, about planting burrowing crops in the dark of the moon and above-ground crops as *la luna* swells, about when to prune so the plant or bush won't feel the cut, about singing to plants to help them bloom. She notices how seldom her descendants read the sky, unaware of the moon's waxing and waning, but in the back garden, she sees the older men painting tree trunks white with lime to protect them from worms and insects, raking even the hard, bare dirt because their fathers did, as the Japanese rake their rock gardens, men who know the old ways, how to watch, how to listen.

She goes to her room, brings out the book in which she writes her thoughts, her recipes and gardening lists. With the ink she scented with a decoction of lemon verbena, she writes, "*Sólo lo barato se compra con dinero,*" only what's cheap, can be bought with money.

Caterpillars whisper on the leaves. Turtles bask in the sun, and my white-haired relatives doze, dreaming they are back in the yards or hills of their youth chasing their siblings through a fountain or under bushes.

I think of Aunt Chole's homes, the first one that my father helped her buy on Stanton Street, and her last house, always cool, tidy and gleaming, the desert light softened by the rose carpet and turquoise and rose sofa and chairs. Little, my sister and I tiptoe in all that quiet, struggle to thread a needle, to stitch the perfect stitches that our aunt pulls smooth as music through squares of yellow cloth. She tries to make each of her homes lovely, even when she's a young girl with no money.

"*Mamá*, will you give me fifty cents? A dollar would be better."
"*¿Pa' qué?* Why do you need money?"
"So I can make curtains for that window."

Chole, a twelve-year-old thin as a sapling, walks downtown alone to Woolworth's, wanders up and down the aisles, looks at SoapsCreamsLipsticksPowderPerfumesNailpolishPursesHose SocksScarvesPencilsGlueTabletsEnvelopesPansCoffeepots KnivesForksSpoonsTowelsScissorsBowsHershey'sOrangeslices GumdropsSourballsCrackerjacks.

Carefully, she picks up a tiny ceramic bird, a dog with a blue collar. She studies the rainbows of yarn, knitting needles and crochet hooks, ribbons, buttons, pins, snaps, yardsticks, thimbles, spools of thread, bolts of cotton and seersucker, the prices. She slides her hand across the dusty-rose satin, the white lace. She buys what she can, an inexpensive organdy, imagines the neighbors walking by, seeing the transparent clouds billowing from the Mora house, like in the movies.

She walks home, clutching her purchase to her chest, enters the smell of onions frying, beans simmering, her mother's frowns.

"*¡Chole, ven te necesito en la cocina!*"

"*Luego voy, Mamá,*" but she ignores her mother's spiny words, takes the sheer material from the paper bag, begins to measure the window that faces the street, to handstitch the curtains.

"*¡Chole! ¡Chole!*" her mother yells.

Chole folds the half-stitched curtains neatly on her bed, begins to walk to the kitchen, returns worried that her sisters might pull the filmy cloth and ruin her work, takes the paper bag out of the trash can, hides her purchase in the bag, under the bed. After dinner while her brothers and sisters play outside, the quiet girl finishes sewing the curtains. She stares at the window, thinks: but if I hang the curtains behind the shade, the people outside won't see them, won't know: this is a nice house, the Moras are a nice family. At night in the dark, she wonders what to do.

The next morning she's up early, before the voices begin, safe in their snoring. She moves a chair to that front window carefully, so no one will hear her, yell at her, laugh at her. She climbs on the chair, removes the shade, hangs the curtains right by the window so everyone outside can see them, smooths the organdy with both hands, then hangs the shade to face inside.

Chole opens the front door very slowly. She unlatches the screen door and slips out without a sound to the sidewalk, turns around to see the window, the window that had the ugly shade. She walks to the front of the neighbor's house, pretends she's not Chole Mora, she's just a nice person walking by. She looks at that window, sees the white gauzy folds. She smiles.

When her family wakes up and sees what she's done, they laugh at a girl who puts curtains facing outside where the shade should be.

"Come, look what Chole did. *¡Qué muchacha tan loca!*"

"I want our house to look nice from the outside, so I put the curtain facing out and the shade facing in, *ee-ee*. Imagine. I think I always have the love of pretty things inside me, *ya lo traía*.

"Here, I found something for you. I don't have much left, but you've been asking about flowers, and I think you'd like these. You like them? They're made of bread dough. Yes, *reinita querida*, bread dough. Your Aunt Carmen used to make some too.

"I'd get a fresh loaf of white bread and pull out the soft interior, mix it with Elmer's Glue and hand lotion until it is smooth. I sit in my kitchen on the weekends or in the evening, mix my paints in different bowls, and then mix the paint and dough and begin shaping tiny *tortillitas* that I curl to make these perfect blooms and tiny buds, shaping each petal with care, tiny roses and lilies. With a needle, I make the veins on the leaves. Take them to your room, *reina*. Anyway, I can't see them. These hands *fueron muy trabajadoras*. I worked all my life."

In the late afternoon light, I read about old-fashioned bouquets called tussie-mussies, messages sent in the elaborate language of flowers, floriography, a custom which may have begun in eighteenth-century Turkey. In the early 1700s, Lady Mary Wortley Montagu, wife of the English ambassador to Turkey, wrote a friend, "fair maidens to the East have lent a mute speech to flowers," and later wrote *Turkish Letters*, an explanation of this communication through blooms. In France *Le Langage des Fleurs* was published in 1819, a handbook of floral language. How the romantics savored the intricate symbolism, aromatically eloquent, silent bouquets; daisies for innocence, lillies for hatred, red roses for desire. The poet Thomas Hood, in "The Language of Flowers" wrote, "Sweet flowers alone can say what passion fears revealing."

Mentally, I design a nosegay for Aunt Chole, starched lace and a coded message, an amethyst for admiration, the central emotion, surrounded by a crown of tiny roses, the reward of virtue; virtuous, this aunt who all day prays for others.

I watch shadows play in the garden, chase one another through the fountain, under the bushes redolent with the new mulches of bark and pecan shells we spread this morning.

Morn - ing has bro -ken, Like the first morn - ing.

Mamá Cleta as always rises early. We hear the *clck, clck,* her rosary beads when she paces round the covered porch, frowns at late sleepers, often repeating a favorite *dicho,* "*Al que madruga, Dios le ayuda.*" She has waited for the first blooms to open, and today begins her annual gathering that continues through autumn, choosing what flowers to dry. She cuts them in the morning or evening when the blossoms' breaths rise warm and heavy; walks down by the *acequia* and the river looking for pussy willows and wild grasses. In a small dark room adjoining hers, wood drying racks will soon have loose bunches of blooms and herbs drying heads down. Berries, pods, and pine cones so useful for the winter flower arrangements will fill one special basket.

"Mamá Cleta, how do you know what to collect?" I ask. Aunt Chole comes to listen.

"I have my favorites—of the roses, Queen Elizabeth, and also larkspur, honeysuckle, strawflowers, and my blue hydrangeas," says Mamá Cleta. "I've learned to keep their color blue by feeding them apple peels. Experience. '*Echando a perder se aprende,*' says this woman who speaks in sayings. "When the snow and cold begin, I'll create small bouquets and arrangements for the house. Gardens, like families, can be timeless—if they're tended, Patricia."

I tell them the old Chinese saying, "If you want to be happy for a day, roast a pig. If you want to be happy for a year, marry. If you want to be happy for a lifetime, plant a garden."

"I like to sit out here," Aunt Chole says lifting her face to the sky. "I hear you, I hear you, *mis pajaritos.* I used to be able to come out and feed these birds in the morning. *Creo que me hacían una fiesta las palomitas y los pajaritos.* They'd scold me if I was late, and when I couldn't go outside at my house alone any more, they were angry for a long time. They counted on me. I sit in there suffering and listen to them, but *ay* what can I do, *mi reina? Son los detalles de la vida.* But birds can be grateful. One day I was standing at the window looking out, only able to see light and shadows, and a bird begins to sing to me, so beautifully. I think he must have come when I could still feed them, and he wants to say thank you."

On Sunday, Mother says, "Look! My Mother's Day present from your sister. A parakeet. It's green, but I'll call it Bluey. That's what your father always called our parakeets."

"You mean the ones whose pink beaks let us know he'd been doctoring them with Pepto-Bismol?"

"Your father! But he was the most wonderful man in the world—even though we did fight for over fifty years. Just listen to this bird, my Bluey," she calls to the family women. "In Spanish I call her *Chiquitina.* She's so smart because she's female. Face it, my dears, females are smarter. We have to be, to survive."

Aunt Chole, Lobo, Aunt Carmen, and Mother's daughters and granddaughters nod as do her grandmothers and great-grandmothers.

Junio / June

Huerta sin agua, cuerpo sin alma.

An orchard without water is like a body
　　without a soul.

THE RÍO GRANDE runs high these summer days,
streams through the irrigation canals quenching the
thirst of fig and apricot trees, *moras* and *álamos*, daylillies
and phlox, agave and ocotillo, mint and basil. In the *jardín*, wa-
ter spills on the old fountain's gray stone surface, glazing the *can-
tera* slides into the round pool that holds the circles of water and
light expanding like silent echoes into one another; the foun-
tain's liquid voice, *ps-slp-plop, ps-slp-plop.*

"Thou shalt be like a watered garden and like a fountain
of water whose waters shall not fail," the words of Isaiah refresh
in any desert. My three when they were little, hands out-
stretched hoping the drops will spatter their palms, stand near
the terra-cotta pots of geraniums circling the fountain like a red
halo.

"*¡Mira qué lindos los geranios!*" Mamá Cleta, her long gray hair
in its soft bun above her head, comes toward us drying her
hands on her floor-length, white apron. "Listen to the flowers,
the garden brimming *como la fuente* with its music. Do you hear
the colors—flutes, guitars, drums, violins, harps." She claps her
hands in a *jaleo*, to the rhythm of a flamenco she alone hears,
lleva la música por dentro. Butterflies brush hanging plants—pink
ivy geraniums and trailing asparagus fern, brush the soft red
mouths of snapdragons.

Since Aunt Chole has promised to tell me the story about the
man on the radio today, I set out to find her but can't resist

watching Mamá Cleta gathering for her potpourri—lavender and roses, pink if possible—now that the sun has warmed the garden's blooms. Scissors in hand, she reads the flowers, floral literacy, grasps their scented promise.

In her room, she shows Christopher, the youngest in the family, how gently to pull the petals off while she brings out her baskets for the drying, the brewing, saves the rose hips for steeping teas, watches the young boy, her great-great-great-grandson smelling the flowers, fingering their velvet.

"*Cuidado, Creestofer. No hay rosa sin espina.* We'll put these *canastitas* in this warm, dark corner. We don't want mildew to ruin our potpourri, do we, *Creestofer?* You can check the baskets every day, and when the blooms dry, we'll pour them into these air-tight glass jars or these tins. Occasionally you must come and shake them. What do you mean you want to go watch cartoons?

"Pay attention and mind your Mamá Cleta as Our Good Lord has told us to mind our elders," she says back and pointing finger straight. "When we have a good mix of blooms, I'll let you help me grind the spices in the *molcajete*—cloves, nutmeg, cardamom, then we'll add orris root to fix the fragrance, dried lemon and orange rind. We can toss the blooms together, and maybe add one of my secret oils. Then we'll store our mix, let the scents dream together in the dark. *Creestofer! Creestofer* come back here!" she complains bemoaning his lack of respect, the family's irreverent habit of calling him Cristo, the absence of religion in today's world. "*¿A dónde se fue ese niño? ¡Qué falta de respeto! Le debíamos de decir Cristóbal, pero se enoja, y peor le dicen Cristo. ¿Qué ha pasado con la religión en este mundo?*"

Mamande sees me standing outside Mamá Cleta's room, watching. My grandmother takes my arm and asks me to go sit behind the house with her under the *mora*. Though I want to find Aunt Chole, I enjoy sitting near my grandmother, holding hands with her in the sliding sound of the *acequia* and the sight of trees heavy with fruit.

"*Mira.*" She points at the gentle curve of a mourning dove's head peeking out from the plumbago. Legends say the female painted her face white and her beak bright red to attract a mate, the red actually the scarlet juice of *tunas,* the prickly pear's ripe fruits.

Biting into an apricot, Mamande looks east to the mountain as she chews the sun-warmed *chavacán.* Who was the man who settled into this redhead's heart? We know she is a young woman in Chihuahua then, and the story is that he's a telegraph operator who has to leave the city. Does work make him leave or is it her stepfamily, the Revillas, who have him sent away maybe because he drinks or because he's not of the right class or because they fear their charge will elope, leave some night, the quiet Amelia take the hand of this stranger and run into her new life.

Leaving her for a minute, I go inside and find the gold leaf. Either he or someone for him, had taken a simple leaf, simple in the botanical sense of a single blade with a smooth edge, and removed the green leaf matter revealing the veins, the delicate structure, leaving only Mamande's initials in an elaborate scroll, a leaf filigree, the entire leaf painted gold, the leaf she kept until her death. Where did she hide it her married years? Why didn't I see it or hear the story until I began to explore this house? The private life of the family women, the chambers of their hearts which they enter when alone.

"He loves me, he loves me not," my daughters sing-song in their childhood pulling off white daisy florets nearby, and I hear Mother's voice when I was little, "Dais - y, dais - y, give me an an - swer, do."

I return to the shade and the murmur of water wondering if white-haired women sip the memory of old loves. Mamande smiles when she sees the leaf, pats my hand, hands me another apricot, soft orange moon, says, *"Qué cara tan querida."*

The young man leaves Chihuahua, but the sober gold eyes go with him, the hint of a smile, until one night unable to sleep, he taps out a message to his love, sends her a telegram. Does it say, *"Amelia, te amo. Por favor."* Does it say where he will be waiting for her? The telegram is probably delivered but never rests in her hands. Does her stepmother, Mamá Nina, shove the envelope deep into the pocket of her long brown dress like the tall stepmother in Disney's *Cinderella* shoves the heavy key? That

evening in her room does Mamá Nina place the words in a dish
and put a match to them, watch the small flame sway, smoke
twirl, paper curl to black ash?

"I think I heard he was an Anglo once," says Uncle Lalo.

"No, not an Anglo," says Mother firmly.

Donde hay amor, hay dolor. As she chews the fruit, does Ma-
mande wonder still what happened to that dear face? Had she
put ivy under her pillow and dreamt her true love, would his
have been the face in her dreams? We have only the gold leaf, its
envelope postmarked May 15, 1915, Hurley, New Mexico, and
her phrase, "*Qué cara tan querida.*"

I decide to write in my room for a few hours before looking
for Aunt Chole, saving her story as a reward. When I come out
to the covered porch later looking for her, I see her laughing to
herself, saying something about radios and shaking her head as
she opens the door to Abuela Tomasa's room. Maybe I'll walk
down to the river and listen to the grackles and cottonwoods
while she visits since she may be in there for hours. I want to
hear the story, but she's only going to tell it if we're alone. Seeing
my mother come out of her room, I say, "Come and walk with
me, Mother."

"But I haven't had breakfast yet, Dear." Mother's smiling,
ready to chat, totally awake and ready to begin her day. I feel my
anger rising, filling me though I struggle to press it into a box I
can lock.

"It's four o'clock in the afternoon, Mother. You're sleeping
your last years of life away. How can you do it?"

"I'm seventy-nine now, hon, and I've earned the right to do
what I want, when I want. Just look at this role reversal. Don't
get old, Pat. You won't want your children telling you what to
do."

"If I make you a ham-and-cheese sandwich and sit out here
with you while you eat, will you walk down by the river with
me? You need some exercise, Mother. You know it."

"Oh, I walk every week when I go to the beauty parlor and
then to the store. You know how I am when I get into a drug-
store. I buy boxes and boxes of Kleenex, cards for my children

and grandchildren—not that I get around to mailing them, mind you. I never did send the valentines I bought this year, did I?"

"That's okay. You can use them next year." Frustrated as I get at her pokiness and sleeping habits, I'm amused by Mom. We laugh together with ease, enjoy one another's company if I can stop my nagging; so alike, so different. Even when I look at my body, I see theirs, my father's feet, Mother's thighs. In habits and tendencies, I'm both my mother's and father's child—his punctuality, eagerness for work, energy, and ability to sleep—anywhere, anytime; her love of books, pleasure at fitting words together, experimenting with their different colors and patterns; and pleasure at public speaking, persuading. From both, I inherited fire: a need for family closeness and a quickness to anger, for neither of my parents had any use for genteel surfaces at home. They flared, often at each other.

"I'll just sit at this table in the shade and enjoy looking at the roses. I never sit in the sun, do you, Pat? If I say so myself, for my age, I have very good skin. People can't believe I'm almost eighty, but it's because I always avoided the sun and used plenty of moisturizer. Do you, Dear?"

I leave her sitting in the covered porch, walk quickly into the kitchen, put together the sandwich, walk back anxious to stroll to the river and look out on the desert mesas, anxious to visit with Aunt Chole.

"Thanks, Dear, but how about some chips? And do we have any of those nice, big kosher dills? I love to eat them at the movies when I'm little. Isn't it terrible how I enjoy being waited on? But I do. Well, I waited on you all for years, so maybe it's my turn." She basks contented in the warmth of the afternoon as I rush to the kitchen, bump into my father.

"She's all yours, honey," he chuckles, freed by death from her aversion to rushing. Like Alice in the looking glass, the elusive spirit shrinks before my eyes into a sparrow, hovers around me, pecks at the chips and pickle. In any shape, my father likes to eat. He flies out with me, begins to peck at Mother's sandwich.

"Scat, scat," she says. "Just look at that bird."

"Maybe he wants you to rush." I shake my head at what I'm

watching. My father could erupt like a volcano at home or work, and I understand. Mother can have anyone who watches clocks gasping for patience, and to a fault I'm one to hear time ticking, like my father, for me, "To be on time is to be late." Often it's afternoon, before Mother gets up, bathes, puts on her make-up, and gets dressed, and then she's up all night. My anger rises again. "Eat up, Dearie. I was hoping to see the river today, not tomorrow. And I've got some things to do."

"Could I have a soda, hon? You know, something diet. I've become a little chub-a-dubs and better watch my weight." Back to the kitchen, the bird too, bouncing up and down on the counter with glee, relishing my frustration.

"I rushed when the four of you were growing up. Didn't I get you everywhere?" Mother asks when I return, hearing my impatient silence.

"Usually late, Dearie." I sigh, but we grin at each other. I'm exasperated but see the humor in her obliviousness to my controlled panting. It's when I try to change her, convinced that it's for her good—she needs exercise and daytime stimulation—that I sour what we have. I think of the prayer that through the years she puts on her refrigerator or by her bedroom mirror, often saying, "I'm such a worrier. I wish I could do what this says,

> God grant me the serenity to accept the things I
> cannot change,
> the courage to change the things I can,
> and the wisdom, to know the difference.

"So in elementary school, you started leaving early on the bus," she says. Not offended, she enjoys the memory of her determined first child, striving so to be prompt, a good girl, a model student at whom those nuns smiled. "That's why I called you 'the sergeant' pushing to get us all up and going. Now what were we talking about? I tell you, my memory's going." The sparrow pecks at her food.

"I guess so, up till three in the morning, sleeping till three in the afternoon." I fidget in my chair, sneak a look at my watch.

"Don't frown, Dear. It will give you wrinkles. I think I'm usually up by one—well, maybe two, but I was always a night owl, too old to change now."

"Eat, Mother, EAT. We were talking about you and your drugstore."

"Oh of course. I have to go get all my medicines. Just look at this crazy bird picking on me." Always, picking on her. "Like your father." Clever lady. "Have I told you how many medicines I'm taking now, Pat?"

"I don't want to know, Mother."

"Well, it's not my fault. My mother used to make me drink cod-liver oil every morning, a huge spoonful of thick *aceite de bacalao*. Mamande programmed me to be a medicine taker." She bites into her sandwich, chews each bite with care, licks the crumbs from the corners of her mouth. "Sorry, Dear, you know I've always been a slow eater."

"Leave my poor grandmother out of this." I tease with her unable to resist Mother's ability to attribute her quirky behavior to others. "I thought she was a saint."

"Oh, she was, she was, but it's her fault I take so much medicine. In fact, I need to call my doctor and tell him I need something for my knee. It's killing me."

"I thought you were supposed to get exercise. To walk, daily, and I'm not talking about your shopping binges." Let's go, I'm thinking, let's go.

"Oh, after I go to the drugstore or the grocery store, I can hardly move for days, hon. Have I told you about that nice man that came to see me? I just love men, don't you? It's your father's fault. He taught me to like having a man around. He taught me that."

The sparrow bites her hand and darts into the garden.

"Did you see that! That dumb bird bit me! Is that you, Raúl?"

I ignore their antics, say, "Wait a minute, wait a minute. You're a drug addict because of your mother and a sex addict because of your husband?"

She throws back her head and laughs out loud. My mother knows how to laugh. "Maybe I'm insane, but you have to admit it's a cute insanity."

"Did you say acute insanity?" I ask.

"Do you think June is a romantic month, brides and all these gorgeous flowers? He's very tall, this nice man, and here I am a shorty. He's taller than Daddy and stands very straight. His Spanish, oh his Spanish is beautiful. *Me encanta platicar con él.* She begins her soft, romantic singing, "*Cuan - do ca - li - en - ta el sol.*" She hums for a bit, *hm-hm-hm-hm-hm*, chews, savoring the food and the memories.

"Have I told you about the nice man that came to see me?" she asks after a bit as if for the first time. "Can you believe someone sold him my name. Why, it's like prostitution!"

"You've told me, Mother. You've told me. I think someone you know gave him your name because he missed speaking Spanish. Eat up so we can go hear the birds by the river. Want to know the names of some Southwest birds?" I try to divert her from her new, favorite topic.

"I want to know which bird you think I am. Your beloved Lobo could be those ravens you tell me about, huge black shadows. I know, I know, but when I'm young your aunt is like a witch in our house. So what about me?" She warms to the topic. "Which bird am I, a beautiful bird, I hope. You know me, hon. I've always been vain."

"All the kids would say to me, 'Your mother is sooo pretty,' " I say.

She smiles, enjoying the taste of the compliment with the last bite of her sandwich. "Did I tell you about the nice man that calls me?" she asks. I sigh. "Now don't worry I'm not going to marry again," she says, "once is enough. But I tell your father, 'Now, Papa, you had your fun before you met me, and I didn't. You were the only man I ever dated so now it's my turn.' If anything ever happens that he shouldn't see, Dear, I'll see to it that he doesn't," says Mother who's approaching eighty, has begun humming tangos. "Not that this nice man has asked me to marry him, mind you, but if he did, don't think I'm leaving my country and my children and grandchildren. No sir."

After dinner, I manage to be alone with Aunt Chole.

"Are you sure we're alone?" she asks. "*Las paredes oyen.* You know how my sisters are. All right, all right, I'll tell you. *Ay*, he was so wonderful, *reina*. He recited poetry on the radio." She pauses. "Who is that? Who's coming?"

"Your sisters, but I think they're going to sit outside."

"Nooooo, I'm not talking about him if they're around." Aunt Chole rises with difficulty feeling her way to the living room. Aunt Carmen guides her to her favorite chair, talks with her about the years they worked together at a department store. I sit nearby, look up at the *viga* and *latilla* ceiling, much like the one in my room, thin wood crosspieces, perhaps saplings, supported by cottonwood beams.

I linger a while and decide my cause is hopeless, that I should visit with my children laughing outside with the family men, then say good-night, go put my tablet up and read.

In the kitchen, I see Abuela Tomasa selecting the softest apricots from the wooden bowl in the center of the table.

"*¿Qué haces, Abuela?*" My father asks from behind me.

"*Nada, nada, querido.*" Tomasa, secretive in her nineties, gathers the fruit in her small, wrinkled hands, scrutinizes each globe selecting only the best, unblemished, the ripest. Hoping no one's watching, she tiptoes away from us, looks around quickly then opens the door to her room. She turns on the radio and whispers to the man in there, the man who croons his romantic songs, "*Bé - sa - me, bé - sa - me mu - cho.*"

She whispers to him, "*Mira, aquí te traigo chavacanes frescos. Pero, por favor, cántame en voz baja.*" She places the apricots behind the radio, the secret spot where she leaves him what she can, last night a piece of *laberintos*, labyrinths of sugar that my father enjoys when she's not looking.

"*Sh, sh, cállate,*" she daily pleads with the stubborn, ardent radio suitor to control himself, not wanting her family embarrassed again by his antics, his endless songs of unrestrained love.

The last recorded words I have of my father he's talking about Tomasa saying, "She'd listen to those love songs and imagine . . ." What would she imagine, Daddy? The dead still move through the house, through our lives, but their audio and videotaping days are over. "No," they say. "No."

Tomasa puts her veined hand over her mouth hiding from the amorous radio man her delight in what he sings. She laughs to herself, savors his passion filling the room, heavy as jasmine. In its fragrance, our great-grandmother dances with his voice.

Women and radios, the longing, the fervent voices that croon their love to us, love us as we long to be loved.

In my room, serenaded by Mother's music and a cricket, I read poet Mary Oliver about noctural creatures, bats, moths, "who do their work in the darkness." The full Rose Moon, 240,000 miles away, eventually pulls us out to the *portal* and garden, tugs us with her gravity as she tugs the tides, the sound of her light irresistible to the moon-drunk, the lunarphilic. Our Holy Mother, the Maya called her, believed she chased her son the sun never quite catching him while the Aztecs told of the Rabbit Moon. Since the combined shine of sun and moon would be too bright, one of their gods tossed a rabbit at *la luna* diminishing its light, the rabbit still visible during the full moon.

"*¿Quién ve al conejo?*" my father asks.

"*¡Ay!* I can't see anything, *nada, nada.*" Aunt Chole whimpers, touches her way to her room.

Acacias and mesquites, green pious nuns, fold their leaflets together like hands in prayer, but I hear creatures more bold savoring the night. Lizards rise dancing *salsa* and *cumbias;* agave open pores they close to the sun. Under the stars, succulent plants open themslves to the desert night, hot nights, red eyes, tongues stretching into thick nectar. Moths heavy with pollen brush against pale blossoms. *Reina de noche* opens her satin throat and stars tumble into her smell. In night's dark, we too, like *el jardín,* do our nocturnal work in our dreams and what has burrowed deep within, appears. For those hours, we lie captivated by our selves.

Waking, I hear comfort, voices, *clk, clk,* Mamá Cleta's morning rosary as she walks round and round, the hem of her dress brushing the worn, red-tiled covered walkway; *sw, sw, sw,* Lobo's broom; Aunt Carmen, watering; Uncle Lalo, raking; clanging of kitchen pots, grandmothers, great-grandmothers, and great-great-grandmothers talking to Aunt Chole as they begin the family's breakfast.

June, the month of Pentecost, *alleluia, alleluia.*

> *Spiritus Sanctus in igneis linguis:*
> The Holy Spirit appeared in tongues of fire.

God spoke in tongues, whirling gusts and trembling fire, symbols of the fullnes of spirit, Holy Spirit. The priest's vestments—stole, chasuble, maniple—red, the Latin phrases and chants rising in us like mantras,

> *Ký - ri - e, e - lé - i - son*
> *Chri - ste, e - lé - i - son.*
>
> *Gló - ri - a in ex - cél - sis De - o.*
>
> *A - gnus De - i*
>
> *Sanc - tus, Sanc - tus, Sanc - tus*
>
> *Dó - mi - nus vo - bís - cum.*
> *Et cum spí - ri - tu tu - o.*

So much violence in the lives of the June saints like poor Saint Erasmas, patron saint of bowel trouble whose intestines were wound on a windlass, and that was after the beating, rolling in pitch, the fire; more appealing to me, the saints with less dramatic lives like Saint Anthony who found so many lost articles for the family all year, except for my note tablet though I continue to offer bribes.

In New Mexico the *acequia* waters were believed to be holy on June twenty-fourth, the feast of San Juan Bautista. People would rise early to bathe in the waters before Mass or at least to splash the water on their faces and feet to insure good health, in procession, carry the statue of Saint John the Baptist through the fields to the irrigation canal for the blessing of the water, "*In nomine patris, et filii, et spirtus sancti,*" San Juan asked to intercede for abundant crops.

Often when a boy and drum signaled that the procession was approaching a house, the woman inside who had prepared her home altar with flowers greeted the group carrying a shovel glowing with coals and incense. If rain were scarce during the growing season, a family might invite friends to join in taking the statues of their saints out through the fields to ask for their help, faith woven into the hours of the day. Saints and rain, songs and rain, usually pale saints, Europeans, a white pantheon of goodness and sacrifice and virtue.

Where are the other holy songs in the family, the non-Christian songs—chants for rain, corn-growing songs, sun-rising songs, harvest songs, hunting songs, heartbreaking songs, hatebreaking songs, healing songs, love songs? What are the names of Indian women and men, part of this family, who sang the songs? Why have only the Spanish names been passed from mouth to mouth? When does the legacy end of cherishing only white skin and *ojos azules, azules, azules?* In this desert garden, when does the *agua santa* heal us, when do we heal our spirits, the soul of the house?

After helping to dry the breakfast dishes, I wait under the cottonwood for Aunt Chole, determined to write the story, for stories, like plants, need attention and protection, this garden, for example, an accumulation of nurtured possibilities. The fruit and shade trees, flowering plants and herbs survive in this desert oasis because of the attentiveness of the family, its seeds, plantings, cuttings, pinchings, feedings, prunings, and endless, endless watering. The green sound carries, shade of mesquites, Chinaberry trees and *moras,* the gray green, gold green, blue green lures lizards, frogs, house finches. Honeybees, moths, and wasps sip the sweet cream of yucca blooms. Occasionally, a pea-cock struts through, *Aayyhh, AAAYYYHHH,* its eyespots mes-merizing our eyes with an optical illusion, the play of light refracted and reflected into glimmering greens, blues, golds.

With her basket of sachets to tuck between the layers of warm clothes and bedding, Mamá Cleta visits each grandmother and great-grandmother busy putting away winter shawls and blankets in her room. "*Buenos días, buenos días*, here are some tiny pillows I made to make our clothes sweet and to ward off insects." The women stop, smell the small cushions filled with rose petals, lavender, dried orange peel, cinnamon, anise, cloves.

I see Aunt Chole open the kitchen door and begin to talk to the parrot, "*Ay, cómo te quiere tu madre.*" I move quickly, but Mamande comes and takes Aunt Chole's arms, takes her to walk for their exercise around the covered porch.

Deciding to drive to a nearby nursery, I walk out through the front courtyard, by the Mexican elder, bee-luring vitex, oleander, the blue humming of morning glory; out the front gate and around the adobe wall to the garage area, where the car is parked amid cars, carts, wagons, and carriages, reflecting the generations that dwell in the house.

"What's this?" The nursery owner who resembles Yosemite Sam looks at the lacy carpet of greenery I'm pointing to in which tight purple buds hide like pursed, purple mouths, a frilly foliage that might work well in a bare corner in the garden.

"Love in the Mist," the beard says.

"Quite a name."

"Just look around here." He points with his wide, rough hand to the tables of lilies, pots of roses, beds of mountain gold alyssum. "Everything about flowers is about sex, the lengths they'll go to be sexed, their amorous, dependent relationships with bugs, birds, bats."

Glancing at yellow Mexican poppies, I ponder his grammatical construction "to be sexed." A woman overhearing him adds, "Yea, just one big singles' bar out there." I laugh, know that botanically the purpose of flowers is reproduction, but I feel uncomfortable, even though the names as I stroll down the narrow rows have a sexual tone: Lady of the Night, Kiss Me Quick, Passion Flower, Maiden's Blush; the roses: Don Juan, Sheer Bliss, Heartbreaker, Playboy, French Lace; but still my companions' humor almost offends my romantic attachment to flowers' aesthetic and ornamental grace, to the innocence of blooms, preferring to be drunk on the white fragrance of pure gardenias than to visualize the sticky maneuverings of bat tongues in petaled throats.

The woman continues. "I grew up next to my grandparents, Italians. They were retired and gardened all day, but they'd learned plant names here and since they mispronounced them, I did too. My mother says I'd run home exclaiming about the 'chrsytansees and nastoortions.'"

I splurge on a scented cymbidium orchid to try in the bathroom that gets plenty of afternoon light hoping the shower steam and my mistings will convince the plant it's still in some *bosque tropical*. Driving home, I plot to pick some ripe apricots for Aunt Chole, find a quiet place for us to talk. I walk through cicada drones and persistent bird chirps of the front courtyard, hear Mamá Cleta and my other great-great-grandmother, Abuela Elena, exchanging recipes for wines—dandelion and rose petal, flowers they brew in the kitchen, fermentings in the dark.

"Use only the dandelion petals and crush the white grapes gently, let them doze in the sugar, stir them softly as they float." Mamá Cleta the Confident. "I tell the young ones, to treat the wine soothingly, never jolting it, imagining if we wake it abruptly from its thick sleep, the deep fruit flavor will vanish, like a dream. We want to pour it in its *sueños*, the sweetened, transformed flavor from our earth, opening in our mouths, ¿verdad, Doña Elena?"

The sensuality of gardeners and cooks. Women who button their blouses to the neck, avert their eyes at bare curves and cleavage across a room or on canvas; such women in their kitchens and gardens release their senses to play. With firm hands, they knead bread dough and smell the drunk steam from cranberries simmering in port, with a tasting spoon sip the crimson concoction. They spread their fingers deep into warm beds they mulch on their knees outside, sprinkle wildflower seeds and their headstrong surprises into the garden, bend into the honeysuckle's gold buzz and place the clear drop of nectar on their proper tongues, watch snails lazily revealing their skin.

Such sensuality is sanctioned, even sacred when performed in the service of others, self-sacrifice a noble path for women, certainly in both Mexican and Church culture. But don't the physical pleasures themselves—tasting the wild orange wind, peering into the hibiscus' open mouth, hearing the tongued trees, smelling the heat of rising dough, stroking the plums' red curves—the private body pleasures also lure women to those kitchens and gardens?

Sexual loves, poetry and song remind us, simmer in kitchens and gardens too, of course, two bodies with eyes, hands, mouths feasting on one another.

These summer months women are intoxicated by the senses, by honeysuckle and loves real and imagined; old and new loves, unrequited.

Love simmers in the June heat like the preserves Aunt Carmen's making in the kitchen.

"Aunt Chole, Aunt Chole, want to sit and have some fruit?" I call.

"Come and smell this you two," Aunt Carmen says. I take Aunt Chole to stand by the countertop sticky with sweet and tart juices from the sliced apricots and lemons. Aunt Carmen stirs the pot of juices tumbling, darkening, thickening; the kitchen floating in an apricot steam.

"I'll freeze some to put on toast or ice cream," she says, her hands bathed in honeyed juice. "But for tonight, I think I'll make a cobbler." Aunt Chole's eyebrows rise in anticipation.

When I gently steer her back outside, a hummingbird zips toward her red top, the sound reminding me of the word for the Tarascan capital, *Tzintzuntzan*, place of the hummingbirds, the word, *tzintzuntzan* that darts as do the gleaming birds. Butterflies also drift through the garden, and for a moment I remember a river's shore again, butterflies landing on my clothes and arms, their legs whispering to my skin.

"*¿Qué es, querida? ¿Qué es el ruidito?*"

"*Chuparrosa, Tía.*"

"*Ay, que mi pajarito,*" she croons to the jeweled hummers.

"*Cómo te quiere tu madre,*" says the macaw.

Arm-in-arm, Aunt Chole and I move into the brightness and warmth of the desert sun, that star of stars. We stop at the old clay water filter, and I hand her a rounded Mexican mug. "Ah," she says, "it tastes so much better, *reina*, water flavored by clay. Don't you taste the difference?" We walk once around the covered porch, and when I stop, she feels for the chair. We sit, silent, listen to the doves, *oo-o-oo, oo-o-oo.*

"Yes, if we're alone I'll tell you about that man. Don't go, *corazón*. I need you. You're like a medicine."

"I need you, Tía. You and your prayers help me." How can I convey to this woman who thinks she's dumb because she had to drop out of school how much her voice and prayers mean, her wrinkled stories fragrant as potpourri. Again, I'm sheltered by an aunt, her undemanding love encircling me like her arms and blessings. Up close, in the rooms of her house and heart, I see and hear her courage and her inventiveness in the dailiness of life.

"When I finish a container of something and need more from the store," she says, "I put the empty container in a special place I have since I can't write a list. What good would it do me to write it? I couldn't read it anyway. I have to think of how to do things, *reinita. No creas, no soy tan tonta.*" Her voice and her words make me cry and make me laugh. Could we have had this relationship sooner, before we were who we are?

"Not a young, beautiful woman and not a young rich woman has been given all the honor and love he gave me with his poetry." Finally, the story begins. "He would recite beautifully on his radio program. It began at five. I had been very sad for a long time. I guess I stop eating, and one day I feel myself and scream, 'My breasts! My breasts! They're gone!' Your cousin takes me to the doctor. They give me medicine and tell me to eat more.

"I start listening to José's program in the late afternoon when the sun comes through a window and warms my chair. His name is José, but he calls himself Pepe. He has traveled. He's an engineer and a pilot, and he has a sensitive heart. He recites so beautifully, *declamaba*, and it makes me happy, so one day I call just to thank him, to say, "*Ud. es un hombre muy humano.*" I don't tell him my name or anything though he asks, '*¿Con quién tengo el gusto de hablar?*'

"He goes on the air then and says that a lovely lady, *una bella dama*, has just called him. For three months, August through October, daily, daily, that man begs me to call him again, imagine. He dedicates all the programs to me, beautiful poems and songs. '*So - la - men - te una vez.*'

"At the beginning, he says that he wants to be my most sincere friend. I know all about him, that he likes food, for instance, good fish, from listening to his program every night. I know that he has never married, that he lives with his mother, that his brother and sister live in Juárez. He says that if I have a family, he will help me. How does he know I need help, *mi reina?* Maybe because I'm so *emocionante*, maybe I cry when I call.

"That man proclaims his love to me, begs me to call him, '*Para esa persona que quiero y adoro*' and '*Te quiero, te adoro, llámeme, hábleme, por favor.*' He says, 'I haven't been a saint. I've traveled. I've known people, but never, *nunca, nunca* have I known such a lovely heart.'

"Well, I don't have a bad heart. I try to be good with everyone. At the end of each program, he would say good-bye to the public, and then good-bye to me. *Fue tan lindo.* So little by little I get better. The doctor gives me that Assure, and I start gaining weight. The man on the radio says, 'This song is for that woman I love and adore.' One day a friend of his calls him and says, '*¡Basta!* Enough!' But that dear man says, 'I want to marry her.'

"I'd wanted to marry in my life, *corazón*, to have my own home, but it doesn't happen. Once I went on vacation to México, and *un señor árabe* falls in love with me." I see her then, tall and well-dressed, careful make-up and perfume, hair in a soft chignon, fake pearl earrings and a string of pearls on her navy-blue dress. "He is divorced and a friend tells me that if his ex-wife ever hears of me, I can never return to México. He calls me every night, very nice, a landowner, but he wants to marry me in secret.

"'NO,' says Isabel, 'not in secret.' *¡Aayy!*

"I tell my brother about the man on the radio because I feel so sorry for him. Your uncle says, 'Why do you want more difficulties?' And can you imagine how my sisters would have treated him. *Aaayyy*, would they have been furious! *¡Lo hubieran haber matado!*

"But, *corazón santo*, I thank God, I thank God that He put that man in my path so that I could know what true love is. I'll be honest. When I'm young I have male friends, but I want to get married and have my own house. It doesn't happen. My wish isn't granted. Twice when I'm young, I think I'm in love. I say *think* because I don't feel what I feel for this man. If I'd had that love when I was young, I would have gone with him. God put him *en mi camino* so that I could know love. *Ayyy*, but how could I marry him, *reina?*"

"Why didn't you call?"

"Why? Why? He doesn't know that I'm not educated and that I'm blind. How can I attend to him? I would only get sick. So I never have the courage to call. What would I do if he wants to marry me?

"He reaches out to me. I think, *qué hermoso*, the beauty of love. On his last program, he sings to me, '*Mi viejo amor*.' How does it go? Wait, wait. It will come to me. '*Un vie - jo amor nun - ca di - ce adiós*.' I remember what he says that day, '*Me despido pero volveré*. I say farewell, but I will return.'"

Para el amor no hay edad. The women in my blood suck warm apricots and hum songs of old loves that never say good-bye.

Julio / July

Al que buen árbol se arrima, buena sombra le cobija.

Seek shade under a worthy tree.

AUNT CARMEN turns on the sprinkler, calls, "Just look how these poor geraniums are drooping." The water arcs, drops patter. I go sit with my sisters under the cottonwood, talk about summer when we're little, running through such a sprinkler on hot afternoons always wishing for a big, blue pool. Our parents buy us the blow-up kind, and we huff and puff until the sides have risen with our cumulative breath. We fill the plastic pool with the hose, stretch out, so safe in our yard, trying to convince ourselves we're really floating, our heads on the blue soft, inflated sides, our eyes scanning the clouds for shapes—dragons, horses, faces. I still catch myself finding shapes, now even in charred wood burning in a kiva fireplace.

In that desert, longing to immerse ourselves in waves of water, we drag the hose up the steps of the slide and sail down the slick, wet, rippling surface. But periodically, one of us decides to produce the real thing, to dig a pool, yes, become Esther Williams in our own El Paso backyard. We dig, but cautiously, afraid we'll reach China and perhaps fall into a strange, other-world of rickshaws and baskets of squirming, smelly fish. Our deepest fear is fire, hell, stench, our small shovels uncovering a blaze leaping from the hole, the intense heat roaring into our peaceful yard, red and orange flames crackling as they had before the frightened eyes of Lucy, Francis, and Jacinta, the children at Fatima. How far is it safe to dig below the surface?

A slightly more practical solution is trying to convert the

front porch into a pool by dragging the hose in, inadequately
sealing the stepped entrance with some board and then sliding
on the red-painted cement until the water seeps, slides down
the two steps into the front grass. We spend hours playing jacks
on that red surface too—onesies, twosies, shoot the moon, little
house, shooting star; a pastime none of my children enjoyed. "I
love the way a golf ball sounded on that porch," Stella says, "that
clear *thump, thump, thump.*"

Summer evenings we play in the front yard, stretch beach
towels out to avoid a night of scratching the grass-green itch.
Until dark, we play statues, hopscotch, Simon Says, watch old
Mrs. McCoy in her thick hose, thick shoes with thick heels,
sweeping her porch across the street, never smiling or waving,
her house full of cats, their round bodies at night curled on her
trees like furred blooms.

"You and I hold hands," Cecilia says, "and we spin as long and
hard as we can, until our hands melt together, until we fall
down, dizzy on the grass, our world spinning around us. We
look up as fast as we can and watch the clouds spinning, tell
each other what appears."

"See that horse over there, Cecilia?"

"No."

"Yes, yes, look, see that big cloud? Follow where my finger's
pointing."

"Everything's still spinning."

"Okay, just keep looking up. See the horse's mouth that's eat-
ing that cloud? See his eye?"

"Oh, yea. And is the right leg lifted?"

"Yes! Yes! Look how his tail is flying."

We run laughing onto the porch, screech if the June bugs on
the screen door fly near us, fear the hard, brown bodies tangling
in our hair. We play Colors with our neighbors.

"What color are you going to be?" Whisper, whisper.

"I'll be red."

"I'll be blue," says Cecilia.

"I'll be green."

Knock, knock.

"Yes?"

"Hello, ma'am, I want to buy some eggs. Do you have any purple eggs?"

"Noooooo."

"Do you have any pink eggs?"

"Nooooo."

"Do you have any blue eggs?"

Cecilia runs out of the porch into the twilight, runs across the front grass, feeling the huge wolf reaching to grab her, its mouth open, teeth sharp as spikes. She runs panting back on the porch to us, safe, safe.

"In a book of children's games, I read that this is a version of an old Spanish game of good and evil," I say. "The game is called *Los Colores* or *Tan Tan* or *La Vieja Inés*. The mother is the angel and the person who comes knocking, *Tan, Tan,* is the devil."

"See!" Cecilia says. "I told you it looked like a wolf!"

Voices weave through the leaves, the July garden brimming with life, seen and unseen, bulbs, roots, worms, the dark life burrowing and brewing underground; blooming cannas, daisies, crape myrtle. Swollen purple clouds rise slowly, the drama of the Southwest summer sky. In the distance thunder rumbles, lightning flashes. I hope for a grand celestial display, the wildness of a good desert storm, this the month of the full Thunder Moon.

Cecilia brings a bowl of apricots to the table under the tree, and Mother comes to sit with us, memories seasoning the family conversation.

"Remember the time Mother caught us eating Mrs. Dyal's apricots outside?" Cecilia asks. "We hide with them where we think she'll never see us. The tree branches had grown to our side of the rock wall, so we figure in a way they're really ours and pull off a few, run to eat them at the side of the house.

"I look up and see Mother's eyes flashing. Oh my gosh! We know what that means. She has her face on; you know the one. She makes us go to Mrs. Dyal's door and apologize for stealing. 'Now girls,' says Mrs. Dyal, 'anytime you want an apricot, you just knock on the door and ask me.' Mother, still furious, makes us sit in a chair in the living room for the rest of the afternoon."

"She probably saves us both from a life of crime," I say. "What about the time we're fighting on Halloween, and she doesn't let us go trick-or-treating? She had ways of getting results."

Mother is born at old Providence Hospital in El Paso, Texas, on August 21, 1916, the first child of Amelia and Eduardo Delgado, the name on her birth certificate Estella Delgado.

"The person who wrote it didn't know that in Spanish Estela would have only one *l*, and my parents didn't notice. Maybe they were intimidated by all the forms in English. I've spelled my name in Spanish the way it appears on that certificate, but I'm thinking of changing it. Maybe it's too late for that at almost eighty, but I like the way it looks, Estela. I think I'm becoming more Mexican every year. They misspelled your grandmother's name on my birth certificate too, put her full maiden name as Sotera Amelia rather than Sotero Amelia Landavazo. At the county clerk's office they wrote her full name as Soteria Amelea. So much for the accuracy of official birth documents."

Mother grows up on Wyoming Street in that "hornet's nest" with four, half sisters, all old enough to be her mother; and, in time, with her two brothers, Lalo and John. She never has a room of her own, shares it with her stepsister, Lobo, as Cecilia and I when we're young share our room with this aunt.

As a child, Mother stuffs cotton in her ears so as not to hear Lobo's grumblings, "*Pero ¿qué está pasando en esta casa decente?*" and later the muttered prayers, "*Gloria al Padre y al Hijo y al Espíritu Santo.*"

"I still remember my phone number, Main 5477. I was jealous of both my brothers' good looks, your Uncle Lalo's golden curls that Mamande doesn't cut until he's four or five and Johnny's dreamy eyes." She laughs. "An aunt of mine would say, 'And then there's Estela.' But there is much good in my early years."

Growing up, Estela is very slender, sighs when she stares at her mother's meals, *comida corrida*, not that tasty since Mamande isn't fond of cooking but prepares a traditional Mexican meal, plate after plate—soup with meat and vegetables, a piece of meat or chicken, *fideo* or rice, maybe *cajeta de membrillo* or cake.

Sundays on the streetcar the Delgado family goes to Mass to hear a sermon in Spanish, then Sunday lunch. If the family goes to friends for lunch or a *merienda*, Estela's father senses if his daughter doesn't want to eat and nudges her with a look. She knows she'll have to taste the *sopa* or *calabazitas* or *empanadas de piña*. She doesn't have to finish everything, but her father's look says she'll have to taste. Papande places a coin in the eager hands of each of his small children, their spending money, their *"domingo,"* a Sunday tradition my father continues with the four of us.

Amelia watches her daughter play outside, shout angrily and then run inside panting. *"Ay, Estelita,* I think you learned English just so that you could fight with the neighbors."

"My mother would let me call for a pint of lime sherbet since we had an icebox, not a refrigerator. While my brothers are outside playing, I sneak in for a while and call, eat the whole pint myself.

"When we're little and my parents can still afford to have someone come and do some cleaning and cooking, Mamande goes shopping and leaves the three of us at home. Poor Alicia doesn't know what to do with us. *'Tres gallos,'* she calls us because of our fighting. She finally gets a broom and chases us which is how Mamande finds us, Alicia gasping about our bad behavior.

"My father would always say the words of Mexico's president, Benito Juárez. *'Hija, hija, el respeto al derecho ajeno es la paz.'* Papande is a very formal man and corrects me because I slip and find it difficult to refer to him using the second-person familiar in Spanish, *tú.*

" *'¿Quiere Ud. café con leche, Papacito?'*

" *'Hija, soy tu padre. No se habla de Ud. Se habla de tú.'*

"He's a very honest and just man. Even when we're poor, if he doesn't think a case is fair, he won't take it. And does he move slowly. When we're rushing to get to school, we're stuck if Papá is moving like a snail down the hall.

" 'Papacito, ¡tenemos que ir a la escuela!'

" 'Yo sé, pero, hija, el respeto a tu padre,' he answers calmly, continues down the hall, one step at a time, no one daring to race past him." Now his daughter, walks at that pace. "Le corre la sangre muy despacio," mutters Mamá Cleta whenever she gets stuck behind her great-granddaughter whose blood moves slowly.

"I have a friend, Betsy," Mother says, "whose father is Mexican and mother is very Anglo so she has all the habits of an American. When my friend bends over, I see her cute panties with lots of ruffles. Mine are so plain, and I wonder, where does she get those? She's always dressed like a beautiful doll. I wish I had panties and dresses like hers."

When the weather turns cold, Stella's mother bundles her up, makes her wear long johns and long socks up past her knees.

"¡Ay Mamá!"

"Sí, sí, sí, señorita. No quiero que te enfermes."

Stella tugs at the hem of her dress hoping the other children won't notice how long her ugly socks are.

"Later on as I get a little older, Mamande takes me to buy dresses at the Popular. The children's department is on the fourth floor by the corset department where Aunt Nina works. A Miss Crenshaw is the head, and I go show her every dress I try on, spin slowly so she can see me. Miss Crenshaw is very stylish, and if she likes a dress, I get it. I'll never forget one dress that I just love. It's one piece but looks like two pieces with a white blouse and a pleated skirt, blues and greens, silky stuff. And then, this is the kicker, it has a, a . . . What do you call those things you put around the neck?"

Mamá Cleta pauses, her hands full of wildflowers, rolls her eyes at Mother's animated reminiscing, whispers, "La memoria de la niñez, dura hasta la vejez."

"A collar? A tie? Bow? Choker? Scarf?"

"Scarf," Mother laughs. "And I think it's the most stylish thing in the world. And I remember another dress that we have made. It's lace and I guess organdy, beige lace and pink organdy. It's just beautiful. I think I look like a princess in it. Mamande tries, she really tries always to have me look nice, but I'm very, very demanding. When I have birthday parties, I probably have to teach my mother what to do because I have to do everything like that, but we serve cake and ice cream, little bags of candy."

"When I'm in one of the lower grades at the end of May we have a festival. Each classroom performs on the playground, and my class is going to do the May-pole dance. All of us, boys and girls, will grab one of the colored streamers—reds, greens, blues—that come down from a tall post and as we dance, we're to weave in and out.

"The girls are to dress like tulips. Mamande doesn't speak any English at all, remember, so I have to translate everything for her. I tell her that I'm supposed to look like a tuuulip," she pronounces each syllable carefully, Mother who liked public speaking and developed the habit of careful enunciation. "I think to myself: *hmmm*, what color is a tuulip?" Again she suppresses a laugh. "I decide that a tulip has petals of all different colors."

"Did you know what a tulip was?"

"Well, I'd seen pictures. Anyway, I think my costume will look much prettier if it has all different colors. A relative makes it since your grandmother doesn't sew much. The day of the festival everyone shows up, the little girls in their outfits, blues and pinks and whites, whatever colors tulips are. Then here comes Stella. I have every color in the rainbow on, and I feel kind of strange really when I look around."

Such exuberance she had, our mother, the child of two such quiet parents, who even as a little one chooses all the colors to wear, unwilling to limit her possibilities.

"Mamande walks me to school every day when I'm little, and my brothers go with us. She looks different from the other mothers, longer dresses, more matronly. One day, I see a mother ice-skating, and I'm beside myself. My teeth almost fall out. Mamande isn't like that. She never wears make-up or short flapper dresses." Stella imagines holding the hand of a mother with bobbed hair, who laughs and calls out, "Come on, honey. Let's skate," and pulls Stella out onto the ice, pulls her round and round everyone turning to watch her and her mother who's like the mother in books and movies.

"I know my mother looks different, long hair that she wears in a bun, reddish but beginning to gray. So anyway, we do the Maypole dance. I'm sure she doesn't talk to anyone because they only speak English. Papá never goes, but I don't think I ever give it a thought. I don't remember if fathers go much.

"We cover the Maypole, and then we sit down to sing some songs. As we're singing, Mamande comes up behind me with a sweater. It's a little coolish so she puts this sweater around my shoulders and says, 'Está haciendo friito, m'ijita. Ponte este suéter.' I just shrug the sweater off and don't say a word to her.

"The boy sitting next to me whom we called Hoot turns and says, 'I didn't know you're a spic.' "

Mamá Cleta doesn't understand the word *spic*, but she hears something in her great-granddaughter's voice. "*¿Una tasita de té?*" she offers that woman's cure for sadness, the warmth of tea.

What is it this child demands who strives both to blend in and to excel, this child who wants to be different, who wants a costume like the other girls and yet wants to be noticed, makes flamboyant choices unaware yet of the degree of her difference and of price of the attention she seeks. In that space between generations and cultures, in that border in which she is Mexican but doesn't look Mexican, does she long to be seen as she sees herself in her daydreams—as we see ourselves in our daydreams—full of promise, demand that her mother strive with her, long to take the mother she loves, pulling the mother with her, to be acceptable in a script written in a language her mother will never speak?

Estela, becomes Stella at Lamar Elementary School, a place she likes because she excels there. "I start kindergarten at seven and in half a year I'm moved to first grade. "*Como pez en el agua,*" says Mamá Cleta about how smoothly this little girl swims through her school days like a fish in water. "I love school because I get to lead the band," Mother says remembering the green and white band uniforms, the thrill of raising her hand in class to answer questions.

"We have a class called civic league. It's held in the auditorium, and we're taught about our government and get to go up on the stage to give speeches. You know I like that part. We pay a one-cent poll tax to vote for class and school officers. It's great. I go to Lamar through seventh grade. There's not eighth grade then so we go right in to high school."

Most of the students at Lamar are Anglo, but Mother says she never feels isolated. Is that because she doesn't give herself time to feel her difference, her energy invested in excelling? Her favorite elementary school subjects are English and arithmetic; her favorite teachers, young Mrs. Crawford who teaches music, and Mrs. Douglas who teaches history.

"Mrs. Douglas is older but feisty. It fascinates me that this little old lady has a younger boyfriend, much younger. She lets me grade papers. One day, I'm sitting in the cloakroom grading, when in walks the principal, Empress Arrington. Yes, that's her name, and she thinks she is an empress. She is racist and disapproves of a child named *Delgado* getting any attention, and I'm always on the stage speaking and winning oratory contests."

"What are you doing?" frowns Empress, staring at the papers Stella's marking.

"Oh, I'm just helping Mrs. Douglas."

"You're grading those papers, aren't you?"

"No, no. I'm just putting them in alphabetical order."

Miss Winberg, the speech teacher, quickly sees Stella's abilities since Stella likes being in school plays, once performs an original dance to music from melodramas in a costume with wings.

"We have a mulberry tree in our backyard, a *mora*, and when my brothers and I have the mumps, we're home from school, quarantined. In those days, they send a nurse out to check on school children with contagious diseases, and where do you think she finds the three of us, our faces covered with mulberry juice?

"If I get mad at my brothers on the way home from school, I run ahead and lock all the doors. Lalo and Johnny bang and bang on the door."

"Open up, Stella. We've got to go to the bathroom! You'd better open up fast or you're going to get it!"

Stella just sticks her tongue out at her brothers through the windows. When Amelia returns home, she frowns at her sons pounding on the door. "*Muchachos, ¿qué pasa?*" Amelia enters the house, asks again. "*Estelita, ¿qué pasa aquí?*" Estela sadly tells her angry, red-headed mother that she had to lock the door because—because her brothers were going to hit her.

"*¡Ay muchachos, que vergüenza! ¡Pegándole a su única hermana!*" The boys cringe at the disappointment in their mother's voice, silently vow to get back at that sneaky Stella.

"My friend and I go buy ice cream sometimes, and we chant together, 'I scream, you scream, we all scream for ice cream,'" Mother says still enjoying the rhyme.

On warm evenings, adults visit on the front porch, while the children play tag, hide 'n seek, run-sheep-run. As they grow older, they run further away in their chases, not afraid to be in the streets and alleys. "But one night," Mother says, "we've been to see *Dracula*. When we start home, we're scared. I say to my brothers, 'Now each of you get ahold of my hand. When I say three, we run to the next corner.' I felt I had to be gutsy."

On Wednesday nights the nearby outdoor theater has what it calls grocery night. A drawing is held on those nights, and the holder of the winning ticket number receives some grocery item. The Delgado trio like the suspense and possibility of returning home with a prize.

"Give me your tickets, Lalo and Johnny, and I'll check them when they call out the winning number," Stella says. Her younger brothers look at one another, hand their sister their tickets.

"Get your tickets out," the man in front says. "What lucky person is going to get to take home this case of assorted sodas? They're gonna taste mighty good on these hot El Paso days.

Ready? The winning number is 07394. Let me read it again 07394."

"I won! I won!" shouts Stella rushing up to show the man the ticket that had actually been Lalo's. They run home for the wagon, and for a week Stella slowly sips the sweet root beer, grape, and orange sodas, occasionally sharing some with her brothers, feeling guilty but not guilty enough to tell the truth.

When the sodas are finished, the three load the case in the red wagon, and before dashing inside to lock the door, Stella says, "Lalo, you really won these. Now don't get mad. I'll let you get the deposit." Then she runs!

"Era sinvergüenza," she says, amused at her young self.

"Did you have a nickname?" I ask.

"Maybe *diablita.* Once as a trick I even made someone a cold cream sandwich. Wasn't I awful? Sometimes, not often, but sometimes, Mamande would say, *'Eres una muchacha muy malcriada, muy malcriada. Qué es eso de que me haces así.'* I don't think I ever answer. I know that my patient mother is right. I can be headstrong. She asks me why I am such a fighter. I had to be, Pat. My whole life I've always had to do the talking, the translating. During World War II when men in uniform come to tell my stepsister, Elodia, so full of life, that her son, Eduardo, has been killed, who do you think has to knock on her door and tell her?"

Some summers Stella goes with her half sisters, Nina or Nacha, to visit their sister Lola in Cuauhtemoc. "One year when I'm about nine, Lola takes us to a ranch owned by her husband's family, the Cuiltys, called Corral de Piedras. Her husband, Gabino, is a bright man, but not very energetic. They say he has all kinds of degrees, in engineering and pharmacy, and that he loans them out to people while he sits and reads. When I visit, he likes to quiz me saying, *'Vamos a ver, Estelita, las matemáticas.'* I think he does some sipping too and not just *café con leche.* I remember that he has a beautiful silver saddle.

"This particular year, as a favor to a friend, Nina also takes Max, the friend's son. He is so stuuupid. He just sits, never wants to do anything, never says much. I write him nasty notes and say, 'Here, read this.' 'You are so dumb I bet you can't even read this.' "

Lola makes *asaderos*, and Estela watches her short, solid half sister, stir and stir the huge pot of milk, until the curds form, watches the white steam rising, scenting the air. Lola winds the white, thready curds into small balls of soft cheese. While they cool, Estela bends over the platter, smells the cheeses that look like unbaked buns.

"Don't eat them while they're hot, Estelita" Lola says, "*te empachas*. They'll stick to the inside of your stomach."

"At night Nacha begins her sex harangues, I guess since that dumb boy's there, as if I'd want to get near the creepy kid. '*Y no quiero verlos tocando. La Santísima Virgen quiere que seas una niña pura, pura.*' I bring cotton with me and stuff it in my ears like I do at home, sing to myself so I won't hear her babbling,

> Some saaaay, the world was made for fun and
> fro - lic,
> And so do I, and so do I.

During the school year, Stella has to come straight home after school, but then can play with neighborhood children who at night gather to play under the big light at the corner; on the Fourth of July, go buy every kind of firecracker from a Chinese man on Missouri Street—Roman candles, snakes, sparklers.

"I never like to go to bed early," says Mother, "and I always like to read. That's why I'm up now till all hours of the night. When I'm little, I take a flashlight to bed, hold a book in one hand and a flashlight in the other.

" '*Muchacha, ¿qué estás haciendo?*'

" '*Mi tarea,*' I fib knowing my mother can't check if I'm doing homework or not. I never really have to do any chores. My mother says, '*Estela, haz el arroz.*' I hold a book in one hand while I stand by the stove supposedly making the rice.

" '*Muchacha, ¿qué estás hacierdo?*' "

Summer vacations Stella reads all she wants and anything she wants. When she gets her adult library card, she wanders the shelves, doesn't know which books to read, picks a book with *doll* in the title. She has never read anything like this and wonders what all the touching feels like, if she'd like it. She watches her older friend, Betsy, go off in a car with a boy.

"I know what you do when you're with your boyfriend."

"Stella, don't say things like that!"

"I read. I know what you do when you go out."

"Stella, you don't know what you're talking about."

"I do. I read *True Romances.*"

Stella's mother studies her independent daughter engrossed in magazines, "*¿Qué estás leyendo, m'ijita?*"

"I play with Bootsie, Lola, and Frances whose mother builds the first apartment on the block. Frances and I both like a boy named Hubert who lives in her apartment building. One Valentine's Day, we each get him a card. He doesn't give Frances a card, but he gives me one. Blackie, a baseball player, lives in the apartments with his wife who works full-time. He's home a lot, has girlfriends."

"Frances," he says, "can you give me the key to the basement?"

"I can't give you the key, but I can get the key. Stella and I will just sit on the ledge and watch."

They sit there, the young girls, watching the man kissing and touching a girl, pushing her skirt up as she pushes his hand away. They wonder how it feels to have a man try to lie on you, put his big tongue in your mouth. Eventually, they tire of watching. "Okay, we're leaving," Frances says.

Another friend, Louise Randall, whose mother is a seamstress, loans Stella party dresses. Stella's brothers go with her to school dances so that her parents will let her go. "So how do I look, Lalo? Johnny?" she asks spinning around in the green, satin dress, seeing her parents watching her out of the corner of their eyes.

"Fine, fine, let's just get out of here before they change their minds."

"*Buenas noches, Mamá. Buenas noches, Papá.*"

"*Buenas noches, hijos. Cuiden a Estelita y lleguen temprano.*"

At El Paso High School Stella begins to enter speech contests, likes standing at the front of a room and seeing faces listening to her, excels at declamation and eventually also in extemporaneous speaking. "I reveled in being out there," she says.

"Oh," Lobo says, "you inherit this talent, Estela, *el don de la palabra*, from your grandmother, Mamá Nacha, whose eyes are so blue, *azules, azules, azules*, whose hair is so blonde that she is lost in the wheat fields. *De tal palo salta la estilla.*"

"I write a speech for your Uncle one time. It's titled 'Fire: Friend or Foe.' Your uncle wins seventy-five cents, and I ask for my part.

" 'But I gave the speech,' he says.

"But I wrote it."

" 'Yea, well, if I'd read Shakespeare's writing would I have had to pay *him*?'

"Our principal, Mr. Davis, often calls on me to speak at assemblies, to warn the students that if they don't behave, the assemblies will end. 'You can lead a horse to water,' I say to all those faces, 'but you can't make him drink. And that's the problem here. We can say behave, but because there are so many of you, we can't make you do it.'

"I never think I'm all that popular and doubt that I can be elected student body president, but I have a plan. I convince the student council that they need a speaker of the house to call assemblies to order and make announcements, so I'm the first person to speak on the PA system at El Paso High School when it's installed.

"One time Miss Duncan, our speech teacher, wants me to prepare a speech for a contest on Texas heroes. I tell her that I've heard about a man of Mexican descent, Lorenzo de Zavala, who was governor in Mexico, and came to Texas, signed the Texas Declaration of Independence, and became the Vice President of the Republic of Texas.

" 'This is it!' Miss Duncan says. 'I hope you can find enough material.'

"I think the guy is a traitor to Mexico, but I don't want only Anglos always talked about like Houston and Austin. I even remember how I start the speech.

Much has been written and more has been said
about the Anglo American in the struggle of Texas
for Independence, but little or nothing has been written
about the Mexicans who fought for this state.

"Two students compete in speech contests with other local schools and then at regional and state. The other speaker, Branch Craig who becomes a doctor, and I usually travel with the track team or the choir. As long as the judges don't know my name, I have a chance, can probably win, but if they hear a name like *Delgado*, I know I'm out. I go to these contests without any money, of course. We have no money. The princial and his wife, Mr. Davis and later Mr. Jones, come for me in their car and bring me home.

"How do my parents let me go? My father isn't well by then, and my mother probably goes crazy with worry; but I just tell them I'm going. Once, we stop for a meal at Lubbock. The sign on the restaurant says NO DOGS OR MEXICANS. I know no one there can tell I'm Mexican, but I feel bad."

Inducted into the National Honor Society her senior year, she savors the thought of being on stage at an assembly in front of the whole school. "We'll be watching," her friends Bootsie and Louise say. The group sponsor, the grandmother of a classmate, points to her granddaughter and Stella. "See, look at these two girls. They are proof that you can be beautiful and smart." Happy walking home, Stella knows that though her parents don't understand the honors she receives, they're proud of her, but she wishes she and her mother were more alike.

Her father's illness and the Depression remove any hope of continuing her education. I think of her, my proud and bilingually articulate mother, listening to classmates talking about college plans, but her salary is needed to help pay for rent and food at the duplex on Wyoming. With a sigh, after graduation she begins working at the department store where her half sisters work, where she has shopped, handed her purchases to salesclerks, what she is now. She earns twelve dollars a week working from eight to six Monday through Saturday plus taking inventory on Sundays for no extra pay.

"What are you doing here, Stella?" her teachers ask frowning slightly when they see her in the lingerie department, hand her the bras and shiny slips they wish to purchase.

She watches the girls who live in big homes but who get so nervous when they speak in front of the class, who think they're better than she is, ask, "Gee, Stella, that was sure a good speech. Uh, do you write those yourself?" Now they see her here, a salesclerk. "Stella! Well, hi, what are you doing here? Could you ring up these nightgowns? Don't you just love these panties with all the lace?"

Stella sorts bras and girdles rather than reading Amy Lowell and Emily Dickinson at the local college. Evenings her mother likes her to go to Mrs. de la Torre's to pray the rosary with her, "*Dios te salve, María, llena eres de gracia.*"

"When I'm little, heck, even in high school," says my youngest sister, Stella, "I think that there's nothing you can't do, Mom. Even when I lose things and am worried, I know deep inside that you will find what I need, or fix the situation—ballet shoes, gym clothes. There's no problem my mom can't solve."

I agree. I'm in bed at night and realize in panic that I forgot to do a third-grade assignment. How could I have forgotten that I need to make a small scene about another country? It's eleven, and my siblings are asleep. I run to my mother's bed, "Mom, Mom," I whisper so as not to wake my father. "I forgot some homework."

Mother listens to my story, pulls herself up. "What can we use?" she asks looking around. We're not a traveling family. "Maybe something your Uncle John sent us when he was in the war." We decide to create a desert scene in the top of a shoebox from her closet, tiptoe as my snoring father rolls over in his sleep.

"We need some sand," she whispers. "Let me get my robe, and

I'll run across the street with a little shovel." She slips out into the dark while I watch from the arched living room window. We plan to create a small oasis since all we have is a small, brown camel from Egypt. We cover the bottom of the cardboard with sand, find a small mirror in the bathroom for our waterhole, carefully tie a white Kleenex to look like a rider on the camel. We look at our handiwork, pleased at the result. I thank her, and we kiss good night again.

My sister laughs now at herself, at the way as awkward youngsters we want to be like our poised, confident mother. "I even loved the way you'd chew gum, Mom," Stella says. "I have this clear memory that I'm in the front seat of the Plymouth with you, and I look over and just admire the way you chew gum, how you can get it to pop just perfectly, and I wonder if I'll ever be able to do it. I'm waiting for certain songs to come on the radio,

> Catch a falling star and put it in your pocket. . . .

Songs from 'The Hit Parade' we watch. They sing and dance the top songs, so corny, but we love it."

The next morning, a Stellar's jay flies into my room where I'm typing, lands on the back of a chair and watches inquisitively,

> Water whispers in fountains, rivers, *acequias*,
> to roots that listen moist in the dark.
> The stories rise green through the stems, open
> in the red mouths of poppies.

"Still working?" Mother asks coming into the room. "Did I tell you that some years ago, after I'm already a grandmother, I'm flying to El Paso. . . . Not that *I* am flying, Dear. The plane is. You know what I mean. Anyway, the woman next to me tells me to stare out the window for a bit and then tell her what I see.

"I look out at the clouds, and I see something. I see a little girl sitting on one. It's me with a bow in my hair, sitting on a cloud, dangling my feet.

"Come and listen to my Bluey. This little bird is a talker, but she usually won't do it if someone else is around. She can say, 'Ay qué chula.' I should tape her, that's what I should do. Watch what happens if I put her on my hand. See? She'll climb up my arm and onto my head. Can you believe it? Bluey likes to sit on the top of my head. That's where my Bluey likes to sit."

On the brink of eighty, Mother stares at herself in the mirror. "I'm the vainest woman in the world. Generations are so different. Mamande wasn't a vain woman at all, never wore make-up or face cream. But you know your mother. I use plenty of cream, always have. Be sure you work it up the neck and face. Don't rub your skin going down, Dear.

"Now what was I talking about? Oh yes, Mamande. She didn't wear make-up, but she'd sit and cream her legs. I think of her when I sit and rub cream into my feet and legs and arms.

"Even now that I'm alone, I spray my hair every night before going to sleep, and don't start asking about what time I went to sleep last night. I've told you that I've always been a night owl. I read the paper, watch the news on television in Spanish because they have more international news. I pay bills, water my plants, maybe listen to a few radio talk shows, and before I know it, it's two or three o'clock. I'm almost eighty, Dear. I get to do whatever I want."

Mornings when I rub cream into my legs after a bath, I think of the women in my family in the rooms of my heart, each rubbing cream between her hands, then up her legs, enjoying the quiet and the feel of stroking, soothing, our own flesh.

Mother surprised me when she said she wanted to be a writer. I flip through a pocket-size spiral tablet of hers, the kind she always had in her purse for jotting down lists and reminders. I have no idea why I have this nor what year she wrote in it. I imagine her sitting under the hair dryer at a Santa Monica beauty shop for her weekly appointment, jotting, "aloe vera—cut piece and use on any sore," and "vinegar helps remove hemlines." I keep flipping through the pages, find the draft of an irate letter to the newspaper for not carrying a magazine insert her son edited, notes for her next doctor visit.

Mother thought with her pen. I keep flipping pages, find two sayings, hard to know if they're original or if she heard or read them. "When I'm good, I'm very, very good. When I'm bad, I'm better!" "Patience is a virtue. A few women have it. But no man has!" I can hear Mother laughing at the words.

She wanted to be a writer. In the notebook, she wrote,

> Oh, dear God, my name is truly Esther. There it is clearly written—right in front of me. It's on my birth certificate. How I came across that paper? I don't know. Yes, I do. I was rooting thru some of my mother's papers. I was & still am a snoop. Esther, Esther. Gee how wonderful! My given name was not Ester as I was called at home but Esther just as I had written it from the 1st day I learned to write in school. Nothing I could do about that last name. It's Mendez. So no matter what I shall always stand out as a - well a what? Let's see. Where race is specified on the b.c. it states Mexican. What kind of a race is that? In school I had been taught there were 4 races—white, black, yellow and red. So what am I? You see at that time the "brown" was not yet a part of the census or interviews for social services. Being born in Texas certainly never would anyone of Spanish or as is now named Hispanic last name be classified as "white." Lord was I insecure! Why me?? I am fair-skinned, hazel eyes, lite brown hair—heck no one will really know. I can pass myself off as white? No danger of Dad showing up at school. He's a busy man, a lawyer by the way and before that had been a Mexican judge. Oh, no I came from no dummy but

Insecure? How early does this little bilingual girl in the 1920s and '30s—how early do children in the '90s—want to push away their names or skin or accent or family or weight or home or language with one hand while they long to clutch tight to the familiar with the other? Torn by conflicting loyalties, insecure in a world different from her private world, Mother took with her the security that came from a house yes, with its own structural tensions, and yet where six adults cared about her, their concern in any language assisting her as she grew to incorporate her pain and doubt, to transform them.

"Mala hierba nunca muere," says Mamá Cleta glancing at the stubborn milkweed I've pulled. In the cicadas' drone, Aunt Carmen and I pull out petunias wilted by summer heat. I'm hot, tired, and welcome sitting in the shade of the *portal* to watch clouds swell over the desert, blue-purple clouds that threatened a downpour for days finally release themselves and the fat drops pelt the desert, the river, the fruit trees, *acequia,* and garden. After weeks of waiting for such drenching rain, we all come out to the covered porch to watch and listen. The great-grandmothers move quickly through the house covering the mirrors so that lightning won't strike.

Mamá Cleta handed everyone a new brown scapular today. "July sixteen, the Feast of Nuestra Señora del Carmen," she'd said handing Aunt Carmen a yellow rose with her scapular, a gift for her feast day. "Appearing on Mount Carmel, the Virgin Mary said, *'Recordarme es más dulce que la miel, y poseerme más rico que el panal de miel,'* promising all who wear the small cloth rectangles under their clothes that she will bring them quickly to heaven's gates."

The sky broods gray and purple. Thunder booms, lightning zig-zags, and the grandmothers, great-grandmothers, and great-great-grandmothers bless themselves. Abuelo Gregorio begins a prayer to Santa Bárbara who protects the faithful from storms, *"Santa Bárbara, doncella, líbranos del rayo y también de la centella."*

Watching the adobe and colors of the hills and mountain darken, and feeling our own parched selves renewed by the blessing of rain, we say little in the presence of the celestial drama. When the rain stops, we listen to the streams pour down from the *canales,* watch drops slide from leaves and petals. Aunt Carmen goes in to make coffee and the chatting begins.

"Las flores contentan pero no alimentan," says Mamá Cleta also

heading for the kitchen to fix a platter of cookies, *orejas* and *cora-zones*.

My children and I walk through the garden with its wet, fallen petals, like damp confetti, and walk out back as the sunlight strikes puddles turning them gold, *ojitos de agua*. Grackles congregate their feathered racket in the cottonwoods, shoot gleaming ebony whistles through the air. The children talk about the kingfishers they'd see where there are lots of carp down the canal and reminisce about tadpoles, filling jars with them after a good rain. We take deep breaths as we listen to the irrigation canal tumble with new life, then walk through the fruit trees down to the fast-flowing river, mesmerized by its slidings and swirlings, looking for minnows or sunfish near the bank. We smell the desert, creosote on its breeze, hear the chatter of sparrows telling their water tales as they settle in the cottonwoods, the *moras* and the Chinaberry tree for the night. Seeing the first night star, we say,

> Star light, star bright, first star I see tonight.
> I wish I may, I wish I might, have the wish I wish
>   tonight.

Since my children were born, all such wishes are for them.

Cissy gently touches the trio of saints carved out of an old tree trunk, their eyes closed, arms stretched high in joy.

"Maybe this was carved after a rain like this," Bill says.

"Or maybe at dawn," Libby says.

"Or maybe at sunset," says Cissy again touching the saints.

"Look!" Bill, our observant naturalist, points to a great blue heron in the river, the large bird that always surprises me in the desert. It opens its wings wide and soundlessly lifts its body from the murky water, like a ballet dancer lifts self and doubt, resists gravity, and flies.

Agosto / August

Goza del mes de mayo que agosto llegará.

Revel in May, for August soon arrives.

I CHOSE HER; she didn't choose me. I'd walk by and see your mother reading in front of her house. I know I'm going to marry her, honest honey. She's so pretty."

"Your dad gives me gifts, and we don't have much at my house. We meet on a blind date, don't we Raúl? One of my catechism teachers calls me and asks if I want to go out with her and two friends. I'm surprised she asks because she's older than I am, but she wants to go out with this French boy who doesn't have a car. I guess he knows Raúl, or maybe your dad sets this up. Do you, Daddy?" she asks my father who winks at me.

"How old is this boy you want to fix me up with?" Stella asks. She's seventeen and soon will begin her senior year.
"About twenty-two."
"That's not a boy. That's a man."
"Don't worry. We'll just walk around Memorial Park. He knows you have to be home by nine, but we can go to The Chocolate Shop for ice cream."
Stella hopes he'll be good-looking. "Okay. I'll go."

"Stella, this is Raúl Mora. Raúl, this is Stella Delgado."
Glancing at him out of the corner of her eye as he drives the group to the park, she thinks: he isn't like the boys I know. Will we look funny walking together because he's so tall and I'm so

short? Is this what it feels like going out with a man? I wonder if he'll try anything? It's okay if he does. I'm curious anyway.

The next time they go out, she thinks: he's funny, always teasing, and he's got a job and money. What's it like to have money? I wish he wasn't so dark. My parents won't like this, but I'm not going to marry him, so why shouldn't I go out and have some fun. I wonder if he'll try anything? I hope he does.

My father chuckles now at his cleverness. "Stella," he'd whispered putting his arm around her, "this is the third time we've been out with these two. Why do we have to go out with them? I'd like to go out with you alone."

"From the beginning your father says, 'You know you're going to marry me.' I think to myself, marry you? Oh yes, Dear. My family's racist about skin color. Sometimes I lie to my parents and say, '*Voy a salir con una amiga y un amigo.*' Daddy's English isn't perfect," she says patting his hand. "He kisses me and I think: this is terrible, but I don't mind it. I read lots of romantic books so when he starts kissing me passionately I think: this must be what it's like. Pretty soon he's stopping by every night. My father, who has had his first stroke by then, wouldn't have approved. Mamande says, '*¿Y ese prieto?*' "

On Christmas Day, a knock at the front door of the Delgado house, delivery of a box for Stella from Western Union. Opening the box as her mother watches, Stella lifts out a black velvet evening bag trimmed in gold with her initials "ED."

"*¿Pero qué es esto?*" Mamande asks frowning.

Stella opens the evening bag and finds a gold compact and mirror.

"What is this?" her mother asks again.

"Raúl sent it."

"This is scandalous, Estela."

Luckily the doorbell rings, momentarily ending the discussion. In comes the doctor, to check on his friend, Stella's father whose left side is paralyzed.

"*A ver, compañero, ¿cómo estás?*" the doctor says. "*Eduardo, ¿me oyes? A ver, di ferrocarril.*"

An hour later the doorbell rings again. "Western Union for

Stella Delgado." In this box, Stella finds a pair of black leather gloves, strokes the smoothness as her mother's frown and silence deepen. An hour later, again the doorbell, Western Union delivering a pink wooden jewelry box. Stella inserts the tiny key, slowly lifts the top. Chocolates. She thinks of sinking her teeth into gooey butter-cream centers, filling her mouth with caramels and peanut clusters, chocolate-covered cherries.

"*¡Es un escándalo, Estela, un escándalo!*" her mother fumes. "*Pero ¿en dónde conociste ese prieto?*"

Stella ignores her mother's sounds, walks through the house wondering what she can possibly give Raúl, opens drawers and cabinets thinking, what can I do? She walks back to the bathroom, stares at the soap, toothpaste, *Sal de uvas*, alcohol, iodine, peroxide, mineral oil, mentholatum, mercurochrome, her father's razor. This might do; the razor might not be bad, she thinks, and wraps it in a scrap of red and green Christmas paper.

My father looks at me and laughs. "Honey, I don't tell her then, but I used to give those safety razors away new to my paper boys when they sold a certain number of papers."

"Imagine. All I can give Daddy is a used razor."

"*Buenas noches, Señora Delgado.*"

"*Buenas noches, Raúl.*" My grandmother, Amelia, watches the tall, dark-skinned young man turn her husband's body, the body that after the stroke can no longer move itself.

"Well, I just keep going out with your father for five years until he finally says, 'Don't you think we should get married?' "

"But our families need our salaries. I don't think they can make it without us, Raúl."

"They'll have to." He shrugs his shoulders, a few days later takes his father with him to ask Señora Delgado for permission to marry her only daughter, Estela.

I watch my father enjoying the old story, grinning at himself. Neither house is happy at first at the news. "Gosh, Stella, what are we going to live on?" her brothers ask. "You know we need your part to pay for the rent and food."

Wondering if she loves this man enough, she goes with him to a jewelry store, chooses a yellow diamond for her engagement ring because it will be larger than a white one. She has her picture taken for the newspaper, *El Continental,* buys a long wedding dress.

"It's a lovely dress," she says, "not expensive because we don't have any money. When your Aunt Chole and her friend Isabel, a wonderful seamstress, see it, they say, 'No, no, no. We'll fix this so it will look much better.' Isabel cuts slits in it and adds other material and makes the dress look really pretty."

Stella addresses the wedding invitation,

Amelia Landavazo Vda. de Delgado
Lázaro Mora
y
Natividad P. de Mora
Participan a usted el enlace
de sus hijos
Estela y Raúl
E Invitan a Ud. y apreciable familia a la ceremonia
religiosa que se verificará el Domingo 25
del presente a las 7:30 a.m. en la
Capilla Santa Rita de la
Catedral
El Paso, Texas, Junio de 1939

Her mother, a widow, still wears black; her maid-of-honor, a long purple dress and a purple straw hat. Carrying a nosegay, Stella walks down the aisle with Lalo, her brother. The priest had asked, "You want a Mexican wedding, don't you? You'll want to bring . . . what do you call those things . . . the white satin rope and the coins?"

"So we got the *laso y arras.* There are supposed to be thirteen gold pieces in a satin bag," Mother says. "We probably use dimes."

My parents are married by Father Swinburne, a priest fixed in Mother's memory because he keeps his false teeth in his suit pocket until he needs them and because he's popular with young people for using words like *damn.*

The day before the wedding, Mother takes fresh flowers to decorate the dining room at Elodia's, her half sister. Delivering the wedding cake before the ceremony, Raúl accidentally dents one side, a detail that Stella frets about hoping her bosses from the department store won't notice as they stand around the table sipping cider. Uncle Lalo and a few of Raúl's friends had taken him to the Puerta del Sol bar in Juárez the night before where they sat and sipped tequilas until the sun came up. Little wonder that my father may have been a bit unsteady as he maneuvered the cake out of the car and up the cement stairs to Elodia's door. I tease my father that maybe he was in no condition to know what he was doing that day.

"Yea, that's it. I'm just a young kid, and your mother traps me."

"What!" she says taking the bait. "I'm not the one who wants to get married. The whole thing is your idea, Raúl, and you know it."

My father shakes his head and winks, pointing his head toward Mother enjoying the pleasure of still being able to irritate her even from beyond the grave.

The bride and groom that stand on the frosting of our parents' wedding cake live in silence among the plates and crystal in our dining room china cabinet while the four of us are growing up. Sometimes, we unlock the glass door with its tiny key and study the couple, a bit of Frosty the Snowman about their shapes, the same curves and cheerful innocence. We study the bride's veil, the groom's black top hat. What made them so fascinating? Maybe that they were there when we weren't, way back then, at the beginning.

Mother hopes for a honeymoon, maybe to Guadalajara or Monterrey, imagines strolling down Mexican streets, a married woman; but instead, one Saturday before the wedding, my father drives her out Mesa Street, turns up the last street at the edge of town and stops in front of a vacant lot.

"Here's your wedding present, 704 Mesita. It's going to be our home."

This? she thinks. This little piece of desert is my wedding present?

"One day you're going to be happy I did this. I got us a new F.H.A. loan, and we can build a house with just $300 down. I've got a builder too, Lowenfield."

"But I wanted a honeymoon. What about what I want? You didn't even ask me. And you mean I don't even have any say about what it's going to look like?"

"It's going to be like my friend César's. We can drive up there, and you can see if you want to change anything."

Once Stella's anger cools, she begins to imagine herself in her own home even if it is way out on the edge of town. She says, "Put a big arch between the living and dining rooms to open things up. And add a breakfast room off the kitchen."

While their house is built, they live with friends, and every morning before going to work at Riggs Optical, Raúl drives to check the construction completed the day before. He kicks the walls testing their sturdiness, admires the curved red tiles above the small front porch. He looks at the desert around him, imagines living in this rock house with Stella and one day, their children. *"Mientras en mi casa estoy, rey soy,"* Mamá Cleta says when she hears this story.

Finally the house is finished, finally theirs, and Stella and Raúl pull into the driveway. He walks with her first to the one-car garage, through it to its side door, *"Mira, Estela.* This will be our backyard. You can raise chickens."

"Ay, Raúl, you and your crazy ideas. I'm not a farmer."

"Okay, okay," he says, "let's go unlock the door to our house." He locks the garage door, and they walk back down the driveway, toward the empty street, to the front of their home, up the two porch steps. Raúl opens the screen door and turns the lock, and they enter the living room, its smell of fresh paint, stand at the large arched window that faces the street.

"We'll plant trees," Raúl says hugging his young wife, "Italian cypress out front and grass and lots of flowers, roses." They walk through the wide arch into the dining room.

"This place is so bare, Raúl."

"Okay, okay. We'll get some furniture. *Paciencia, mujer.*" They walk through the swinging wood door into the kitchen, then through a small arch into the yellow breakfast room.

"It will be nice to sit in here and have coffee, look out the window," Stella says.

"Let's see the bedrooms." He winks and puts his arms around her, but she shrugs herself free. "*Ay, Raúl,* can't you think of anything else?"

"But we're married."

"I don't care. We came to see the house, to walk through it *como gente decente* as my family would say." She pulls him back through the swinging door into the dining room then through the swinging door that leads to the hall, a bath and two bedrooms.

"We'll put the big bed here by the windows," he says, "and one day the smaller room will have the crib."

"Don't start talking about babies, Raúl."

"Okay, okay, just come into our bedroom and think of how nice it will be to lie here together with the windows open, and no one else in the house."

Stella walks slowly around the room, her own house, no honeymoon, but she has her own rock house.

"Are you quiet because you want to stretch out on this floor and pretend there's a nice bed under us?" Raúl asks, his voice dropping.

At Riggs Optical Company, Raúl grinds, cuts, and mounts lenses, and with his pay checks, Raúl and Stella furnish their house, a bedroom set, a sofa and chairs, curtains, carpets, tables, lamps. Every day Stella cleans the entire house, dusts, sweeps, shines mirrors. In the late afternoon, she sits down, brushes her brown hair back from her face, studies her home, drags herself up to straighten a picture, a mirror, a venetian blind.

"I visit Mamande a few times a week, but I never share anything intimate with her. Your father pays his mother to wash our clothes since we don't have a washing machine. I don't think she approves of our buying the house and mutters something about people who buy houses when they don't even have underwear. Well, I don't know where she got that since we do too have underwear!"

Sundays both mothers and Lito, my paternal grandfather, come to visit. My father stretches out in the bedroom and falls asleep.

"It's not fair, Raúl. They're your parents, and you just fall asleep and leave all the visiting to me."

"*Ya, ya, ya, Estela. Déjame en paz.*"

Mother's quick temper flares, and she slings a plate at the wall. Our parents were not ones to hit or spank us, but Mother would, if really angry particularly at my father, throw her keys. One time it was her engagement picture, tinted in glass, the sophisticated photo that now only exists in shadow and light from an old newspaper clipping, her short, brown hair brushed back to reveal a clear widow's peak above a long nose; dark, thin penciled eyebrows, slight smile from the burgundy lips.

Her husband opens a small grocery story in South El Paso for extra income that he calls *El Surtido* across the street from Sacred Heart Church. One of his sisters runs it for him, and she and her husband live in the back. Since Mother has to go help some afternoons, she's relieved when Raúl closes the store.

"I'm happy when I can finally stop waiting on people, Dear, but we bring all the canned goods home. I never want to see another can of Spam as long as I live."

Two years pass. Stella spends each day cleaning the house. Finally, Raúl says, "Don't you want to have a family? We have a house; we have a car. Don't you think we should stop using that thing and have a baby?"

"A baby?"

"Yes, it's time. You need something to do."

"Stella, what's the matter?" Raúl asks a month later seeing his wife's face as she comes out of the bathroom.

"My period. Maybe I'll never get pregnant."

Wind rustles the cottonwood above our heads, and when I turn to say something about the moving shadows to my father, he has disappeared again, no accounting for the rhythms of spirits.

Mother and I hear *sw, sw, sw,* Lobo's broom sweeping the *portal,* and Aunt Carmen and Uncle Lalo talking about what shrubs to move in the garden before winter, maybe a boxwood and an oleander. Turning the sprinkler on chrysanthemums that will soon bloom, float their fall scent into the air, my aunt asks if I'll get up early with her tomorrow and help pick the ripe figs before the sun gets too hot.

August. The feast of Saint Augustine this month who wrote, "Paradise is a place where there are trees," especially in the desert. Mamá Cleta cuts wildflowers to place in vases throughout the house—cornflowers, larkspur, goldenrod. Gardeners create small places of paradise, the root of the word itself, Persian for "walled garden." We sit in the play of shadows listening to *las voces del jardín,* fountain, breeze, cicadas, braided in conversation.

"When I decide to have a baby," Mother continues, "I'm bitterly disappointed that it doesn't happen immediately." I've looked at the black-and-white picture of Mother standing by a car in 1941 in a maternity dress, the first picture of me. Safe inside her.

"You were born at Southwestern General Hospital at nine at night. My doctor, Jesson L. Stowe, gives me something called twilight sleep, something so the mother won't suffer. I hate it because they wake me and say, 'Mrs. Mora, you have a little girl,' and I remember nothing. You're purple around the lips which is probably caused by the medication. I never have it again."

At the hospital a week, Stella thumbs through *Life,* ten cents a copy, while she waits for Raúl to visit during his lunch hour, arriving in his gray fedora and overcoat anxious to go see Patsy. The magazine cover shows a man, completely covered except for his eyes, holding binoculars in his thickly gloves hands, the caption: North Atlantic Patrol.

Bored, Stella glances at the pages of liquor ads, and the ads for Cashmere Bouquet Soap, Vicks Vaporub, women who solve their "bridge-supper problem" by serving pork and beans. Oldsmobile says it's not only producing its "Hydra-matic" car, but also is "engaged in the mass production of automatic cannons for fighting planes." Roosevelt is shown addressing Congress. "The words he used, the figures he cited were enormous, staggering, beyond anything ever attempted by any nation on earth." Churchill, visiting the White House, poses in a zippered air-raid suit, boasts, "I can get into it in half a minute."

Not that body, Stella thinks flipping through pages of bombed Nazi battleships, a Midwest blizzard, Hollywood and the War—Clark Gable, Myrna Loy, Cary Grant shown planning how to do their part. The dairy farmers are too, according to their ad showing cakes and baked potatoes that says, "5,000,000 dairy farmers are helping to maintain Nutrition Defense. Plenty of Butter Makes 'Economy' Foods Taste Better." She pauses at the pictures in an ad captioned, "The Happiest Job in America!" What does he do, she wonders, reads that he sells hearing aids, the Sonotone man.

A second World War and a baby, she thinks. What will I do if they take Raúl?

"When we bring you home, I keep going to check that you're breathing. I'm afraid you'll suffocate. Your father says, "But she hardly has a nose." He warms oil and gently slides his oiled fingers down your nose, lengthening it he thinks.

"In the kitchen, I listen to our old little green radio, hear the news about the war. I take you with me to Our Lady of Guadalupe Church and pray that your father won't be taken. We're lucky. Because he's making glasses for the military, his work at home is considered part of the defense effort. During the war, your father decides to raise chickens."

Among my earliest memories are chicks and incubators. I think the first time I walk is to touch the small, moving bodies. I remember lights in the garage to keep the noisy feathered creatures warm.

Mother begins her story about the day I point to a pair of eye glasses and say, *antiopos*, my parents as proud of my version of *antiojos*, as if their first child had invented the seeing device. "You're just a little thing, and you run around the house naming things," Mother says, with the pride my parents openly show throughout their lives. Naming things, the interest continues.

When I'm little, Mother often takes me to Mamandé's. "You're the love of her life. That's why she has a tiny pink and white bracelet made for you when you're born."

"And what about the rest of us, Dearie?" her daughter Stella asks patting Mother on the shoulder. "What about your other three? What are we, chopped liver?"

When Mother leaves me and my toys at Mamandé's, Mother and Aunt Carmen go window shopping downtown, look at the new hats, purses, skirts. Alone with me, no one else to hear her, my grandmother releases her voice, softly sings as she bounces me on her lap.

> Ri - qui - rrán, ri - qui - rrán,
> las cam - pa - nas de San Juan.

Mother also takes me to Lobo's who likes to have me visit her room at the boarding house. She buys me small glass bottles of milk, spoons me the cream on the top. I see my aunt, her face a smile, spinning her finger above my stomach to make me laugh at the impending poke, "*Lanza, lanza, pica la panza*" or pretending she's putting money in the palm of my hand saying, "*Pon, pon, pon, dinerito en el bolzón.*" Early I learn to put my arms up to her, ask her to dance, "*¿A bailà?*" as years later she dances with my children, with both hands lifting the skirt of her dress up a bit in our kitchen, pointing her toe, dancing to "*Las Chiapanecas*" or "*El Jarabe Tapatío.*"

My sister, Cecilia, is born a year and a half after I am, then Stella Anne who always jokes that our parents were hoping for a boy, and then Roy Anthony, the joy of a boy, my father returning from the hospital that July night with his gray hat on backwards.

"I'd use birth control," Mother says, "and then those missionary priests would come into town and convince us that's evil, and I'm pregnant again." The baby years for our parents. Daddy carrying us in his arms when we're sick singing, "Ole man ri - ver, he just keeps roll - in." Mother giving her teething infants tiny white candies to suck that she'd give me too, small specks of sweetness on my tongue. Dr. Bennett, our pediatrician, is often at the house, squeezes my throat that's already sore and asking, "Does that hurt?" We're like living pincushions, regularly punctured by injections.

Sundays we all go to Mass, of course,

> *Dó - mi - nus vo - bis - cum.*
> *Et cum spíri - tu tu - o.*

and then out for lunch often to Juárez or outside in the backyard. My father, who usually doesn't know the words of the songs he likes, puts on his Caruso or Mario Lanza records and sings along just faking much of it, loving the music but especially enjoying the resonance of Caruso's voice, "*Ri - di Pa - glia - cio, la - la - la lalalala.*"

In 1949, he opens his own optical business on Myrtle Street, names it the United Optical because it's across from the United States Court House. We're all expected to help. Mother handles the payroll, frets over the bills for the business and the house in which now four children and our grandmother and aunt live. When we aren't in school or doing homework, my sisters and I go to the optical and clean the desks or wash finished glasses, but there's always a reward, a stop at the Oasis Drive-In if we go with Daddy at night, the waitress bringing chips and foamy strawberry ice-cream sodas on a tray she clamps on the car window.

"Daddy makes me wash the finished glasses over and over until they're really clean," Cecilia says. "Whenever he gets mad, I just stop breathing. He's so demanding and just works and works and works. When he gets mad, all hell breaks loose. He yells, and Mommy throws her keys at the wall, and we go to our rooms so afraid they'll get a divorce."

If we work Saturdays or on summer days, we get to eat at Luby's Cafeteria with Daddy, all those choices, and desserts—cheesecake and strawberry shortcake, and we receive a pay envelope Mother prepares like the other employees, a number of them our aunts or cousins, all working as fast as they can before my father starts booming out impatiently again, insisting that we all work faster. "*¡Ándenle, muchachos! ¡Ándenle!*"

Off we rush delivering glasses to Dr. Dickson, Dr. Schuster, tiny, white-haired Dr. Hill who invites a Dr. Webber, a doctor of homeopathy, to share his office. To our horror, my father trusts this Dr. Webber probably because he promises to cure my father's gall bladder condition with herbs instead of surgery.

Needless to say, those herb drops don't work on those stones. My father's moans at the post-operative pain shake the hospital we're sure. "Only that pretty Sister Teresa can quiet him," Cecilia says, and we see the pale nun gliding into his room in her blue habit and starched white-winged veil pointing to heaven. She takes my father's hand, "Now Mr. Mora, Mr. Mora, what's the matter? Mr. Mora, I know you don't want to bother the other patients, do you? We're going to give you the pain medicine again as soon as we can. Mr. Mora, I'm going to say a special prayer for you right now. I know God will help you to bear this pain and to offer your sufferings for the souls in purgatory."

Unfortunately, Sister Teresa isn't available to calm my father on a permanent basis. At home, how we dread to hear his angry voice on the phone, "Who's been on for so long? I need one of you down here. Now."

During the fifties he decides to have a basement built, a fallout shelter, he thinks, in case of an atomic blast, a large room where we eventually put a Ping-Pong table and an adjoining small room for a freezer and refrigerator.

Mother, our chauffeur all those years, drives us to school, piano lessons, to the library, to the pool and parties and movies, to deliver glasses for my father's business. She plans birthday parties for each of us, taking friends to the movies, or at card tables, rolling dice, calling out, "Bunko."

"My favorite Holy day of Obligation," Mother says, "is August fifteenth, the Feast of the Assumption. I know that summer is almost over, and soon the four of you will be back at school."

Some summers my parents pack all of us and Lobo in the car and take us to Redondo Beach, California. "One day we're going to live here," my father says licking his cone of purple-people-eater ice cream. On a hot Arizona night, my parents search for a motel with any vacancy, finally spot one and Mother in pedal pushers runs into the lobby. She returns furious, slams the car door. "Let's go. They say they don't rent to Mexicans." My sister, Stella, looks at Mother and thinks: how did they know? They must have looked in the car.

Mother rushes to take us to school, to P.T.A. meetings, to help my father, to fix dinner, to help with homework, until one of her migraines sends her to burrow into the comfort of her bed in a darkened room, Mamande's remedy of Bayer aspirin and black coffee never enough. Mother feels her heart beating too fast, is sure a tumor's growing in her brain. Taking Cecilia and a flashlight to the bathroom mirror, she studies her pupils as she turns the light on and off, watches the black circle contract, more proof of her terminal illness. "Look, honey. Watch what happens to Mommy's eyes when I turn on the light."

"Doctor, I don't know what's happening to me." Dr. Leo suggests she visit another good doctor he knows, a psychiatrist.

She gets all dressed up for the visits, a luxury she can now afford, purple dress with matching heels and feathered hat, earrings, gloves, a gold glove guard on her purse. She dresses the way she does when she goes to the symphonies and concerts she likes so much at Liberty Hall or sometimes in Juárez, events she takes us to as soon as we're old enough.

Mother watches the quiet, stooped psychiatrist, his careful writing. "Why do you write down everything I say, Doctor?"

"I study it later for patterns, Mrs. Mora." Weeks pass. "I can now tell you that nothing is physically wrong with you, Mrs. Mora. You are not going to have a heart attack; you do not have a brain tumor. But you do need an outlet for your emotions. Let's continue talking." Mother finds relief in the slow, calm words of the doctor who speaks such correct English, who asks interesting questions, who reads, a man who understands her, a man she thinks is refined, cultured, cultivated. And she thinks he must find her intelligent and attractive, look forward to her visits. She begins to learn to like herself, to admit that what she later calls her perfectionism is unnecessary, damaging.

"Raúl, the doctor says I need a creative outlet."

My father knows his wife took piano as a child, that while his children now take lessons, it's his wife who practices at the upright, plays the duet with them, taking the hard part in their first piano book, *Thompson's Teaching Little Fingers How to Play*, her fingers reaching where theirs can't yet, tackling the chords, her hands stretching and reaching, their voices rising, together, "Home, home on the ra - ange." Raúl likes it when his wife sits at the piano struggling with the notes, likes to raise his hand conducting as she plays.

One evening my parents go to a concert downtown, and soon after my father hears the same piano music coming from a ballet studio around the corner from his optical business. He follows the music, introduces himself to the pianist.

"Hello, I'm Raúl Mora. I have an optical company right around the corner on Myrtle. I heard you playing. Very nice. Would you like to teach my wife piano?"

"I don't teach, Mr. Mora."

"Just meet her. I'll tell you where she is."

Stella goes to the pick-up window at the United Optical, asks the reddish, short gentleman what he wants.

"Mrs. Mora?" he asks very properly in an almost British accent.

"Yes."

"May I come in?"

"Well, yes, I suppose so," she says turning to make sure her husband is in the building.

"Mrs. Mora, I want to talk to you about piano lessons."

"Piano lessons?"

"Mrs. Mora, your husband has spoken to me about teaching you piano. Would you like that?"

"I don't have any idea what you're talking about," Stella says smiling graciously at this refined gentleman while plotting to murder my father. "RAÚL!"

"Would you like to take piano?"

"I don't have time. I have four children."

"All the more reason you need piano lessons. Mrs. Mora, let

me hazard a guess about you. You seem like a woman who worries about unimportant details. When you go out to a nice restaurant, you worry so about which spoon to use, that you don't savor the food. I'd like to help you learn to savor life more. You'll be a different person. I can tell. You are very bright."

The classes begin, and Woody becomes my parents' one close friend during those years. Like most children, we resent the attention Mother gives someone else. Though sophisticated, a Yale music graduate, he lives out in the country and often arrives in a beat-up green pickup, proud of his calloused hands.

"Just look at these gorgeous roses I brought you, Stellah." Secretly, we all frown at this man who drops in whenever he wants with his airs and East-coast vowels, sipping sherry or Scotch, the sound of glass tinkling in those glasses frightening my sister, "What if they drink too much? What if they have a wreck?"

Woody insists that Stella play on a grand piano so she first takes her lessons at his sister's ballet studio, then at his home where Raúl goes with her and enjoys listening to his wife play, sipping Scotch, and later enjoying Woody's green enchiladas. Finally, Woody convinces Raúl to buy a baby grand piano.

"Stellah, Stellah, my deah, come, come, come. We're here to create muuuuuusic. Let's try that Mozart Sonata again. No, no. Repeat the first measure without blurring the notes."

We're furious at this man who dares to criticize our mother. Hours she practices, plays Beethoven, Chopin, Schubert. When she plays "Für Elise" or the "Moonlight Sonata," her music scents the rooms of the house, drifts out through the windows and doors, all seems right with our world. Our pug dog sits under the piano howling his accompaniment, *ahooooooo*.

Woody convinces my parents to take some literature courses at the local college, Mother thriving on *Jane Eyre*, my father in his own way enjoying the discussions though failing every test, but wanting, I think, to be there with his wife.

Woody begins to teach me too, pinching my cheeks, saying, "Paht, Paht, don't drop your wrists. Let us hear those feelings when you play." Though Mother suspects he likes men, she thinks he likes her too, is enamored of this former concert pianist. Mamande glares at *el americano* who arrives with his mouth and hands full of roses. "*¿Qué no sabe que eres casada?*" Annoyed, Mother says, *"Ay Mamá,* as if I'm going to hide the flowers. Raúl will see them." Lobo mutters, "*¿Y quién es este hombre tan feo?*" and we fume in our bedrooms. "Why doesn't he go pester another family? Does Daddy know he's here all the time?"

Years later, after Woody dies, I ask, "Mother, do you think Woody was gay?"

"Well, Dear, I guess he was pretty happy, all that money and no children to worry about."

"Gay, Mother, gay!"

"Oh," she says laughing until she's gasping for breath, my mother who enjoys a good laugh, and with whom I so like to laugh.

My father continues the long hours, moves his business to Texas Street. Even though the bills increase, he puts a ten dollar bill in the collection basket on Sunday, hires any man who has a family and needs work.

"But Raúl," Mother says furious at the sight of another employee. "You're just not a good businessman. We cannot afford another salary."

"But he has a family, Estela."

My father yells louder, works faster, but he can't outrace the larger optical companies that take his clients. Seeing the unpaid bills, Mother begins to teach Spanish to Peace Corps classes at the university and at public and Catholic schools, works at a Green Stamp Store, but finally my father has to close his business. He wants to mortgage the house to keep the optical going, but needs my mother's signature.

"No." It's the one thing the creditors can't take; she has to protect her children. Because her father had not understood the homestead law, Stella and her family had lost their home when she was a child.

Raúl, who may never have traveled alone before, boards a Greyhound, to Houston, Dallas, and Gallup looking for work, living at YMCAs, sending money home to his family, the good financial days over, the which-dress-do-you-like-I-don't-know-I-can't-decide-well-just-take-both days. Finally Uncle John who'd learned the optical business from Raúl calls and says, "Come to L.A."

Working for American Optical, my father begins what he calls troubleshooting, sent in to increase the productivity of a particular optical lab, walking into each lab with all his old energy and drive, "Come on, come on, these are rush jobs. You people have to learn to hurry. ¡Ándenle!"

Mother visits, and they begin to look for an apartment in Santa Monica.

My sister, Stella, begins frantic prayers to Saint Raphael the Archangel, patron saint of travelers, protector against eye trouble and monsters, a saint with whom she's had experience. She inherited Mamande's statue of Saint Raphael after our grandmother's death, the statue that still has its price, $3.50, under the base; the blonde, barefoot angel with light turquoise wings and a green toga, his delicate hand raised in peaceful blessing. No peace for this angel in our household, though.

"I'd pray to Saint Rafe for silly things," my sister says, "like passing an algebra test or being asked out on a date. I'd write what I wanted clearly and place it right before his eyes, *Please have Richie ask me out for Saturday night. Please.* If I don't get what I want, I turn Saint Rafe's face to the wall. 'Thanks, Saint Rafe. Thanks a lot. I even said lots of prayers this week, and you know it. I thought you were my friend, that I could count on you. We'll see how you like staring at this wall.'

"Poor Daddy. I am so terrible to him when we sense we'll have to leave El Paso. It can't be happening, I think. I write him these awful letters,

> Please, Daddy, don't do this to us. Don't make us move.
> Please, if you love us, you won't make us move.

"And I pray to Saint Rafe, of course. When I hear we're really moving, that we're going to have to leave our house, I pick up Saint Raphael, grip him hard in my hand. I lift him and bang him hard against a table. See here. His hand broke off. I think he is one heartless saint then. 'You're not my friend any more, Saint Rafe. I'm going to leave you here in El Paso. Good-bye.' I put him in the closet and close the door.

"Mother, Roy, and I go by train to California the summer of 1964. You're married and Cissy's finishing college so you two don't have to go. It's just us four out there. The last day in our house, I'm crying and crying at leaving. I ask Uncle Lalo to walk through the house with me one last time. He puts his arm around me, and I'm crying and crying as we walk through the living room, dining room, kitchen, breakfast room, bed-rooms, and then out back where I was so happy singing on my swing."

Mother had sold what she could including the car and piano, packed what she could, and left. We're never sure what happens to our old party dresses, our Madame Alexander dolls, the *Childcraft* I so loved. Maybe the next family uses what we valued and didn't take. In retrospect, we're not sure why or who made the decisions. Often we discard in life for the person we are. How can we make wise decisions about what to save for the person we're becoming?

Stella and Roy ride the train through the desert with Mother, and when they arrive in Los Angeles have their first trip on California freeways, an experience anytime my father's at the wheel and Mother's navigating. When the four arrive at their Santa Monica apartment, my sister, Stella, looks at her bedroom that doesn't look or feel like home. A few days later, she opens her closet, and there he is, the long-suffering survivor of this family's travails, a battered Saint Raphael and his smashed hand and broken nose, patiently staring down at her.

"At the time, I'm sure it's a miracle," Stella chuckles now, "but I turn his face to the back, banish him anyway to the closet for months. 'No, you're not my friend anymore, Saint Rafe. I'm not going to talk to you.'"

"Saint abuse," I say.

"We arrive in June," Mother says. "Coming from our desert, I think it's freezing, think: and this is sunny California!"

My sister and brother finish high school in Santa Monica, become Californians. Mother, without a college degree unable to pursue a career equal to her intelligence and talents, works parttime at a stamp redemption center, as a teacher's aide in a bilingual class, translates and interviews for UCLA's Institute for Social Science Research.

Working in California's optical business for almost thirty years, my father in his seventies opens his own dispensing business, a small place that he can go to every day in a suit and tie and see his patients, his perhaps the last generation with little interest in retirement, defining themselves through work. My parents remain in that first apartment complex the years they live in Santa Monica.

"It's as if half of me is gone," Mother says after my father dies. "I was married to him for over fifty years and go out with him five years before that. He's really the only man I was ever close to. I hope I told him enough how much I loved him. I feel him near me. A neighbor who's Bahai says your father is, not his body but his spirit, that I should learn to feel it, so finally I say, 'Well, Daddy, just put your arms around me lightly.' Maybe, very lightly, I do feel something."

A few months after my father's death, Mother says, "Oh your father is at it again." She finds the cards.

"Let's go look at them, Dear," she says to me now. "Let me hold on to you, hon. I feel steadier that way. I say I'm *tembelereque*. It's not really a word, but it sounds like a good description of how unsteady I am, don't you think?

"I'm cleaning a cabinet the day I tell you I find these romantic cards your father gave me. Oh, we fought for over fifty years, but he is such a good man. So sweet of Stella to get them framed like this. They look nice here in the living room." The sparrow flies in and lands on the rim of the frame, peers down at the cards.

12/24/36 Greetings monkey. To my sweetheart
on Christmas, With all my love to Estella

8/21/38 To my darling Chango - I love you,
dear, and I wish you joy.

"He called you Chango?" I ask. Mother grins and keeps read-
ing. The card dated 12/24/38 is a religious card, an image of
Christ as a young man.

Wishing my darling Chango a very merry Christmas
and may this help to brighten your New Year.

Mother says, "He put a hundred dollar bill inside, and we
were very broke. Look at this one dated 8/21/40."

To my darling wife
Wishing my 24 year old wife a very happy birthday

"Was he cute?" The sparrow takes a bow. "Awful penman-
ship, but look how he scribbled in the words 'young and beauti-
ful' on this card that says 'Birthday Greetings To My Wife.' "
Mother and I read the rhyme printed on the card out loud to-
gether as the sparrow follows the rhythm with his head, con-
ducts us with his right wing,

> All the other fellows,
> Must find it pretty hard,
> Each time their wives have birthdays,
> And they have to send a card,
> Because they can't say these words,
> And mean them like I do,
> "To the dearest girl in all the world,"
> Because you see that's YOU!

My father who must have signed the card in a hurry using his
work-day signature, writes, "*Happy Birthday, Raúl A. Mora.*"

Hot summer mornings I'd kneel in front of the cedar chest in
my parents' room, remove the books or clothes on top, open the

heavy lid, lock the side hinges so the lid will stay open while I peer into my parents' past, see my father's rushed writing on these romantic cards, the kind the rest of us seldom give—too mushy. I read the papers and valentines we wrote in kindergarten.

"Oh how I finally started to cry," Mother says, "when in his own scribbly handwriting I saw his words, 'To my beautiful young wife.' And what about that grocery bag I gave you. Have you got it?"

I bring the plastic bag in which I save his writing done on a brown Mar Vista Market double-strength grocery bag, the red printing on the ordinary bag, a heart and letters.

"We'd been to one of those bargain markets. You know your mother. When we come home I'm putting things up, and I see your father sitting at the dining room table, writing. 'Raúl, what are you doing?' When he finishes, he just hands the bag to me.

LOVE
It was so wonderful I loved every thing &
every one it was a very new experience,
my heart is full of joy & thankful
of this experience

HOPE
I see so much misery around
me & I try to be compassionate &
thankful, & there is so much need for
help that I seemed to fit some
place here on earth.

CHARITY
I gave a small part of my fortune
but I felt I was not giving I was
receiving a thousand fold
they have so much to give but we
can not accept what they give to
us because we do not accept charity
as our way of life

Luckily I put the bag up that day. You say I'm a pack rat, but sometimes it pays off."

"Every time I read his words," I say, "I think, Daddy wrote that?" Why do the words my father wrote surprise me? Maybe because when I'm growing up he seems a man of few words, the man up early to leave for work, the man calling in anger to ask, "Who's been on that phone? I need one of you to come and help me," the man fixing the air conditioner on the roof yelling down, "Patsy, try the switch now," the man working at night or falling asleep from exhaustion, from all the verbal pushing to get the glasses finished on time. "*¡Ándenle! ¡Pronto! ¡Pronto!*"

What terror I feel when he climbs the ladder to go up on our roof, not perhaps when I'm little and he takes me with him, lets me survey the neighborhood, look off into the desert; but when I'm old enough to fear death, know that he can fall, his body, vanish; the same cold fear I feel when he lights any pilot light, afraid he'll yell at me if I plead, "Don't. Don't. It's too dangerous." I watch my big father put his face close to the gas jet terrified that the mountain of flesh I so need will be blown away.

"Well, I don't know what fortune he's talking about because I sure never saw any of it, certainly not when he lost the business in El Paso, but he was a good man. Your sister says I've made him into a saint.

"*Shoo-shoo*. Why does this dumb bird keep trying to peck me?"

"Maybe he's trying to kiss you," I laugh as she shoos the sparrow from her face. He lands on the rim of the frame again, head thrown back as if laughing.

"So your sister says that I've forgotten all the fighting. I'd get so mad that one time I start writing on the walls with toothpaste, have I told you? And what about the time I actually leave, go to the store and call your brother to come and take me to a hotel. Of course, in my anger, I've come off without anything so he has to take me back to get a gown and toothbrush. I have to laugh, I walk into the apartment and say, 'I'm not back!'

"I pack a little suitcase, and tell your poor brother, 'Now you go into the hotel room first to be sure it's safe, and I'll lock the door when you leave.' I'm sure he tells your father where I am. Well, the next morning it's raining, and I think: I don't want to walk in this. I'd better call Dad before he leaves for work.

" 'Hello.'

" 'Raúl, this is Stella. It's raining.'

" 'Yes. Where are you?'

"I tell him—as if he doesn't know.

" 'I'll be right there,' he says.

"He comes for me and I say, 'Will you be home for lunch?' We don't mention my leaving again. But why was I telling you all this? Your Aunt Chole said something nice after your father died. She thanks me for taking care of him those two long years. I say, 'It was my job.' What were we talking about? I always forget where I'm going. I talk in circles."

"You were talking about the day you find all this."

"Oh, yes. So I find the cards and say, 'Daddy, why don't you leave me alone?' And then I find this grocery bag and get teary again. I read his words and stare at the plain, ole brown bag, and then I burst out laughing because printed on the bag in red, see here, is a big heart with the words 'Bagged with Loving Care.' I'd never noticed that before so I say to your father, 'Listen, Daddy, kind of cool it a bit.' He just won't let me forget him." She touches the bag. "This is *mi carta de amor*."

"Your *bolsa de amor*."

I head for the back door, hear voices in the kitchen beginning dinner, the grinding of spices. Aunt Carmen's digging kitchen scraps—rinds, peelings, eggshells—into the garden to enrich the soil while Uncle Lalo adds leaves and garden clippings to his compost heap. In his small prayer room, Abuelo Gregorio prays to the August saints, to Santa Clara and Santa Rosa who both liked to kneel and plant in their gardens.

> *Asciendan hasta Ti, o Señor, nuestras preces,*
> *perfumadas con la suavidad de la bienaventurada*
> *Virgen Rosa; para que, refrescados en la tierra*

con los manjares celestiales, disfrutemos de la
dulzura del banquete eterno en el cielo.

Behind the house, rows of sunflowers bow their heavy heads, and I watch gossipy butterflies whispering their secrets from blossom to blossom, sit in the patient voice of shade that invites rest in her, listen to pods swaying, doves' *ooo-oo-ooo*, sparrow chirps, corn rustle, water slipping over the *acequia's* stones. High above the desert, a red-tailed hawk glides the hot air currents.

Hummingbirds shimmer in the sun, tiny beings the Maya said their gods shaped from scraps—bone, flesh, multicolored feathers left after making all the other birds, patched beauty. When the gods called the other creatures to celebrate the small creation, the sun for its gift shone on the small, delicate bird's feathers setting them dancing with light.

From the wide, desert sky, light flows down to us, day and night. Atmospheric turbulence, astronomers tell us, alters smooth starlight, breaks it into its twinkling; the cold, white sight we gaze at with such fondness and awe. Turbulence in the heavens, turbulence in our homes, both probably inevitable and unavoidable, the play of solitary bodies moving through space whether in proximity or at a distance, the pulls and tugs of gravity, the root of the word from *gravitas*, heaviness, the weight of solitude, the sparks that can fly when we rub against another, and then, in the distance of time, gaze at the small flares with fondness because we were there.

Mother begins her marriage with a degree of doubt, wonders, "Do I love him enough?" For years, she argues with my father, who's in many ways so unlike her, cares for him his last two disoriented and disorienting years, resentful, angry, aching at seeing her six-foot tall, two-hundred pound husband altered, become a barely breathing silhouette on their bed. Then one night, after years of I-can't-take-it-anymore and He's-driving-me-crazy, Raúl slips away on his last breath, leaves her.

Two years after his death, she's set him in her firmament. "I've canonized your father, Dear. Why should the Pope be the only one who can canonize people? He was such a good man. I talk to him every day. I tell him, 'Papa, you take care of our kids from up there, and I'll take care of them from down here.' "

We gather outside her window, wait until almost noon this August day to give the night owl her birthday serenade. *Aaayyy, AAAYYY,* even the peacocks tune up. We begin *Las Mañanitas,*

> *Qué lin - das son las ma - ña - nas,*
> *cuan - do can - ta el rui - se - ñor.*

Mother's whole family, living and dead, sings and waits for her to pull aside the window curtains. She surprises us by coming outside.

"*Feliz cumpleaños, Estelita,*" the *guacamaya* squawks. I can't tell if my father taught it this trick or if it's my father in all those feathers. Mamá Cleta hands my mother, her great-granddaughter, a bouquet of fresh flowers from the garden, roses, daisies, dahlias.

"Take your time, Dearie," her daughter, Stella, says hugging Mother. "In the late afternoon we're having a party out under the mulberry."

"*Cada chango a su mecate,*" says Mamá Cleta sending each of us to our tasks. *Aaayyy, AAAYYY,* peacocks strut, shimmer by. *Aaayyy, AAAYYY.*

"Noisy *pavos reales,*" Mother says. Without a sound, Mamá Cleta transforms herself into a peacock and leads the birds to the back gate.

By the time Mother has had her coffee, bathed, dressed, put on her make-up and new pant-suit, we've started the grills, hung a piñata from the *mora,* and started the music, mariachi tapes, the Gypsy Kings, Paco de Lucia, Los Lobos. Mother arrives at her party holding her son's arm, and Uncle Lalo asks her to dance as he asked Lobo, his half sister on her ninetieth birthday. We clap at our tall, straight uncle bending a bit to lead his sister carefully under the trees.

"Your dad was a good dancer just like your uncle, kids, but

I've always been terrible," she says. "And now that I'm *temble-reque* and wobble, I'm even worse." Her face flushes, glows.

"*¡Estelita, qué bonita!*" the parrot squawks. Mamá Cleta whispers, "*Lo bailado, nadie te lo quita.*"

For a few, brief moments, Mother hears the anniversary waltz, "Oh, how they danced, on the night they were wed," and she's dancing again with her husband, Raúl.

Septiembre / September

De lo hermoso, hermoso es el otoño.

To speak of lovely, speak of autumn.

UNCLE LALO pulls out a small notebook and records the time of the sunset. "It's just a habit. I have a little weather radio, Patty, and like to jot down the time the sun rises, and the time it sets. It's interesting to see the days lengthen and then to see darkness return; like during the summer solstice, I jotted down that the sun rose at 6:00 and set at 8:14. That's a long day of light. Now here we are at the fall equinox. Soon we'll see that nice, big Harvest Moon."

I wake in the night to coyotes howling in the desert and wonder if my father, the old trickster, is running on four legs with the pack.

The next morning, I go sit and listen to Uncle Lalo in the *portal*. "When I was a little guy, a tiny guy, we used to go out in the back yard, the three of us. The big deal is to put on our bathing suits and squirt water at one another. We have a metal tub, and we climb in. I have a green bathing suit, and across the top it says, 'Baa baa black sheep.' "

"You had a bathing suit with a top, Unks?" my children ask feigning amazement. "Boy, you *are* an old timer! You're even older than we thought."

Uncle Lalo laughs. "I remember the little sheep on there. Maybe I was beginning to read because I remember the words."

The young people leave for the day, and my uncle, who's in his seventies, fit and trim from his daily routine of morning exer-

cises, mentally sharp as ever, tells me about his life, this humor-
ous raconteur who chuckles at his past, like most of my family.
Although his parents have been dead for years, I've sensed he
misses them, his voice changing when he speaks of them, a
hard-won resignation.

Relaxed, enjoying watching his wife painting at her easel
nearby, he runs his hands through his thinning gray hair, re-
members Sundays when his family went by streetcar to Sacred
Heart Church and then had their Sunday dinner. "Even if we
finish our meals, we have to sit there until my father nods to say
we're dismissed." The family goes on outings to the park, zoo or
Juárez horse races, his mother crushing a lucky dollar in her
hand. Papande buys his three children bright colored felt hats
they plop on their heads, later roll and stuff into their pockets.
"I'll trade you, Johnny," Lalo says. "Give me the blue one.

"When we're old enough to go to Mass alone, my brother and
I skate to church right down the middle of the street since there
aren't many cars then. We throw our skates over our shoulders
during Mass and then skate back home."

What a transformation a quarter of a century made and has
made again between the El Paso he and my parents grew up in,
the city I grew up in, and the El Paso my children called home.
They find it hard to believe that when I'm little, my father drives
to the nearby college and rents a horse at the riding stable, rides
the horse home on Mesa, now a main El Paso street, lifts me up
into the saddle with him, takes me riding in the desert by our
house.

The young Lalo goes with his mother and one of the neigh-
bors to Consumer's Ice in the evenings where a frozen block is
lifted with huge tongs into his red wagon, then at home placed
in the icebox with the drain pan underneath.

"Sometimes to save power, the city had Moonlight Saving
Time. If the moon is really bright, the electricity is cut off for
the evening, and we play outside and get ready for bed all by the
light of the moon.

"Did I ever tell you about Nieves Delgado, Snows Delgado?" my uncle chuckles. "We used to have problems with tough kids at Lamar School, the elementary school your mother and I go to. There is a guy who goes there who lives back of us a ways. His name is Nieves, a big, powerful man who has probably been in school a loooong time. The fact that I am Delgado and he is Delgado, I think pleases him. Well, when I become president of the student body, we have a council. School offenders come before the council, and we tell them they have to do some punishment like pick up paper or rocks.

"There are two brothers, kind of Western type kids, you know, American boys. Tough, I mean tough little guys, and they are always gettin' in trouble. So they come before the council, and nobody wants to say their punishment. It's my duty as president to tell them they have to pick up rocks and all this good stuff.

"Well, of course, they don't take kindly to this so when I'm leaving school one day, here they come, both of them, after me. They're goin' to beat me up, right there close to the school. About this time, good ole Nieves shows up, and BAM! he knocks their heads together. 'Bother him again and I'll beat your brains out,' Nieves says.

"Never again did I get bothered when I was student body president. Then one day Nieves comes before the council." My uncle's soft laugh rises. "Payback time. I just say, 'Now, Nieves, you shouldn't drop papers on the school grounds.' Ole Nieves gets off with extremely light punishments. He isn't troublesome, you know. After Nieves, boy, I am the law. I have a back-up.

"But let me tell you about the adventure of my life. At fifteen I decide to go to Mexico, to Chihuahua, to see and know the places my father and mother always talk about. We don't have any money, but your mother gives me four or five dollars for my big adventure. I go with a cousin who is a Chrysler dealer in Chihuahua. We go in a 1934 Teardrop Chrysler. This is super stuff!

"I had never been to Mexico's interior. We get in the car in the morning, drive through the desert and through little Mexican towns, and finally arrive in Chihuahua. Early the next morning, my cousin drives me to my half sister's, Lola's, to the small town of Cuauhtemoc that is San Antonio in those days. Now on the way, I see lots of really dark people, and I say, 'Gosh, what are Negroes doing over here?'

"My cousin laughs and says, 'Those aren't Negroes. They're Indians.' I mean I didn't know much, but I do remember that my father had taught me a few words in the Tarahumara language since he had worked up there. Eventually, we get thirsty, and we park, and I follow my cousin into the hills. It rained the night before, and water collected in some rocks. 'Drink some of that,' he says.

"When we finally arrive in San Antonio, we're dying of thirst. My cousin and his friends take me into a big old-timey bar. Warm beer, that's all there is. They take me to one of those phones that you crank, and I call Lola. She's out at a ranch called Ojos Azules because there are two blue ponds in front of it. She can't believe I've actually arrived for my first visit to Mexico.

"A relative who's about to be married suggests that until my sister returns for the big wedding, I stay at his future home that's presently vacant. Everyone knows everyone in the little town. The house is right at the base of a hill called El Picacho. No streetlights and no indoor facilities. At night I see lights, fires really, coming from the caves where the Tarahumaras live. When I get up in the morning, I see an Indian come up to a prickly pear, take out his knife, cut off the fruit, scoop it out with his knife, enjoy the bright red pulp and walk on.

"The groom's family that loans me the house owns a general store, and they're busy getting ready for the wedding. I don't have any clothes for the wedding, of course, but I'm ready to go in my gray pants and old brown coat.

"The day of the wedding, Gabino, my sister's husband, knowing I can no longer stay in the bride and groom's house, takes me to put my things in another house where I'm to sleep that night after the reception. We go to the wedding and the dance, but, of course, I'm just a kid and pretty soon I'm tired and say, 'I'm going to go back and go to bed.'

"Now the streets are completely dark, black, black. I walk along and I come to the house where I'm to sleep, find the bedroom, take off my clothes, and climb in bed. I'm just gettin' to sleep when I hear something stirrin'. I listen in all that dark. I hear a whimperin' and pull the sheet up close to my chest. Suddenly, a baby starts crying—at the foot of the bed.

"I think: my God, I'm in the wrong house! I jump up and start pullin' my clothes on, and the baby's crying and crying, and me trying to shove my arms in the shirt sleeves as that baby cries. I'm tuggin' at my pants, sure someone is going to come in and find me half dressed. Probably shoot me and ask questions later. I somehow button my shirt and race back to the wedding.

" 'Lalo, I thought you'd gone home,' my brother-in-law says staring at my misbuttoned shirt.

" 'Ay,' I say, 'I got lost and went to bed in the wrong house.' Gabino starts laughing and laughing, slapping me on the back. He thinks it's really hilarious, my narrow escape from death, and starts telling others at the reception. Laughing and slapping me on the back, he finally takes me to the right house.

"In the morning, everybody is laughing and laughing at my mistake. '¡A que Lalito!' It looked like the same place to me, but I kept wondering what would have happened if Don So-and-So had come home and found me asleep in his bed."

"What if Doña So-and-So had slipped into her bed?" asks Aunt Carmen.

"Another night while I'm visiting, they let me take two of the little guys to *la placita*. The small, town square has the only electric light in town and is enclosed with a high wall that has entrances. So I'm walking along holding the hands of these two little guys when a voice hollers out, '¡Cuidado, muchachos, el toro!' I turn around, and I see a bull coming at us. I tell you it's constant adventure.

"How I never get sick . . . as a matter of fact one of the young men in his twenties—who seems a real old guy to me at that time—gets diphtheria because of the water and dies. They filter

the water, but they don't boil it. I think the particulates are fil-
tered out, but not the bacteria. Maybe it doesn't bother my *tío*
and me because, even though I'm so young, he keeps giving me
beer."

My uncle chuckles again. "But I've always looked back and
thought, maaan, that is my adventure! Your mother may not
even remember it, but she finances it with about seven dollars.
My poor dad and mother don't have any money.

"That's Part One of my great adventure. Then we go to a real
old-timey ranch, Ojos Azules. I mean it has towers with slits
where people had shot at Indians. It's enclosed with the well in-
side and a big door. The windows have no glass. There's a
chapel, but they don't let me go in because it has been closed for
a while, and snakes tend to go in there.

"From there we go to another ranch, Corral de Piedras. We
get in an old Dodge touring car, and my brother-in-law says
he'll teach me to drive. All the gears are reversed, I remember. I
start the car and gun it. 'No, no,' my brother-in-law says, 'You can
only go five miles an hour, in low.'

"That night we get to this big, ole ranch, old as can be, a hun-
dred and ten and two weeks or somethin'. In the front are the
quarters for the *vaqueros*. I sleep in a huge room, as big as this
house. Now all this sounds crazy, but it really happened. I'm
asleep in my room one night, and the moon comes out. It's so
pretty. And I wake up to a terrific noise right outside my win-
dow. I look out, and I see two bulls in a terrific fight, thudding
and thudding. I'm okay because there's a big adobe wall between
us. I see the *caporal* come out and they're raisin' hell and yellin',
'¡Los toros se están peleando!' They finally separate the angry bulls.

"Another day, my brother-in-law takes me up to a little hill
and says, 'Look as far as you can in any direction. All that land
belongs to us.' This is part of the Luis Terrazas land that the
Cuiltys are part of. I think, 'My gosh!' as I look out on endless
miles of rock wall encircling the land called, Corral de Piedras.

"Then they take me to Rancho Viejo where they have a huge
warehouse where we go buy huge sacks of beans. We go by the
Mennonite camps that are the neatest, prettiest places you've

ever seen. I mean, they really keep them nice. We go into one of their houses where a man wants to sell a rifle since it's against his religion to keep it.

"Soon it's time for me to go home, back to school, but the rains come. I mean this adventure never stops. I mean the rains come! It rains like crazy. So now my brother-in-law can't drive me back. He says I can ride his horse to the train station, but it's four or five hours away—by horse.

"He gives me his black horse with a big, beautiful, Mexican saddle, a slicker, one of those that covers you up, and a big *sombrero*. I put them on and climb aboard the horse, about 3 A.M., mind you. The guy that's going to lead me is up in front, and he has my little ole bag tied to the haunches of the horse that's in front of me. It's dark when we start. We trot and we gallop, and when we come to an *arroyo* we just raise our legs like this, and the horses just go through the *arroyos* like nothin'. I'm on that horse for about six hours.

"This guy knows how to pace the horses. The one I'm on is a great big black animal that doesn't give me any trouble. When we gallop, it's kinda nice; but when we trot, man that is hard. We get there ten minutes before the train that takes me to Chihuahua where my aunt is.

"When I get up the next morning, I can hardly move, and it isn't just my rear end; it's every muscle in my body. All that shaking and jarring up and down. I stay there a few days, and in the meantime, your mother has gotten together another two or three dollars which she sends me to get back. This is my greatest adventure. I'm gone about three weeks. In fact, I've got a copper coin I found in an *arroyo*, a treasure. You know me," he laughs. "Always looking. I've kept it all these years."

He laughs again, "Just like I've kept a picture on my desk to remind me of someone who's about as smart as I am. Let me show you." My uncle returns and hands me a photo of a donkey he calls Don Profundo, then he continues his story.

"During the Depression, when my dad becomes ill, we have to move into a smaller house on Octavia Street. The rooms in the house have kerosene heaters, but when they start to smoke we have to open the windows to let the smoke out—that is, the rooms that have windows. At bedtime, my brother, John, and I change near the warmth of the stove, then dash to get under the covers of the back porch where we sleep. The porch has no windows, just canvas curtains to keep out the cold."

"But what happens if it snows?" I ask.

"We get cold," my uncle chuckles. "When we're in high school, my brother buys an old Chevrolet, a touring car, no roof, no nothin', just spoke wheels and whatever, but when you're young, it doesn't make any difference. We're going to go to Cloudcroft, drive a couple of hours into New Mexico and enjoy the forest. When we get there, I break the only molar that I'm missing. Man, it starts to hurt. I'm maybe seventeen or eighteen. So some smart guy says, 'Oh what you gotta do is just take a little whiskey. Don't drink it, just let it sit on there, and it'll kill the pain.' Well it does, but I keep swallowing the whiskey!

"And it starts to rain, so we get under the car, mind you, the ole automobile. When it quits raining, Willy, one of my friends says that we were going out to Billy the Kid's cave, or some goofy thing, midnight ride. The moon's supposed to be out. So even though I'm hurtin', and I'm about three sheets in the wind, I'm gonna go.

"They give me a horse named Cheyenne. I remember that this guy says, 'This horse is kinda mean, but they say you know how to ride, and you won't have any trouble,' so I climb aboard Cheyenne. The moon's out, the sky's cleared, and it's pretty, you know. We're off on our moonlight ride to Billy the Kid's cave. Well, since I've been drinkin', I fall asleep on the horse's back, and the horse wanders over some place and stops. And everybody keeps goin'. When I wake up, the moon's gone down, and you know how dark it is in a forest.

"The horse has his head down, and I do too, and it's black, solid black, and I think, 'Oh my God!' So I move the reins a little bit. I don't want to startle the horse, and the horse kinda raises his head, and I guess he thinks, 'Wow, man!'

"In the meantime, my friends have gone to the cave, and on the way back Willy says, 'Where's Lalo?' They realize I've disappeared, and they have to find me. Well, you know how when you're kids, you always have a special whistle, so Willy starts whistling real loud, and I hear the whistle way in the distance, so I answer. He whistles, and I answer, and I move that horse a little bit toward his whistle until we get together.

"Back at the stable, the man says, 'That horse give you any trouble?'

"No," I say. "I guess he was too tired, and I was too."

"One day, I was walking with a boy whose family had money, and I pointed to our house. 'That's where I live,' I said.

" 'You don't live there,' the guy said. 'You exist there.'

"To myself, I vowed that I'd get back at him for being so mean. Now he was more myopic than I was, so the next time I saw him at school, I hid my glasses. He noticed, of course, and said, 'Where are your glasses, Eddie?'

" 'Oh, I went to see this doctor who put drops in my eyes, and now I can see perfectly. I don't need glasses.'

" 'Really! So what's the doctor's name?'

" 'No, I won't tell you.'

"And every time I'd see him out of the corner of my eye," my uncle chuckles, "I'd hide my glasses.

" 'Come on, Eddie, tell me that doctor's name.'

" 'No, I won't tell.' "

"Yea, I wanted to go to college. I had aspirations to be an engineer, believe it or not. We have a high-school teacher who lives on Brown Street. Her name's Mrs. Duncan, and we all think she's the most beautiful girl in the world. She likes me. I'm kind of a loner, and after I graduate, I take my twenty-two rifle and go walk up the hill there and shoot cans.

"Eddie, Eddie," she calls to him. "Are you going to college?"

He looks down, then smiles, "I can't afford it, Mrs. Duncan."

"But you're so bright, Eddie. I know someone up at the college. They can get you a job as a janitor working in the gym. I think that'll pay for your tuition."

"Thanks, Mrs. Duncan, but I can't. I've got to take care of my mother. You know, rent, food. What am I gonna use for money to take care of my mother?"

Our uncle, bright, funny, responsible, becomes an accountant, teaches himself computer programming, works with numbers, he says, because they don't lie, our hard-working uncle who can't afford to be a janitor at the university at which, years later, I become an administrator.

Perhaps because he's fair-skinned, he seldom experiences discrimination, but is questioned about his name. "I don't think he was a mean man," Uncle Lalo says. "I think he was trying to help me, to tell me the way things were."

It's a cold winter day during the Depression when Lalo goes out to the local army base, Fort Bliss, with a group of other men hoping to be chosen for the Civilian Conservation Corps.

"Let's move, Men," the sergeant barks sending the shivering men into a tent to put their clothes into bags they place around their necks, then have their physicals. With little money in the house, Lalo needs the job. The wind pushes against the men as they stand outside later, dressed and at attention, hoping not to hear their names, not to be eliminated.

"DELGADO," the sergeant calls and my uncle steps forward hoping: it's a mistake. Maybe he made a mistake.

The sergeant glances at him and frowns. "I said DELGADO!"

"I am Delgado."

"See me later in my tent."

Lalo walks against the wind into the tent, nervous, not knowing what to expect, why he has been singled out. He clears his throat.

"Just change your name, Delgado," says the sergeant glancing up, "and you've got a job."

Lalo doesn't know what to say at first. His family's counting on this job, but how can he surrender his father's name, his father, the judge who recently died. Lalo can still hear the dirt he'd thrown on the coffin, his duty as the eldest son.

"I can't, sir," Lalo says looking hard at his shoes.

"Up to you," the man in uniform answers gesturing for Lalo to leave.

How am I going to tell them, he asks himself thinking of the house with the bare cupboards as the desert sand stings his skin. Lalo takes his few cents and goes downtown to the Wigwam Movie Theater, sees "Red Sails in the Sunset," slides low in his seat, watches singing heroes to avoid walking into the question on his mother's face.

"Not looking the way some people think a Delgado should look is a problem a few times when I'm older, but it doesn't cost me a job again. In '41, I'm on the streetcar coming back from Juárez and show the immigration agent my birth certificate. He makes me get off saying I'm not a Delgado. There I sit angry and frustrated in an office with only Anglo agents when the only Hispanic working for Immigration then, a guy I know named Torres, sticks his head in. 'What're you doing here, Lalo?'

"They don't believe I'm a Delgado."

" 'Let him go. I know him. He's a Delgado.'

"Another time when I'm older, I have a problem at my bank. Because I'm older, I get really irritated. Every time I go to this one bank teller, who's herself Hispanic, she looks at my check and sneers, 'You're Delgado?'

"Yes, I've told you."

" 'I need to see identification, please,' she says her voice full of doubt.

"Finally, I get sick of it and speak to her boss. After that, she and I get along fine. It's just annoying that people think we all have to look a certain way. Even some of us think that."

"My first job out of high school is printing some signs at the warehouse of United Incorporated. I help a guy who's a commercial artist when I'm twelve or thirteen. He makes the signs and does lettering for the movies like 'King Kong.' Mostly I wash paint off, but I do a little sketching. I'm never any good at it, but I do it so they put me in what they call their printing department, making signs. I'll show you."

My uncle returns with some beige cardboard rectangles advertising men's coats and hats for fall, fedoras, the hats he and my father wore. "I'm paid a dollar a day, but, for twenty cents mind you, I can get a feast at Pop's Hamburger Joint, two hamburgers, a soda, and a piece of pie. We have to be at work every day of the week including Sunday even if all we do is go outside and pitch balls, so when Roosevelt comes in with that forty-hour week, man, we're in heaven!"

During World War II, Lalo's hired by the Cable Landwire Censors' Office in part because he's bilingual. "We sit at the phone company all day and listen to any call made to a foreign country for security reasons. Most of the calls I monitor are to Juárez." He grins. "They bring people in to do the listening who don't understand phrases used on the border.

" 'Eddie, you better listen to the conversation we recorded, talk of a submarine.' "

My uncle and I begin to laugh as we think of our dry landscape and of the Río Grande.

"I listen and start to laugh," he says. "Some voice in Spanish says they're bringing something across the border *por submarino* meaning it will be hidden, smuggled. 'Relax, my friends. No submarine attack on the Rio Grande today.'

"My eyesight keeps me out of the war. I know all the vets will have a better chance at jobs, so I learn shorthand and become a stenographer for Immigration, then a property clerk for the Border Patrol. I climb those tall towers along the border, full of bees and spiders, to inventory radio equipment."

From 1948 to his retirement in 1979, our uncle works for the Boundary Commission, begins as an accountant, then an auditor, and finally becomes the chief financial officer.

"For years, I'd have to take these long trips along the border auditing the books, say, at Falcón Dam. Sometimes my boss travels with me, and we go to dinner at some little place across the river. He tells me that if we have a double tequila before dinner and another after, we'll never get sick in Mexico, and we don't. He picks up a six-pack on the way to the motel, and all night I hear him popping open those beer cans. In the morning, they're empty. Anyway, on those long trips, maybe I'm odd, but I tell myself stories. . . ."

"Okay, you two, enough talking," Aunt Carmen says, "Let's put the grills up out back and roast that bag of green chiles."

Fall in the air, its soothing breath stroking our skin. Roses still bloom, trees sway green, and yet late at night the ground has begun to cool, to dream of its long sleep. Such autumn days are a relief after summer in the desert, the rain last night cleaning the air that tastes the lavender of blooming sage, tempting us to walk and walk, over the *acequia*, through the trees out back, to the soughing of cottonwoods, down to the river, the ribbon of light.

From a halo of steam, Mamá Cleta says from the kitchen, "I'm simmering these chamomile heads for an hour in last night's rainwater. The liquid will bring out the golden highlights in Elizabeth's and Cecilia's hair."

Aunt Chole listens to the ticking of the clock. "Don't tell my sisters, *corazón*," she whispers, "but my vision got worse yesterday. You know how I get up early? I pray first with my eyes closed. When I went to have my breakfast, all I could see was brown, like mud and water.

"No, why see the doctor, *reina*, why spend the money? I just waited all day." She chuckles, "*Ee-ee*, guess what I did? I fixed my lunch, and by mistake I put my hand in the soup, *imagínate*. But what I can see came back. My eyes are normal again. The Holy Spirit helps me so much. He tells me what to do. I tell my *Diosito*, 'I'm ready to go whenever you want.' I want to go before I can't take care of myself any more."

She whimpers and raises a hand to bless me. "I pray for you, *querida*. More than once a day. *Que Dios te llene de bendiciones, que te guíe y que te ilumine, que te ayude en tu trabajo.* I'm not sure what you do, but I pray for you. Take the time to enjoy things like you enjoyed living in Santa Fe. You say the dirt is red there. Imagine. *Trata de disfrutar, mi querida.*"

Lobo takes my arm saying, "*Ummm,*" follows the green smell of roasting chiles through the back gate and out near the fruit trees. As we walk, she tries her riddles on me, *adivinanzas.* "*Agua pasa por mi casa, cate de mi corazón,*" she says.

"*Aguacate,*" the old answers rising as from a deep well inside me.

"*Lana sube, lana baja.*"

I grin. "*La navaja.*"

She laughs, pleased that I still remember.

"I don't get them," my children say.

"They're word play," I say, "the answer embedded in the hint. You have to listen very carefully."

"I've got a riddle for them," Great-great-grandfather, Nepomuceno says getting his hands ready. An old-fashioned name, Nepomuceno, from San Juan Nepomuceno, the Bohemian saint born in Nepomuc in 1383, patron saint of confidentiality, who even when tortured would not reveal the details of Empress Jane's confession. A story says that when his coffin was opened in 1719, his tongue was perfectly preserved because he had honored confessional secrets.

Great-great-grandfather begins to tap his fingertips together as a clue to his riddle. "*Ahora, pónganse a pensar.* What flaps its wings in the morning like a butterfly?"

All of us flap our hands together trying to divine the answer as Uncle Lalo turns the chiles on the grill, the smell making us all hungry.

"*¿Qué, Papá Nepomuceno?*"

"The tortilla maker," he laughs.

Lobo pats her hands together in the shade enjoying the clever conceit, saying, "*tortillitas, tortillitas,*" and imagines huge monarch butterflies filling our kitchen with their silent, orange flutters.

"I've got a joke for you kids," their uncle says. "A young girl in Mexico fell in love with an Anglo. A bit embarrassed, the young woman said, '*O señor, yo no soy señorita,*' to which the young man replied, '*No problema. Yo no soy señorito.*' " Aunt Carmen laughs at the joke she has probably heard a hundred times.

Aunt Carmen rises early even in retirement to work in her garden. She's born in Pachuca near Mexico City, her mother Altagracia, a Mexican, born in Zacatecas, and her father, Conrad Veal, a British engineer who works in the mines in Mexico. Even as a little girl, Carmen sews with her *abuela*, makes dresses for her dolls. In the twenties when foreigners are sent out of the country, the Veal family has to abandon their belongings and come with nothing but their ingenuity to El Paso. Carmen is nine, a round-faced pretty girl, who speaks no English, attends Saint Patrick's School briefly, Morehead, and then El Paso High. In a church group she meets Eduardo Delgado, Lalo, her husband now of over fifty years.

"This fig tree belonged to my father," she says, "the apple tree too. I got my love of gardening from him. Because she hated the sun, Mama didn't like to garden. It was my dad, my daddy."

Carmen and Lalo date to "Sundown Serenade," "Stardust," "Begin the Beguine." In Lalo's car they're Jeannette McDonald and Nelson Eddy singing "The Indian Love Call": "When I'm call - ing you - ou ou ou - ou ou ou."

"I don't start gardening until after I get married. I don't want to spoil my skin. My parents were young, happy. They love picnics and dancing, not serious like your grandmother," she tells me of the woman with whom she lived for years. "When I move into your grandmother's duplex, at 1419 Wyoming, a very small duplex, I can't stand how bare everything is. There's nothing in front, and I want to liven up the place. I think it's horrible, horrible. It looks so baaad. I ask my dad, and he says, 'Here.' He has some poppy seeds so they're the very first thing I plant. Maybe that's illegal now with drugs. I don't know, but they're the most gorgeous poppies. We fertilize the soil, and I turn the dirt over. People just stop and look at them, orange and red poppies. Beautiful! I want color!

"I like to be out in the garden by 5:30 or 6:00 A.M. The sun you know, honey. I take good care of my skin. My favorite plants really have been roses, geraniums, begonias, and of course my bougainvillea that I've had for forty-five years. Yes, ma'am! I've carried it, transplanted it into umpteen pots. I buy it as a tiiiiny little thing at Black's nursery, and from there it's been nursed through all this time."

She'd sew for us, singing to herself, "O so - le mi - o," as she makes us white eyelet pinafores, crochets turquoise knit dresses with tams to match, lines coats with velvet collars, sews doll clothes filling a small blue metal trunk for Christmas, a rag doll I call Esper. Our tall, handsome aunt spends her days then selling ladies fine dresses at the White House Department Store with Aunt Chole.

She models there when she's young and later helps coordinate the fashion shows smiling at customers from El Paso and Mexico. At night with her sewing machine and quick hands she makes her versions of the dresses at the store, through the years fills her closets with carefully measured suits and outfits of bold colors, magenta and purple, buys purses and shoes to match, a self-stitched, fashionable woman smelling of Shalimar, the walls of her home covered with her paintings. "It's my outlet."

We loved to visit our aunt and uncle's home, the rooms cool, the drapes drawn to keep out the desert sun, the pink bathroom decorated with lace and shells, always the bottle of perfumed Royal Secret, expensive cream we rub into our hands and wrists.

Her hands crocheted and knitted, gardened, cooked, still do. "I'm fine, Honey, fine," she says in her seventies firmly avoiding sounding like her complaining friends and relatives.

After taking the toasted chiles to the kitchen, Aunt Carmen takes her husband out back to tell him her plans for redoing the grotto to Saint Francis, the statue she brought from Mexico that has been spared the blows inflicted on poor Saint Raphael in this family.

"I tell you this yardwork never ends," Uncle Lalo says. "I had to trap another squirrel this morning. I think that makes fifty. They get in the garden and eat the leaves and build their tunnels so I made a red wooden trap. Carmen makes a little peanut piñata we hang in there to lure the animal in. I take the wily squirrels down near the river and let them go. A friend of mine teases me that it's the same squirrel I've caught fifty times.

"Yesterday morning, I was out early, and I saw a small bobcat on that adobe wall. He looked at me, and I looked at him, at his brownish gray fur and the tufts on his ears. He stared and then he walked on."

"Have you seen the turtles?" I ask.

My aunt and uncle laugh. "You mean Primera, Segunda, and Perdida?" Aunt Carmen asks. "The three were born in this garden, honey. Soon they'll be hibernating again. They disappear about November through April. We try to feed them meat or dog food, but they're not interested. They like sweets like bananas and figs. Sometimes your uncle goes out, squeezes a banana between his fingers hoping to lure them out."

What would they say, I wonder, the shelled creatures and their dark secrets, their tiny eyes, the safety and danger of all that protection, their persistent pace? I'd stare at the tiny ones Cecilia and I would buy at a downtown dime store when we were little, watch the moss-green turtles move up the ramp toward a palm tree of the clear plastic container. I'd study the box turtle that lives in our back yard when my children are young, lumbers across the grass to eat the dog food placed on the back patio as a lure.

> The time of the singing birds is come,
> and the voice of the turtle is heard in our land,

says "The Song of Solomon," a slow voice that carries its own echo.

Sitting in the shade, I listen to my uncle savoring the stories he told himself, when he's a young man, takes the twenty-two rifle his brother won and sits in a cave, respite from the heat, wonders about the welcome breeze at his back and begins to create an explanation, to spin himself a yarn about a boy like he was, going down into a such a cave with friends, finding . . . the storyteller pauses and drops his voice, "a mastadon." I see the immense animal the boys name Oscar staring down at me without blinking, his eyes frozen wide. My uncle braids his life and his character's life, the author creating, leading the way, and then following as the character begins to live his own life, this character and others my uncle creates through the years as he drives across Texas, watching the flat, gray highway yet seeing a caravan winding its way between Chihuahua and Santa Fe in the 1800s, seeing a man named Martín Brady and the old Indian woman whose blanket protects him.

My favorite uncle, a man I think I know well, and yet I never really knew the difficulties in his life, didn't suspect this creative habit of story making, reworking details for his own private pleasure, enriching his secret, adult life with his invention. The view into that well-protected interior space, an *in sight*, a gift of the house, the quiet and space it gives me to listen to the awe in his voice when I ask if he likes to read as a child.

"Oh gosh yes!" he says in almost a whisper drifting back to the pages of *Dr. Doolittle* at Lamar School's library, again anticipating weekends with James Fenimore Cooper and Jack London. The life of readers, our solitary, indescribable pleasure different from reading for facts, data, theories, no, the deeper, more sensory joy, black proper letters apparently stiff, silent, still; yet latent with movement and promise that mysteriously enter us, stimulate our taste buds, rub against our elbows, sing and echo in our skin, their scent more overpowering than nostalgia.

"Lalo!" his wife says shaking her head at the power of these stories in her husband's life. "Pat must be starving, *pobrecita*. Come into the kitchen both of you. I've made us a nice chicken enchilada casserole with some of those chiles and baked some pumpkin slices like Mama used to with lots of brown sugar. Come on. You can finish your stories later." She's singing softly to herself when we come in to join her, "Gra - na - da, tie - rra so - ña - da por mí."

The last few years thanks to the stories I've been following, I've had a few such meals alone with my aunt and uncle. "Let's not go out this time, honey. I'll fix us something good here," her words and the plate she hands me, measures of comfort. Somehow, the feel of the time with them—he's sitting at the table remembering and she's moving from refrigerator to stove, pouring iced-tea, stirring a pot, adding to his memories, basting slices of pumpkin—and I'm pre-adult again, pre-responsibility, in that private family world with two older people who care about me and have known me since I was born, watching a woman who understands kitchens, whose hands dice, slice, sauté, pare, stir, blending ingredients and serving them on scrubbed dishes, a woman who, when she finally sits at the table, tastes and ponders what she cooked, adjusting mentally, a pinch more pepper next time, a little less garlic, seasoning what she serves us as her husband seasons the stories he tells himself.

"*Cada cabeza es un mundo,*" says Mamá Cleta listening in the shadows. She's right again, of course. Do we ever know another person, the unseen chambers into which they can retreat?

Wind rattling windows wakes me before sunrise. I step onto the porch, see chile *ristras* by the doorways; in the distance, hear an owl, feel a hint of fall in the air. Out the front gate, I study the silhouette of the mountain as that first wisp of light begins behind it. Crickets lull the sleepers in the house, and the steady rhythm of their breathing and the hidden crickets send me back to bed. At the first pale sun rays, Mamá Cleta begins to pace her prayers, *clck, clck,* the rosary she murmurs round the *portal,* "*Dios te salve, María, llena eres de gracia.*" She pauses at dewdrops glistening on fine spider webs that sway in the morning breeze, wishes she could heal the broken hand of poor San Rafael's statue before the saint arrives, on this, his feast day, September twenty-ninth, feast day of all the angels, "*prontos a la voz de su palabra.*"

She invited him, a few of the family saints and Our Lady of Guadalupe, of course, to join her for *café con leche* before the family rises. She covers a small table with a yellow cotton tablecloth in the *portal,* so the fountain, *ps-slp-plop, ps-slp-plop,* can serenade us, she thinks. Bringing out the blue and white dishes, a tiny vase, spongy *conchas*, pitchers of steaming milk and coffee, she tastes the sugar she's flavored with rosebuds, buried the tiny blooms in layers of sugar she set in the sun for months to perfume *la azúcar*. She savors the grains openly like a child, the taste like arches, and looks out at *el jardín*, its winged and petaled pleasures, its visual and fragrant solace.

How strange this would have seemed once, entertaining the saints, welcoming them into the family's walled world. How little we understand when we're alive, she thinks dusting sugar bits off the tabelcloth.

My father appears, quick to smell the coffee. Mamá Cleta struggles to hide her frown. After all, she has just finished her rosary, dedicated her day to the honor and glory of God, and is preparing for heavenly visitors. No time to be selfish, but . . . she had hoped for a private visit with the saints, maybe a slightly more elevated conversation about faith and grace and fate than will be possible if all the family spirits are going to appear.

"*Buenos días, Don Raúl. Buenos días.*"

"*Buenos días, Mamá Cleta. ¿Qué pasa?*"

She tells him about the early morning gathering, tries to make it sound dull, lots of formalities, the need to dress appropriately. Her strategy works. My father studies the heap of sugar-crusted, shell-shaped rolls, takes the biggest, undoing her symmetrical bread mound, but then he drifts away, munching.

"*Gracias a Dios,*" she whispers.

"*Gracias a Dios,*" blares the parrot.

Frowning in the direction of the kitchen and the rude bird, she redoes the bread platter, hears wings behind her.

"*¿San Rafael?* she asks turning slowly. And there he stands, his clear eyes smiling down at her, his wings, immense. She blesses herself and nervously pours streams of milk and coffee at first missing his cup. The angel lifts the bottom of his mother-of-pearl wings to arrange himself in a curved rawhide chair. Taking the offered cup, he smiles and nods his thanks, takes the cup with both hands, closes his eyes, and inhales deeply.

"*¡Rico!*" he says with satisfaction when, about to take his first sip, he quickly puts the cup down and rises to greet Saint Martin and Saint Cecilia. In the midst of their *abrazos*, they hear the courtyard fill with birds and smell the red perfume of roses, turn to see Our Lady of Guadalupe moving toward them waving gently. She stops at the parrot cage, digs into her long, pink dress and brings out a handful of pumpkin seeds.

"*Gracias, Virgencita, gracias*," the parrot squawks.

Approaching the group on the porch, she slowly hugs each being standing near the table, pats their left and then their right cheek twice, looks into their eyes. She pulls Mamá Cleta up from her knees and gently hugs her too, the scent of roses thick velvet on my great-great-grandmother's palms.

Quickly, Nuestra Señora reaches for the *pan dulce*, sinks her teeth into the sweet bread, says as soon as she's swallowed, "¡Ay. qué delicioso! Forgive me," she laughs licking the last bits of topping from her fingertips, "I just couldn't wait. *Pan dulce* is one of my weaknesses. Please, sit, sit. Doña Anacleta, how can I help? How kind of you to invite us into this wonderful garden on the feast of San Rafael."

Once Mamá Cleta sits, Our Lady does too, nods a greeting at the birds of every color that cover the trees, their songs a morning serenade. The group sips their coffee in silence, mesmerized by the feathered music and fountain's melody. "*Mira no más*," Our Lady says pointing toward the garden entrance, toward them trudges a disheveled Santo Niño de Atocha. The Holy Child hands Mamá Cleta his staff and basket, climbs into His mother's lap. She looks at the soles of His shoes and shakes her head, incorrigible child, wearing His shoes out night after night on His errands of mercy. San Martín quietly goes to fill the Child's gourd with fresh water while Our Lady hands him a roll that he stuffs into His mouth. "*¡Jesús!*" she exclaims.

The child smiles at Mamá Cleta who is too amazed to either drink or chew. Speechless that He is here, in the garden, she fills His small basket with bread, never taking her eyes off His face. Our Lady begins to hum and the voices in the garden—water, wind, birds, crickets—braid in polyphonic song. Santa Cecilia directs, with her long fingers gestures silence to peacocks and parrot. The weary Boy rests his tired head on His mother's breast, lulled to sleep by *las voces del jardín*.

The kitchen noises begin, the stirrings as the mountain to the east blushes a golden pink, and saints nod their thanks to Mamá Cleta, slide an extra bread roll into their flowing gowns as they drift away. For what seems like days, Mamá Cleta stands perfectly still, unable even to blink. *Sw, sw, sw,* Lobo's sweeping begins as does the raking of dirt out back. *Sw, sw, sw,* morning rhythms, restoring order to this desert oasis.

Convinced that no one's watching, Mamá Cleta bends and picks up a long glowing feather *de San Rafael* from the tile. She strokes it and tastes a delicate whiteness on her tongue, crisp like a host.

Octubre / October

La que anda entre la miel, algo se le pega.

Honey clings if you're surrounded by it.

MRS. MORA, MRS. MORA, may I see you for a moment? Patricia, you just stand by the door while I speak to your mother. Remember, while adults are speaking, we keep our distance to be polite and respectful, don't we, Dear?"

Dear seems an odd word in the mouth of my ten-foot tall, three-hundred pound second-grade teacher, a nun with thick, black eyebrows and lashes, green eyes big as headlights, a slight mustache, and a voice piercing as metal across smooth tile.

"Mrs. Mora," says immense, green-eyed Sister Eleanor Clare. "It's not easy to teach this combined second and third. You know, I have two Patricias in the class, your daughter and Patricia in third who's just a little talker . . . Excuse me, Mrs. Mora.

"RICHARD!" Sister's voice even makes Mother jump. It's the sound in the movies when two cars without brakes smash into each other. That's how loud Sister's voice is when it smashes into the air.

"RICHARD! YOU COME RIGHT BACK HERE AND WALK DON'T RUN OUT OF THIS ROOM!"

"I'm so sorry, Mrs. Mora. Now where was I? Patricia, you just continue standing right there by the door. It is not easy, Mrs. Mora, as you can imagine to teach some of

these children proper behavior. Now after lunch and re-
cess to calm the class down, I have them put their heads
down and rest."

"Class, please put your arms on the desk and your
heads on your arms. Now, Richard! Fine, fine. Sister is
going to sit down here at her desk and begin a new book
for us today, *B Is for Betsy* by Carolyn Haywood."

I listen to her voice, happy that Sister's not screaming. I
shut my eyes so I can see what she's reading about Betsy
who's going to her first day at school, "that strange new
place," about her teacher, Miss Grey, and her new friends,
Ellen and Billy, about Betsy's furry koala bear.

BAM!

"PATRICIA!"

I jump when Sister calls my name. What did I do?
Why is she angry? I look at her scared that I'm in trouble
when I only closed my eyes to see the pictures. I see Sister
lift the book over her head and bang it on the desk as
hard as she can, her face so red I can't see her mustache.
But she's not looking at me. Her green headlights are
flashing at the other Patricia, Patricia in third.

"Now, Mrs. Mora, I'm just trying to teach that other
child to behave, and sometimes I may raise my voice
slightly, but your daughter just jumps out of her skin
when she hears me say her name. I've told her, though,
not to worry. You don't think she's scared of me, do you,
Mrs. Mora?

"Patricia, Patricia, come over here," says Sister almost
blinding me with her eyes. "You're not scared of me, are
you, Patricia? You're not scared of Sister Eleanor Clare?"

Uncomfortable with journal writing, I make myself sit in a
wide-armed chair to drift to these early memories, sink back
to what has become real/reel in my mind since we compose
the stories of our lives not only for others, but for ourselves,

through repetition perfect certain scenes and moments unable consciously to retain all our joys and woes. Opening the journal, I read the Nahuatl word, *ninoyolnonotza*, and its meaning, "I address myself to my heart." I reread the vignette I started last night, then drift to sleep thinking of pumpkins and the moon swelling these crisp, leaf-scuttle nights. Autumn wind skims the heavens, the mountain, and the rounded corners of the adobe house. I begin to worry about frost, time to bring the house-plants back inside.

Comfortable under the covers, hearing the wind still weaving its *canto hondo* through the willows and cottonwoods, I wake and hear Lobo out early, *sw, sw,* the falling leaves this month requiring steady vigilance from the keeper of order. October second, the feast of Guardian Angels, those gentle beings who after years of neglect have reappeared, golden on stationery, wrapping paper, and calendars, suggesting our longing in this turbulent world for benevolent beings floating unseen down our streets, walking beside our schoolchildren, hovering behind us at our computers, under the stars circling our homes ever ready to guide and protect us. As Lobo sweeps away leaves, dirt, disease, disappointment, debt, despair, danger, *diablos, divorcios, demonios y dolores,* she repeats the comforting prayer she says to the winged guardians at night,

> *Santo Angel de la Guarda,*
> *mi dulce compañía,*
> *no me desampares,*
> *ni de noche, ni de día.*

"Boys and girls, boys and girls," Sister Alicia, my first-grade teacher, says her face and words shining. "Today is the feast of our Guardian Angels. Please fold your hands together like this, fingertip to fingertip. Press them together, now place one thumb over the other. Good, now let's close our eyes and say our prayer together in a nice, clear voice. Our Guardian Angels are right here with us, boys and girls. They're watching to see whose hands are together perfectly, whose eyes stay closed. The angels are listening, and if we are very, very quiet, maybe we can hear

them too. Now let's say our prayer together so perfectly that all
the angels in the room will smile.

> O angel of God, my guardian dear,
> To whom God's love entrusts me here,
> Ever this day, be at my side,
> To light, to guard, to rule, and guide.

I know I need to go outside and help lug in all the house-
plants that have been on the porch since spring. "Sorry," I say to
the ficus, miniature orange tree, crown of thorns, asparagus
fern. Inside, I hear Mother saying, "October gave a party, the
leaves by hundreds came," the poem we learned in elementary
school, a poem she recites every fall.

"I'm reading some old books about fragrant plants," I tell my
husband who, as he risks a hernia moving the bougainvillea, re-
ally doesn't want to hear about more plants.

"Don't you think we have enough?" Vern asks.

"An oxymoron, enough plants. I ordered some paperwhite
narcissus and some hyacinths, but these books suggest plants
like ginger lilies, sweet olive, and gardenias. Maybe I should try
to find a lemon tree since they're supposed to be so aromatic.
Remember how in Greece even the leaves smelled wonderful?
Don't worry, don't worry. I may not find any of these. They're
just ideas. You know me and my winter garden.

"But did I tell you that scents are classified, really, scientifi-
cally. Look here at the categories in the eighteenth century: am-
brosiaca, fragantia, aromatica, graveolenta, tetra, and nauseola.
You laugh now, but wait till the nauseolas move in. Unless you're
anosmic." I laugh. "You'll have to look it up," I say before Vern
can ask the definition. We love words.

"Think how nice it would be," I continue, "to scoff at artificial
aromas and to walk into a room in December scented by what
Bacon called the 'breath of flowers,' say lillies-of-the-valley.
Don't you want their breaths sweetening your winter days? And
think of the historical aspect. You're an academic. The Ancient
Greeks planted the most fragrant plants near windows because
of the salutary benefits, and monks in Medieval times planted

herbs near their infirmaries believing the sweet scents would benefit the patients."

"*I'm* going to need an infirmary if you keep buying more plants."

"The problem is, you live in your head. Cultivate the senses."

My sister, Stella, comes to help me lift the crown of thorns cactus. We complain to one another about backaches and headaches. "No pleasing us though," I say, "Now we complain about our bodies, and one day we'll complain about not having them."

She takes a deep breath. "Doesn't fall make you think of our old back yard?"

"It was my safe place," Cecilia calls out to us.

What a haven the imperfect, rock-enclosed back yard was for the four of us. We turn cartwheels, hang by our knees on the trapeze or swing-set bars, beautiful and limber we see ourselves in the private, protected space, climb backwards up the slide, push each other on the wooden merry-go-round my father has made for us one Christmas. Without horses or mirrors, the spinning device was a square of four wood boards, a few feet off the grass, attached to a central turning piece. On each corner are four raised wooden rectangles for sitting high. The four of us put our hands on these seats and begin to push, run faster and faster, then leap on and as the merry-go-round spins, we fly.

Cecilia and I make pretend meals with mud and sticks, fill japonica leaves with damp soil, our tiny tacos. We collect cocoons, crunch the dry, brown leaves where our dogs through the years like to sleep. In what we called the alley behind our house, two sloping, scrubby, vacant lots; we watch ants, beetles, horned toads, and lizards hiding in the shade under the creosote.

"Uh-oh," says six-year-old Cecilia, "I caught the lizard with Mom's tweezers, but it ran away and left his tail. Now what do I do?"

We, and later our younger sister and brother, build forts of rocks or bricks in the vacant lots or nearby hills, shape spaces for ourselves, take our peanut butter and jelly sandwiches for picnics.

"I can't imagine my life if I didn't sing," says Stella. "I'd sing all the songs from *The Wizard of Oz* on our swings, 'I would while away the hours, conferrin' with the flowers.'"

"*La que canta, sus males espanta,*" says Mamá Cleta from the shade where she sits with the grandparents and great-grandparents.

"I liked being in that yard of ours," Stella says, "especially in the fall, *ummm*, the leaves crackling, chrysanthemums almost wild, the big pomegranate bush by the merry-go-round, cocoons hanging from branches, and Daddy's fussing with his roses, Peace, his favorite. I like to be outside with him. I'm swinging, and he's working. I hear him, 'Did you ever see a dream walk - ing?' That's where he pulls one of his tricks on me."

"Have you ever seen the little people?" he asks. Stella runs over to where her father's working. "Oh, they're everywhere," he says. "They're the cutest things."

When he goes inside, the chubby brunette in her purple shorts and white-and-purple striped top, begins looking under the rose bushes. She kneels on the grass and peers at the leaves, inside the pink and yellow blooms, around the roots, with her fingers carefully brushing the curled, brown leaves away, longing to see perfect miniature people scurrying in the aroma of roses, making tiny twig beds, knitting petal quilts, kneading bread dough, slicing berries, stirring pots and baking cakes and berry pies with crimped crusts at miniature stoves, rocking in small chairs of dried leaves, swaying in spider-web hammocks, wee children clasping bitty hands, singing and spinning to "ring a - round the ro - ses." The stuff of grand, old children's stories—tiny, private friends.

"Too bad you didn't know the old superstition that if you gather thyme where the little people live and put it on your eyelids, you can see the little ones," I say.

"I didn't even know what thyme was until I started cooking. Finally, discouraged, I went in and said, 'I don't see any little people, Daddy.'"

I can see him glancing up from his paper, his mischievous look when he confesses that the mini-creatures don't exist.

Later, when I sit at the kitchen table and return to my journal, I hear the wind chase itself around the garden, and I hear singing, Lobo and Schubert's *"Ave María,"* my father and "Old Man River," Stella and "I'm off to see the wizard," again and again, as Mamande whispers her prayers, *"Angel de Dios, Angel de Dios,"*

I'm in my parent's bedroom, maybe four years old, enjoying being in there alone. From the dresser, I pick up the photograph of my smiling mother. I look at the perfume bottles, pick them up carefully, smell the glass bottles without opening them, glancing to make sure Mother isn't coming. I listen. I hear her singing to my sister in the kitchen, "Shine lit - tle glow - worm, glim - mer, glim - mer." I tip a perfume bottle, pretend I'm putting the smell on like Mother does. Touch behind my ears and on my wrists.

I look at Mother's lipsticks, very slowly slide off the top, smell the dark, red smell, the smell of Mother's lips. I turn and look at my parent's white bedspread, how bare the white looks, all that white like a giant piece of paper, a lonely, bare piece of paper. I walk to the bed holding the dark, red lipstick, and I draw a line on the white, but it's not smooth like paper. I press to make the lipstick mind me, reach as far as I can with my red to draw a river flowing across the bed. I . . .

"Patsy! What are you doing? Give me that lipstick! Haven't I told you never, never to play with the things on Mommy's dresser?"

I begin to cry, the tears rising like a wave I can't stop, spilling down my cheeks. Cecilia peeks out at me from behind Mother, begins to cry because I'm crying.

"No! No! No! The bedspread is ruined, Patsy. It looked so pretty, and now it's ruined. What will your father say?"

"Just listen to that wind howl," says Mother coming to sit with me. We watch my nephews, Gil and Christopher, clowning to Belafonte's "House built on a rock foundation, it will stand, oh yes." I fix us a cup of tea with lemon and honey, enjoying the wind, one of my favorite sounds, perhaps because other than during my school years, I know that desert wind within the protection of walls, hearing its power and exuberance around me, but from a home, an eye in the storm. I have known good havens.

Clouds brood blue in the late afternoon. I'd push through fall winds in grade school, walk up the hill from the bus, arms heavy with homework, the wind almost tipping me into the agave thorns in a neighbor's yard. A mulling season, autumn. Houselights come on earlier in the late afternoon as the daylight diminishes. I peer in windows from the bus on the way home from school and wonder: what do those people do in there, what are they eating as they sit around that oval table? Are they happy?

Growing up, my children would say, "Mom, want to drive by and see your little, old house?" My childhood home seemed neither to those who lived in it. When it was for sale a few years ago, I returned to it, walked up the two steps, could see us sliding on the red porch, our pool on summer afternoons. I opened the screen door and entered the living room. Walking through the rooms was like seeing someone who has lived hard or has been neglected for over thirty years. The frame is there, but the layer we see has aged without grace.

Hearing the sound of pans and chopping, Aunt Chole comes to sit at the table.

"I had my secrets in the kitchen, *reina*. Like my pineapple upside-down cake, plenty of brown sugar, but the secret was my *sartén de fierro*, the cake pan I gave your daughter. My sister would make the same cake, good, but it doesn't taste like mine.

"When you're little, *ee*, your parents bring you to me on Sunday. At first, I sit you on the bed. You like to eat, and I want to please you. Then you start walking and talk, talk, talk. I used to make special lemon cookies for you. Do you remember? I make them so they won't be too greasy because you are little, *reina, muy chiquita*. People ask me for the recipe, but they don't know my secret. I moisten a small piece of thin paper and place it on the bottom of a glass, press the dough on that to make the cookies thin, browned at the edges."

Thin cookies, lemon hosts, placed on my tongue by my single aunt.

Hearing the screen door bang out back in the wind, I return to my journal.

"Who banged that door?"

We freeze at the sound of our father's voice, spiny as cactus. I was chasing Cecilia who took my favorite paper dolls, Ethyl and Gordon, and started running. I named her Ethyl because I love the smell of gasoline when my father fills the gas tank. Gordon is for the movie star Gordon McRae, his brown hair always perfect, the deep voice booming out when he croons to pretty girls, "By the light, of the sil - ver - y, mo - on." Ethyl likes to get dressed up and go out with Gordon. Very carefully, I cut her dresses, skirts, and blouses. She looks really nice, likes it when Gordon holds her hand.

"WHO BANGED THAT DOOR?"

"Raúl, what are you yelling about?" Mother asks pushing through the swinging kitchen door. She sees me. I point to the front screen door and gesture that I let it slam shut. She shakes her head and opens both hands. Nothing she can do.

My father's really angry, and he can easily get really angry. So can Mother. Cecilia ran out the front door first so it's her fault too, but I ran out last and forgot to catch the door.

"I did, Daddy," I call back trying not to breathe, imagining him stretched out on the double bed of my parent's room, reading the newspaper in his slacks and T-shirt. I feel the tears welling,

"Open and shut that door a hundred times, Patsy! How many times have I told you not to slam that door?"

"Okay, Daddy," I say as loud as I can muster.

"WHAT?"

"I said Okay, Daddy," I say trying my hardest not to sob.

My sister tiptoes back near the red porch and peeks at me hiding behind the japonica so our father won't see her from his bedroom window and ask her to do the same.

Mortified, the tears beginning to slide down my face, I open the screen door and close it softly, say every number out loud, not daring to skip any.

"One."

"Two."

"Eleven."

I see Mamande open the kitchen door and look at me, suffering.

"Nineteen."

"Twenty-three."

"Lobo's coming," my sister whispers and runs to meet my aunt, to tell her. Maybe she can save me.

"Thirty-four."

My aunt makes as much noise as possible as she walks up the two porch steps in her black dress and low-heeled, shiny patent shoes. I can tell by her lips that she's ready to make my father repent for his cruelty. Cecilia clings to the back of Lobo's dress.

"¿Qué pasa, querida?" she asks me, her voice brimming with compassion. She looks over and glares at my father's window.

"Forty. I can't talk now, Lobo," I whisper trying to look as pitiful as possible, sighing so she can hear my breath wheezing through my broken heart. "Come on in. I have to do this until I get to a hundred. I'm only on forty, and I'm so tired and hungry." I pause. "Dice mi papá."

"Paaaatsy," I hear my father call. "I don't hear that door."

Lobo's glare in the direction of my father's room could melt our blue Ford.

Why can't that man just stay at his optical, Lobo wonders. He's probably lying in there without his shirt on and with young daughters in the house. *¡Qué ver-guenza!* That's what happens when women from nice families like ours marry people like that. They're not cultured. And now this, torturing this sweet, innocent child. He'll suffer for it, in Hell if not before. And where's this poor child's mother? Why isn't she in-terceding? I think Patricia will faint soon. She looks so pale.

Lobo kisses the top of my head and points to the paper bag she has, as always full of Hersheys, Milky Ways, But-terfingers, Archie comics. I nod stoically. Her displeasure stronger than her perfume, she strides toward the kitchen to find Mother, Cecilia waving to me with one hand and clinging to Lobo's dress with the other.

"Sixty-seven."

I hear Lobo and Mother arguing in the kitchen, strain to hear talk of my salvation as I count. *"Pero esa pobre niña. . . ."*

"Seventy-four."

The kitchen door opens a bit, and out of the corner of my eye, I see Lobo, Mother, Mamande, and Cecilia suffering with me.

"Supper's ready," Mother calls, her voice tight with anger.

I wait for a reprieve, think of cheese enchiladas, beans, rice, neopolitan ice cream.

"Espérate. Let Patsy finish," my father calls.

"Raúl, these enchiladas will be ruined!"

"Let her finish," my father says slowly, too clever for the ploy.

"Eighty-nine."

"Es un hombre pero feo, feo, feo," Lobo mutters going to the bathroom to wash her hands.

Cecilia tiptoes in and sits very quietly on the edge of the sofa, here to keep me company though I glare at her for getting me into this mess by yanking Ethyl and Gordon right out of my hands.

"Ninety-five."

I hear my father getting out of bed.

"Ninety-six."

I hear him walking down the hall and into the dining room.

"Ninety-seven."

Lobo walks by him muttering about "*la pobrecita inocente.*"

"Ninety-eight."

My frightened sister looks up at my father who fills the archway to the living room where I've endured my penance.

"Ninety-nine."

"Raúl!" my mother says shoving the kitchen door open unaware as yet that I've survived.

I open the screen door one last time very slowly and close it as gently as possible.

"One-hundred."

"Okay," my father says. "Let's eat."

We sit and all bow our heads, together say, "Bless us, O Lord, and these Thy gifts, which we are about to receive from Thy bounty, through Christ, Our Lord, Amen."

I hear the screen door banging out back in the wind. Banging doors remind me of my father. I live in the same rock house on Mesita from the day my parents bring me home from the hospital in January, 1942, until the day I marry in July, 1963. Because Mother's convinced we'll receive a better education in Catholic schools, I attend Saint Patrick's from kindergarten through eighth grade.

"But there's a perfectly good public school right near us. Why can't they go there?" my father asks Mother though I think he too likes to see his four wearing uniforms, at church singing, "*O sa - lu - ta - ris Hos - ti - a.*"

Annually we memorize answers to: Who made us? Who is God? Why did God make us? For high school, my sisters and I attend Loretto Academy, an all-girl school. My daughters cringe at such a thought. "Nuns and no boys?"

"I loved it," I say thinking of the cool, hushed marble chapel, of the sisters of Loretto in their black shoes, black hose, black habits, long rosaries, nuns who in the early years wear wonderful, starched black veils shaped like the letter *M*. How I want to wear those garments, symbols of goodness and purpose.

"When was I dressed like a nun?" asks Libby when she's little holding a black-and-white photo.

I laugh. "That's not you, that's me. When I graduate from kindergarten, we are to have a full graduation with white caps and gowns, and three lucky children will be allowed to dress like priests and nuns—one will be the bishop, one a priest, and one will wear the habit of a Sister of Loretto. Oh how with all my heart, I long for that moment of slipping on the secret layers of the black habit and stretching my neck with the starched white collar. Until I'm about seventeen, I never consider being anything other than a nun, Sister Mary Jude, the name I'd chosen, Saint Jude the patron saint of the impossible.

"Wouldn't you know it, my friend Martha Ann is picked to be the nun by Sister Margaret Ann, the kindergarten teacher I remember fondly because she too loved licorice in spite of the fact that her mother would tell her that it was made by mixing the dregs of all other candies.

"Not chosen. The beginning of life's little disappointments, *los detalles de la vida* as Aunt Chole would say. But, but Martha Ann gets sick, and guess who gets to have that sweet habit, smelling of purity, on her little body?"

I hover near my proper, energetic, and oh-so-holy sisters of Loretto—SisterMargaretAnnSisterAliciaSisterEleanor ClareSisterAndrewSisterJustinSisterErmalindaSisterEugene-MarieSisterGodfrey, and that's just elementary school. How I long to please them, take the early morning bus to be standing in front of Saint Pat's when they arrive in the morning in a taxi, ready to straighten desks or clean blackboards or dust erasers, mortified when I can't spell *once* in a third grade Friday spelling bee, when I miss 4 x 7 in fourth grade and have to go to the end of the line.

I buy red albums and fill them with holy cards, collect them like some people collect baseball cards. One album is for the many manifestations of Mary alone, the Immaculate Conception, Our Lady of Lourdes, of Fatima, of Sorrows, of Loretto, of Light, of the Assumption. No names in Spanish, as I remember, at the Madonna Shop near my father's optical business where I'd go down the steps and study what new saints had come in, no *Nuestra Señora del Carmen, Nuestra Señora de Atocha, Nuestra Señora de los Angeles, Nuestra Señora de San Juan de los Lagos, Nuestra Señora Refugio de Pecadores, Nuestra Señora del Sagrado Corazón, Nuestra Señora de Guadalupe.*

Somehow my parents tolerate me when arriving home from school, I often put a black mantilla on my head and line up the dining-room chairs like pews, play nun by myself for hours, clicking the orange Halloween frog clicker signaling to the invisible students to genuflect in unison, lecturing them, as the Sisters lecture our classes, about saints, sacrifice, sacrilege, sacraments, scapulars, salvation, and sin—venial and cardinal; about martyrdom, miracles, mysteries—joyful, sorrowful, and glorious; about relics, rosaries, redemption, and resurrection, about creation, creeds, commandments, crosses, confession, contrition, communion.

"Boys and girls," I say to my imaginary pupils, "remember that when you see the priest open the small window in the confessional, you're to say in a nice, clear voice, 'Bless me, father, for I have sinned.' After the priest gives you absolution, you are to say your Act of Contrition. Let's say it together, 'O my God, I am heartily sorry for having offended Thee, and I detest all my sins. . . .' "

Cecilia says, "I couldn't think of any sins, so I'd lie about some and then I'd have to confess lying."

"I'd press rounds of white bread between my fingers to make hosts," I say.

"You did what?" my three children ask. It seemed perfectly normal to me.

"Stella, come over here and tell the kids about the time you confused a movie theater and a church, about the popcorn," I say. "You'll see how much religion was a part of our lives," I whisper to my children.

"Now don't you guys laugh at me," Stella says. "We used to go to this beautiful downtown theater called the Plaza. We go on the bus or Mother takes us. We go look at the alligators at the *placita*, and then walk to the theater to buy our tickets. This theater has a big lobby with lots of velvet curtains, and inside where the screen is, the ceiling is like a huge sky with stars that twinkle.

"I'd go to the movies with my friend, Loretta, since my older sisters don't give me the time of day then. So this day, Loretta and I buy our snacks and go in. The movie has already started so the theater is dark. I go in first, and when I find a row we like, I just calmly turn, hand Loretta my popcorn and Coke, and genuflect."

No matter how many times I hear this story, I burst out laughing at that image of my sister automatically genuflecting before entering a row in a movie theater as we'd been trained to genuflect before entering a row at church. Cissy asks, "Mom, what does genuflect mean?"

Early I sink into stories, Lobo's first, though at the time I'm unaware of her luring, unaware that stories are essential as water. I take books home from school and public libraries, join summer reading clubs, read biographies of Clara Barton, Amelia Earhart, Betsy Ross, read *Dolly Madison: Quaker Girl*, *William Penn: Friendly Boy*, *Jim Bowie: Boy with a Hunting Knife*. I read Nancy Drew books, Bobsey Twins, Pollyanna, and every book by Laura Ingalls Wilder, whom I discover in the *Ws*.

Although I love school and dislike being absent, I also enjoy the days when a cough and Lobo's whispered admonitions to Mother keep me home, and I can stay in bed all day, read the *Childcraft*, play with storybook dolls, Mamande coming to pat my hand. When I'm older, staying home sick means getting to listen to the soaps on the radio—Ma Perkins, Stella Dallas, Helen Trent, listen to enthusiastic commercials for Oxydol and Vaseline Petroleum Jelly.

Saturday mornings, Cissy and I wait in bed for the radio music that signals the show "Let's Pretend," the theme song we still remember transporting us to castles and cottages, feel the pleasure of lying under the covers and hearing that small gritty voice boast, "Rumplestiltskin is my name!" We hear the commercials for Cream of Wheat, and my sister says, "Ugh. All those lumps."

The one story my father tells me when I'm growing up is "The Grasshopper and the Ant."

"Patsy, Patsy, come in here, honey."

"Yes, Daddy?"

"Lie here on the bed next to me, and I'll tell you about the grasshopper and the ant. Once upon a time, there was a little hardworking ant and a very lazy grasshopper. Now this grasshopper would just stand around and sing, 'Oh, the world owes me a living, tra - la - la - la - la - la. . . .'"

Stories, sights, scents, from our youth return us to the younger person nested inside of us, songs like "It might as well be spring," and "The bells of St. Ma - ry's." I'm not sure how old I am when I see the movies *State Fair* and *The Bells of St. Mary's* with my parents, little though, and those songs make me nostalgic; though I'm not sure for what, perhaps for that time when I sat small in a dark theater between my mother and father.

Clk, clk, the rhythm of beads. The grandmothers, great-grandmothers, great-great-grandmothers, and aunts sit together, pray the rosary, candles lit before an image of the Virgin Mary, Mother of Christ, conceived immaculately, who appears everywhere miraculously, on the top of desert mountains, in grottos, on water tanks, on brick walls, on screen doors, on tortillas.

"October seventh is the feast of Nuestra Señora del Rosario," the women say, frowning that I'm not joining them. When young, I wrote reports and gave speeches about the word, *rosary,* that originally connoted an enclosed rose garden. In the late twelfth century, prayer beads—the pattern of decades of Hail Mary's separated by an Our Father—prayer garlands, became popular with European Christians, and the word acquired its devotional connotation, roses not only heavy with perfume but with mythological and symbolic meaning, the rose of Sharon, and the roses that bloomed in the footsteps of the Holy Family as they fled to Egypt. In the writings of anthropologist Jack Goody who studies relationships between plants and people, I read that *perfume,* from *per fumum* in Latin, means "through smoke," suggesting an early religious connotation, offerings to heavenly beings.

The family women murmuring their beads may not understand my pleasure in listening to their rhythms and intonations of the joyful, sorrowful, and glorious mysteries, their voices, *"Dios te salve, María, llena eres de gracia,"* rejuvenating as the voice of the fountain.

Standing in the covered porch, wind drumming in my ears, I watch clouds gather, the promise of rain, holy water, *agua santa,* that will seep into the garden's soul, this frame of rooted variety, its life both visible and hidden, the roots braided, like this family. In my room I light candles and read again an interview with Ingmar Bergman who says, "The doors between the old man today and the child are still open, wide open. . . . I can move from my bed at night today to my childhood in less than a second."

The wind sweeps over the desert, the *río,* the fruit trees, the *acequia,* swoops into the garden and spins round the *portal* as I write once more in my journal.

My father is stretched out on the living-room rug reading the Sunday paper on this, the one morning of the week that he's at home. He chuckles over the funnies. I stand in the wide archway between the living and dining rooms watching him, hearing Mother behind me finishing the breakfast dishes in the kitchen. Maybe I'm five.

My father looks up at me, opens his arms, and I run into them, smell his warm skin. He rolls on his back and sits me on his chest where I bang on him lightly.

"Patsy, *mira*," he says, "I'm going to teach you how to fall, so you won't hurt yourself. Pull me up."

I jump off and tug and tug until I've pulled his six feet up.

"Help me move the coffee table." My father pretends I'm really lifting, really helping.

"Raúl, what are you doing?" Mother asks walking through the dining room drying her hands on a dish towel, slight irritation in her voice at seeing her carefully kept house disturbed.

"I'm going to teach Patsy how to fall. Help me put some of the sofa cushions in front of the sofa. *No, no*, not like that, like this, near the sofa so when she falls she'll land on them."

"I think my way was better," Mother says.

"*No, no, no, mujer.*" I know what I'm doing. Okay, Patsy, now climb up on the sofa."

I look at Mother who has taught me not to climb on furniture.

"Take off your shoes first, honey," she says. "Let's keep the sofa nice. Want me to help you?"

"I can do it. Watch." I unbuckle my shoes and look up to see my parents both watching me, then barely nodding to one another. My father gives me his hand, and I step up on the pale rose sofa cushions, feel the pleasure of their sponginess beneath my socks. I rock back and forth, heel to toe. Mother sits in the chair across the room, watching. "Careful," she says.

"Okay now, Patsy," my father says. "Watch me."

I look over at Mother.

"Patsy. Watch me," my father says firmly. "Open your hands like this, see. Have your palms facing me, *así, así.*"

"Like patty-cake?" I ask.

"Now," says my father, "see the cushions on the rug? You won't hurt yourself, so just fall forward, but catch yourself with your hands. I want you to learn to catch yourself. Okay now, just fall forward."

I look over at Mother. "You can do it, honey." To my father she says, "Don't rush her Raúl! Give her time."

I look down at the cushions. All the way down. I want to do what my father asks, but my feet are glued to the sofa. They won't budge.

"Just fall, Patsy," my father says. "You need to learn this, better to hurt your hand some day than to break a shoulder or get your face all scratched up. *¿Lista?*"

I want to fall forward, but my feet are stuck.

I look at Mother. "Come on, Patsy," she says. "You can do it, honey. Just do it once today, and then we can go out back to the swings." To my father she says, "She's scared, Raúl. Don't rush her. You're so impatient!"

"Okay," my father says. "*Yo sé. Yo sé.* I'll sit in front of you, Patsy, and you first fall into my arms, Okay?"

He sits on the cushion and opens his arms. I fall right in.

"Great! Great, honey!" Mother says clapping.

"Now do it again, Patsy," my father says, "but keep your palms open. Let your palms hit my chest, *aquí.*"

I put my palms stiff in front of me, check to see that Mother is watching. I wave at her with the tips of my fingers.

"Patsy," my father says, "ready? Now pay attention. Fall and land on your hands."

I look at my hands, glance at Mother, look at my father and back at my hands.

"Fall, Patsy! Fall here," my father says his arms ready to catch me.

I fall forward, my open palms hitting his shirt.

"Great, great!" Mother says.

"Now," says my father giving me his hand to help me climb back on the sofa, "I'm going to stand up, and I want you to fall just like that on the cushions. It won't hurt, Patsy."

"Don't you think she's done enough for today, Raúl?" Mother asks. "What's the rush?"

"She needs to learn this. *"Se va a caer afuera y luego se lastima. Mejor aquí."*

Do it, I think. Put your palms up. Fall on the cushion. I put my palms up. I rock on my feet to unstick them from the sofa. I close my eyes and fall forward. Roll, when I land on the sofa cushion.

"That's fun. I want to do it again."

"*¿Ves?*" my father says, "Didn't I tell you? She wants to do it again. But Patsy, this time, really land on your hands. Catch yourself."

"Just one more time," Mother says. "And Raúl, she'd better not do this when the table is in place. Just look at the sharp corners. Patsy honey, you can only practice this if Mommy and Daddy are with you, understand?"

"Okay, Patsy," my triumphant father says, "Put your hands up and fall. And keep your eyes open. *¡Qué muchacha!*" he chuckles, shaking his head, pleased that he's taught me to take care of myself, to catch myself, to fall into my own hands.

Noviembre / November

*La primavera se hace ligera, el invierno se hace
eterno.*

Spring breezes by, while winter seems eternal.

NOVEMBER FIRST, All Saints Day and *Día de los angeli-
tos*, a day to remember children who have died. The
month the living and dead ponder one another. *"Whoo,
whoo, whoo,"* calls an owl. Who is living, who is dead?

In the morning dark, we hear winter wind ignoring calendars,
arriving on a whim, flinging tumbleweeds down the road. Lobo
and I step out onto the *portal*, and the wind stings our skin,
shoos us back into the house.

Later when the wind vanishes and the sun warms the garden
and porch, Lobo sweeps under the wood frame of the old, clay
water filter that will be silent until late spring. Slowly she
sweeps the rest of the porch circling the garden with her *sw, sw,
sw*, while I water the large pots of orange and black pansies by
the front gate.

Though unsure she likes the custom, preferring to leave al-
tars to the officially holy, saints and angels, Lobo agrees to help
me build a small *ofrenda* in the *portal* for the family babies who
died young, Edermida, Saúl, Manuel, Lázaro, Elodia, Eduardo
Octavo, and the little ones whose names have been forgotten.

"I took care of her," Aunt Chole says as we cover a table with
a white tablecloth, add tiny coffins made of hard sugar—purple,
blue, pink; sugar skulls staring at us with their foil eyes, minia-
ture plates, breads, candy baskets, bananas, flowers, candles.

"She was retarded, Edermida. Such a good baby, my parents'
last, retarded. She only lives a few months. I sew the tiny dress

for her funeral, *mi hermanita tan chiquita*. We bury her at Evergreen Cemetery, go in your father's Ford. My mother crying and crying, always crying and crying. Yes, *reina*, yes. She did bury four of her babies. Maybe more."

"So many babies died back then," Lobo says. "My parents had two friends who had little girls about the time I was born, 1889. I am the only one who lives past infancy. Every year on my birthday the other couples give me a gift and call me *hija*.

"My sister, Adelina, almost dies as a baby too, my mother's third child, sickly since birth. She is almost buried alive there in Guerrero where my Uncle Urbano Zea is the mayor. Your aunt is baptized by two persons of good station who have no children, Don Miguel Enríquez and Manuelita Paredes who is so white, pretty, rich—but no family. Months later, their godchild, Adelina, comes down with bronchitis, and in one of the terrible bouts, her breathing stops."

I hear prayers flutter like lost butterflies through that hushed Mexican house, "*Salud de nuestras almas, médico incomparable, no desprecies nuestras súplicas y concédenos las gracias que te pedimos por las lágrimas de Tu santísima Madre. Amén.*"

The doctor arrives in a black carriage, examines the still baby and shakes his head. He declares Adelina dead. The family bows its head, tries to pray but tears dissolve their words.

"Her godfather, Don Miguel, cannot believe the news," Lobo says. "In those days it is the custom for someone to stay with the deceased whether child or adult until the coffin is constructed. While Adelina's small box is being made, her body is placed *en una mesita*."

Lobo is seven years old, and she and I tiptoe into the room of sighs and tears to watch the child's still body on that little table. All day we whisper, hear that at five in the afternoon people with the small coffin are to arrive. How can they bury a baby, close the lid and place her deep inside the dark earth? How do the dead breathe?

Dreading that terrible hour, Don Miguel rushes into the house at about three or four and goes straight to the kitchen, asks for a small spoon and glass of warm water sweetened with sugar. The godfather approaches the table on which the still body lies and with tears in his eyes begins to drop sweet liquid on the child's lips, praying she will sip. Prayers flutter, *"Salud de nuestras almas, médico incomparable."*

The man places drop after sweet drop on the child's blue lips. *"Salud de nuestras almas, médico incomparable."*

The man places drop after drop on the child's lips. The baby's eyes open. She begins to cry.

"Cuando Dios quiere," whispers Mamá Cleta, *"el agua es medicina."*

"Don Miguel lunges at the doctor," Lobo says, "grabs him by the lapels, hurls insults at him, and wants him thrown in jail. My father, trying to calm his irate friend says, '*Pero mira, compadre,* the miracle happened. God inspired you to come and care for my tiny daughter, and her life returned. Let's just leave things as they are. Adelina is with us, new, alive. Now we are deeply worried about our second daughter, Elodia.'

"God had another sorrow for my parents. My sister, Elodia, such a cute little girl who loves to dance the 'Can-Can' and the '*Jarabe tapatío*,' is very sick with scarlet fever and almost dies." Lobo sighs. "About midnight one night, as my parents fret about her, our brother, Eduardo Octavo, becomes ill with a terrible meningitis. Within two hours, my parents' only son is dead."

Re - quies - cat in pa - cem.

November second, *Día de los muertos*, All Souls Day. On a wall of the *portal*, we place of map of Mexico and the United States, photographs of Northern Mexico and El Paso in the late 1800s and early 1900s, a painting of Mount Franklin at sunrise. We sprinkle sand from the Chihuahua desert on the floor to create a desert garden around a series of small altars to family who have died. *"Whoo, whoo, whoo,"* the owl calls.

We scatter marigold petals, creating a path from the front

gate, through the front courtyard, to the house and garden gates, down the worn tile of the *portal* to the *altares*, around them arrange narrow-leafed yucca, ocotillo, sotol, agaves, lechugilla, mesquite, creosote, cholla, prickly pear, claret cup and barrel cactus. On the tiered altars, we sprinkle handfuls of orange and yellow marigolds, originally called Mary's gold, *cempasúchil* in Nahuatl, flowers of the dead, that stain my fingers, their scent a lure to spirits, the ancient Mexicans believed. We add *pan de muerto*—bread skulls, skeletons, sweet bones we'll chew, and small sugar skulls made of *alfeñique*. As the sun begins to set, we light the wicks of almost fifty candles, place them on the *altares*, watch the smoke curl and rise. Shadows, *sombras del pasado*, arrive.

I hear my father's voice as he waters the garden by hand, "*Voy a bus - car, un rin - con - ci - to en el cie - lo, don - de lle - var a mi a - mor.*" He turns off the hose and walks toward me.

"What are you doing, honey?"

"Making *altares*, Daddy, honoring the dead, luring you elusive spirits back on this night of the year when all of you hover closer to the earth." I watch the smoke. "Look at that breath."

"*¿Cuál?*" he asks looking around.

"The smoke. Pueblo Indians say that smoke or steam or clouds are a visible sign of the cosmic breath. In Tewa the word for that breath of life is *powaha*, the water-wind-breath that flows in us all, in all aspects of the universe—trees, mountains, rivers."

"My relatives, *los indios*, believe that?"

"The Maya believed that in caves the earth god's daughters grow cotton that when struck by lightning becomes rain-heavy clouds, and the Aztecs that in caves are clay pots filled with clouds, seeds, lightning. When you die, you became a cloud, a rainmaker."

"Interesting, very interesting," my father grins walking around the altars, then rises with the wisps of smoke becomes a heavy cloud sailing above the garden.

Listening to the breath of this house and garden, I think of the Tewa idea of a grand breath in which we all exist, in which we will continue. I breathe with it and in it in this dream house in which our souls gather, the living and dead gather ourselves, the bodied and disembodied communing within these adobe walls.

For months I've stared at a picture I clipped from a *National Geographic*, a photograph of tiny igloos, each with a candle, *luminarias* of sorts in the snow, a Japanese festival, the igloos miniature shrines to the water gods, the *suijin*, asking for a good harvest. I taped the picture to the refrigerator unsure of my fascination. Maybe later we'll float candles down the river, glowing spirits weaving through this desert.

"The dead are lured back by what they love, sweet temptations, Daddy," I say as my father returns in a somewhat cloudy form. "The Egyptians, like the Maya and Aztecs, believed that nourishment needs to be provided to ensure life after death, supplies placed in the tomb, the house of eternity."

"*Llegando al camposanto, no hay calaveras plateadas,*" says Mamá Cleta who understands death, the unflinching equity enforcer.

"I like that idea of the supplies, honey," grins my father. "I'll make a list of what I want, maybe a ham sandwich, but don't think I'm staying in any place *allá abajo.*"

"No. In Mexico, the belief was that *las ánimas* would come to savor what they could consume, the scents, lured back by their favorite aromas."

"Scents, *ooooo, me muero de hambre,*" my irreverent father laughs.

"*Oooooo, me muero de hambre,*" the *guacamaya* screams.

I continue, ignoring their antics. "In some villages, people take their offerings to the cemetery."

"Is someone going to the cemetery?" asks Lobo joining us. "I used to go, remember Raúl, and wash the family's gravestones this day, buy chrysanthemums to decorate their graves."

I show them a book of *el día de los muertos* in Mexico, homes and cemeteries glowing with candles and marigolds. My four grandparents come close to look. "In some villages, they have a picnic at the cemetery," I say, "enjoying the food, remembering their loved ones."

"*Otra vez,* no one's listening to me," my father says. "Doesn't anyone want a ham sandwich? But I'm not having a picnic in any cemetery."

"*No, ni yo,*" the others say, shaking their heads, these cautious spirits afraid of spirits, so at home in this house, this garden, in its rhythms, its major and minor keys, its refrains and incantations, their earthly sanctuary. The rest of the family drifts out.

"Why are you all talking about death? You know what Mamande used to say," Mother laughs, " '*¿De qué se murió? De lo malo que se vió.*' "

"You don't think Mother was talking about me, do you?" Uncle Lalo chuckles, settles into a chair and the rest of us sit too in the candlelight. "I got close once maybe, thanks to ether. Remember, Carmen? I was looking for a new job, and I got sick. One morning I throw up my breakfast, have a bad pain in my side. A friend of mine just had his appendix out, so I go see his doctor. He says my appendix is badly inflamed and will have to come out and that I have a hernia that needs repairing.

"I go home and tell my mother and family and everybody gets shook up, and I call Carmen. I have $125 in the bank; that's my fortune. I go to the hospital, Hotel Dieu, and I get a big room, I mean to tell you, four dollars a day, but I get a big room, I mean two windows with a view of Mount Franklin and all this good stuff.

"They give me ether, and what I remember is that it gives me a sensation as if I am on a turntable, spinning, going *hnnnnnnn-hnnnnnn-hnnnnnn.* Finally, I'm out, and I have the strangest dream.

"They say I'm never in any particular danger, but I have the sensation that I come up to a curtain. I'm there, but there is no body. I mean there's just me, but there's no physical part to me. The curtain's like a mist, a heavy mist. And I stand there, and I'm very comfortable. The thought crosses my mind, 'If I penetrate that mist, I'm not coming back.' "

My father, Lobo, grandparents, and our other spirits look at one another. Candles flicker in the twilight.

"I don't want to cross; I don't not want to cross. I'm just waiting. My spirit—because there is no body—is just waiting. And then I hear somebody say, 'He's coming out of it,' and BANG, they hit me with that ether again."

My uncle remembers that when his mother dies at the hospital, a tear slips out of her eye, and he softly dries her cheek. He thinks of the parents he buried, how they still move through his days, active dead in this house.

"I've still got my father's derby," he says. "He had one of those capes like Dracula. You know, red inside and black on the outside. I mean they dressed with the high hat. I've got that too. I mean they really dressed elegant when they were still living in Chihuahua.

"My father would tell about the time he and some *amigos* go out to have a few drinks or whatever. On their way home, walking of course, they start telling a ghost story. As they pass a cemetery, this one guy says that he's not scared and to prove it, he'll go to the far end alone and come back. His *amigos* say, 'Well, how will we know that you reached the far end?'

"So one of these guys gives him a cane and says, 'Now, when you get to the faaaar end over there'—they bet him so much money—'you stick that cane into the ground, like this, and then you come on back. Then we'll all go, and we'll know that you were there.'

"So the guy goes, and he doesn't come back, and he doesn't come back, and he doesn't come back. And they're all wondering what happened to him?"

"*Pues ¿dónde está nuestro amigo?*" The men laugh, but nervously, the cold, fall wind howling, whipping their capes.

"*Vamos a esperar poquito más. Quizás nos quiere asustar.*" They laugh again as they wait a while longer, but nervously, hoping their friend is just playing one of his jokes. The well-dressed men look around, try not to gaze too long at the cemetery, at the gray and white stones, at the dry leaves scuttling over the graves.

Finally, my grandfather says, "*No, mis amigos. Querer o no querer, tenemos que ir a buscarlo.*" Trying to comfort one another with their comaraderie, the small group sets out into the wind, across the graveyard, wrapping their black capes around themselves for warmth and protection. They stay close together, walk carefully through the cemetery not to step on any grave. At the far end, they peer into the darkness for their friend. Nothing.

"*¡AY!*" screams one of the men startling the others. "*¡Aquí!*" He points down to their friend sprawled out cold on the ground.

"*AAAYYYHHH, aaayyyhhh,*" the peacock cries making us all jump.

"Now what happened," my uncle chuckles, "is that the first man had on a long cape, and when he stabs that cane into the ground, he plunges the cane into his cape. When he turns to leave, he can't, feels something—someone—pullin' at him from the grave, and he's so scared, he faints."

"In Northern New Mexico," I say listening to the wind begin to moan, "they used to talk about *El Hombre Largo* who is seven feet tall, very thin, and wears a cape and top hat. He appears out of nowhere and with his long, skinny legs can chase and overtake anyone, those legs stretching and s-t-r-e-t-c-h-i-n-g." I drop my voice watching the faces of my relatives. "You can probably hear his bones rattling in his skin coming after you," I say grabbing my father's arm.

"*¡Ayy!*" he cries, "don't scare us, honey."

"*Me la debes,*" I say quoting one of his favorite phrases. "You should talk, all those times you scared poor Aunt Chole when she's young, putting a sheet over yourself the night of any funeral and wailing, '*Oooooooo, oooooooooo.*'"

No one wants to get up and move among the shadows. "Up in the New Mexico hills," I say, "they'd also tell not only of *brujas y espantos*, of *La Llorona* who wails by water, but also *La Tuerta* who stalks her victims with her evil eye, *La Jorupa*, the humpbacked woman who chases children out at dark, *La Malogra*, the huge cotton monster who suffocates her prey, and *La Larga* who brandishes her sickle as she chases her victims with huge strides anxious to add their dismembered parts to the huge, black pot simmering in her dark cave.

"¡*AAAAYYYY!*" my father yells making us all jump.

"Stop it, Daddy," I say.

"Stop it, Daddy," squawks the parrot. "¡*Raúl! ¡Como eres malo!*"

"I'd better stop this," I say, hearing the wind running through the *portal*. "I'll be terrified all night. Threats of those creatures out roaming in the night probably did send kids scurrying home by dark."

"Just tell us about one more," Bill says.

"Well, there was a witch Cleofas Jaramillo writes about named La Chon. She'd sit smoking her cigarette by her fireplace when she wasn't out transforming herself into a dog or cat. In the secret room that only she could enter, pumpkins are in a corner, drying herbs hang from the ceiling. She'd sail through the night in slivers of pumpkin rinds. In fact, she may be sailing near us right now, cackling to herself, deciding which of us to visit tonight. One time, two girls who live near her sneak into her secret room and what they see sends them wailing from La Chon's house."

"What is it?" my uncle asks.

"There she sits, on a pumpkin, the wrinkled old woman in black, grinning and grinning. And what do you think she's holding?"

"¿*Un gato?*" my grandfather asks.

"Noooooooooo, La Chon is holding . . ."

"Tell us, tell us."

"She is holding . . . her own two . . . eyes."

"¡*Ay no!*" cry the great-grandmothers standing to leave the group.

"Yes, there she sits staring ahead with daaaaaaark, eeeeeeempty sockets."

Aunt Carmen laughs and tries to lighten the mood. "My grandfather used to tell a story like Uncle Lalo's. My grandfather had gone to the cemetery to visit his wife's grave. He has his cape and cane too, and when he goes to leave he feels someone pull at him. He's sure it's his dead wife pulling him into her grave."

"¡AYYYYYYYYYYYYYY!" yell my father and the parrot loud enough to scare the dead which they do since all of us, living and dead, jump and then laugh though looking at the shadows around us.

"We need peony seeds that were carried to ward off evil spirits," Mamá Cleta says. *"El dicho dice, 'El muerto a la sepultura, y el vivo a la travesura,' pero con Raúl, el muerto sigue en su travesura."* No, not even death tames my father's antics.

"That's why I never use a cape or a cane, honey," my father chuckles.

"Oh, yes you did, Daddy," Stella says. "When you were a Knight of Columbus you used a black and red cape plus that funny hat and a sword."

"I think they may be the Knights of the Americas now. Columbus is out," I say.

"Bah," my father says, *"pobre Colón."*

"Don't waste your pity on him," I say.

"Don't get Pat started, Daddy," my sister says.

How strong my father looked lined up in church with the other Knights, sword tips touching, under which the priest and monstrance would pass, *"Tan - tum er - go Sac - ra - men - tum,"* the smell of incense, "Holy God, we pr - aise Thy name." Intoxicating.

"Yea, but I wasn't dumb enough to wear the cape to any cemetery," my father says. "I don't know why all you want to do is talk about cemeteries when we could be eating that ham sandwich. I guess I'll have to make it myself."

Mamande's mother, Mamá Cuca says, *"No hay mejor salsa que un buen apetito,"* and signals that she'll go make my father something in the kitchen. I wish we knew more about her. Even her large photograph was forgotten for years.

Wind wails through the night, that wild desert wind that follows its will, a sound I love. Tonight, are spirits even more elusive than those of this house sailing down roads and round houses, slipping into familiar rooms? In dying, were they transformed, and now return to this earth and images of their bodies as we return to old homes and wander the chambers, touch the ledge of a favorite window, stare at a favorite arch, stretch out on a bed in which we dreamed, open closet doors and see what we wore, who we were, the self that continues in us as our dead do. How do the dead breathe? They breathe in us. In this season of contemplation, the garden folding into itself to dream of spring, possibilities, do spirits rub the shoulders of those who cry for them? Do spirits open books that once released spirits into their bodies, suggested what we can't seem to grasp: the universe is more than matter.

I slip into Aunt Chole's room, sit close to her. She hands me a persimmon she's been saving for me, this aunt who years ago would peel this sensual fruit for me to taste.

"Yes, yes, I've been listening to the radio tonight, *mi corazón*," she says. "I'm not sick in my body. I'm sick in my mind. It's not very strong, but I think I'm getting better. I've gained fifteen pounds. I'm going to take that Assure *hasta que me muera*. And my sister has improved one-hundred percent, so nice to me.

"Those *trios* from México help me, *reina*. And now I hear 'La Hora Azul.' It's not this new *chaca-chaca-chaca* music. They play the old orchestras. They don't exist anymore. *Ayyy*.

"The music makes me happy before I go to sleep, *música buena, no música corriente*. I always make sure I'm clean now before I go to bed. Ever since I had that *ataque* a few years ago, I try to be ready. Luckily, I was clean when I had that stroke, but now I bathe in the morning and take a sponge bath at night. Bad enough that I'm blind. I don't want them to find me dirty too. *Ciega y luego mal arrugada no está bien*."

She rubs cream into her hands. Looks at the fingers she cannot see. "I wish they had been beautiful, *corazón santo*," she sighs. "But my hands were always ugly. My mother would boil our clothes behind the house, and I had to help her. The strong soap and steaming water ruined *mis manos. Aaayyy, los detalles de la vida.*

"You want me to pray for something? For what, I need an idea of what you want. I'll pray to the Holy Spirit. I pray to Him in English. He's so wonderful to me. I get in trouble, *querida.* People who can see get in trouble so I get in more trouble, *ee-ee.* But I know that often when I pray for things, they happen. I know this inside me, but I don't say anything because my family would just get mad at me. They're jealous I think and don't want to believe what I say, *ya sabes, ya sabes, mi reina.*

"I want to be cremated, don't you think? I've been alone so I'm going alone. No need for people making trips, you know, to my grave."

I hug her good night, the once-tall woman of perfect posture now a frail woman in my arms, the body bent by osteoporosis and grief; but not the spirit, the gleaming spirit that keeps the body pacing day after day to keep the blood moving, alive in that thin skin.

Under the covers, I listen to the wind spinning around the fountain, around the garden, around the house. Late at night, I wake to a humming of sorts. I pull aside the curtain and see a phantom glowing in the patio. Years I've seen her, moving slowly, back straight, the Indian Dolores, circumambulating the *portal,* then suddenly peeking in a window hoping to startle us like she startled them, the glowing figure chuckling to herself. I watch her until my eyes begin to close.

"*Aaahh, sí,* I remember," says Lobo when I mention Dolores the next morning. "One night, there's a wonderful full moon, so bright its light fills almost half the room I share with my three little sisters. My father must be away on a trip. I wake to a slight humming, the sound moving closer, closer. Frightened, I wake my sisters, and we sit up in our beds and there! a figure comes toward us, gliding, glowing, shining from head to foot. A ghost! *¡Un fantasma!* We gasp and run terrified from the room and out

of the house, run, fly to the nearby home of our teacher, Doña
Marinita Terrazas.

"*¡Doña Marinita! ¡Doña Marinita!*" we wail, banging on her
door. She and her sisters put their arms around us to calm us,
smooth our hair, soothe us saying, "*Ya, ya.*" They go with us,
trembling I'm sure, back to the house. And there stands Do-
lores, laughing. She added phosphorus to tortilla dough and
spread the *masa* all over herself, her face, her arms, her legs. The
woman shines. Doña Marinita scolds Dolores, tells her it is in-
deed an original idea, but that she can't frighten us that way.

"*¡Qué Dolores!* She plays with us as if she is our age. Maybe
she's twenty; I'm twelve. My poor younger sisters are terrified
that night, but I sort of like looking at Dolores all covered with
masa, going *para allá y para acá.*

"Doña Marinita and her sisters give us each a spoonful of
sugar water to counter the fright, then tuck us in. We fall asleep
seeing Dolores glowing as she glides from room to room, room
to room."

I see her here too, Dolores shining as she paces the *portal* on
a windy night, still laughing.

I wake, hear soft footsteps moving through the house at
dawn. I look out and see Abuelo Gregorio, raising his voice in
morning praise,

> *Bendita sea la luz del día,*
> *Bendito sea Quien nos la envía,*
> *Bendita sea la claridad,*
> *Bendito sea Quien nos la da.*

He carries a small clay pitcher of *agua bendita*, holy water he
sprinkles room by room. He whispers, "*M'ija*, tell me if you see
any flying objects. Spirits and their mischief, *tú sabes.*"

I hear Mamá Cleta humming in the next room. Last night
before beginning her evening rosary, she said she'd be up early to
work on her potpourri and the small organdy sachets she'll give
each female at Christmas. Nothing like a project to make the

woman happy. When I enter her room, I enter the furnishings of the 1800s, sunlight streams through the mica window onto Mamá Cleta's old, leather chest. Without a word she fills her hands with dried roses, lavender, lemon and rose scented verbena and offers the scents to smell, a wonderful way to wake, bending into my great-great-grandmother's sweet-smelling hands.

"*Buenos días te dé Dios,*" she says. "When I smell this, I feel a soft blanket in my hands, do you? *Para los hombres,* I'm making small pillows we'll fill with pine and bayberry. Smell them in that basket in the corner." I take a big whiff. Now I'm awake.

"Remember this *alabado, Patricia,*" she says, a reminder of the futility of seeking meaning in silver and gold,

> *¿De qué te sirve afanar*
> *por juntar la plata y oro*
> *si el verdadero tesoro*
> *no lo procuras buscar?*

Noticing I'm looking at a box near the basket, she says, "*Es otro secreto, Patricia.*" She lets me open it and see the flowers and leaves she has been pressing to give as bookmarks to the family. She laughs and points at the heavy rug which serves as her flower press. After I've studied the violets and pansies, she motions for me to return the box to its place, "*Un lugar para cada cosa, y cada cosa en su lugar,*" she smiles at me, this tidy woman and her *dichos.*

Outside, I see Aunt Carmen in her straw hat watering the bushes, the Indian hawthorne, pyrocantha, bottle brush. Uncle Lalo putters in his workshed among the paint cans, nails, hammers, and saws, until his wife comes in to check on her geraniums and bougainvillea in the green house.

We'll retreat from the yard these next few months, let the garden rest as writers retreat from their work for perspective, many the similarities between gardening and writing. Like the gardener, the writer stores scraps below the surface, allows a complex and mysterious process to transform the compost into nutrients, enriching the muck with which we work, composed of all that lived before, layers of visible and invisible bodies. The life of a poem or story often begins in the dark, in faith, rises a green, delicate, hopeful song, requires as plants do, attentiveness, pruning, protection and yet the willingness to trust, to free the fingers to play knowing the gathering or harvesting can never be predicted. The gardener/writer works alone in old clothes, the solitude allowing a listening, ear to the earth, hands busy planting, digging, mulching, weeding, fingers cultivating a feel for the soil, the clay, its moods, seasons, demands, never in total control; annually surprised by what bursts through.

The Aztec poet-king Netzahualcoyotl sang,

> We become as spring weeds, we grow green
> and open the petals of our hearts.
> Our body is a plant in flower, it gives flowers
> and it dies away.

Whoo, whoo, the owl asks these nights.

"*Oooo,*" honey" Aunt Carmen says. "Just look at these red blooms. This sun is making my plants happy! Pat, Pat, come and look. See how well the geraniums do in the greenhouse."

"They look great, Aunt Carmen. I can't believe it's almost Thanksgiving."

We begin to plan the menu. My children join us, volunteer to make our favorites: cranberries with port, sweet potatoes with pecans, sour-dough biscuits, pumpkin pies with real whipped cream, what my youngest when small mistakenly called "whole made," instead of home-made. "Not *my* favorites," Cissy says now. "I don't eat turkey, and I don't like cranberries or sweet potatoes," says this vegetarian daughter who when she was little would cover her face so as not to see the turkey baking in the oven.

At the end of the day, after helping to dry all the silverware, whistling her *wh, wh, wh,* Lobo every year sits with a glass of *camote* and adds a bit of milk, her sweet reward.

My three children sit with their grandmother enjoying the afternoon desert sun. She smiles remembering her young self. "I

always wanted to have turkey for Thanksgiving when I was lit-
tle, Dears. Mamande didn't really know how to cook one, but
she'd have it prepared at a restaurant that made a delicious
turkey in *mole*. I thought that's how everyone ate it."

"Bad enough turkey," Cissy says. "But in *mole*! Who'd want to
eat a sauce of chile and chocolate? I just don't get it."

"I remember that one year I'd eaten lots of turkey with *mole*,"
Mother says, "and I know that my mouth has a big ring of the
dark sauce. I don't wipe it off because I want to run outside so
all my friends will see what a wonderful meal I've had. Of
course, I don't realize that they won't have the vaguest idea what
the ring around my mouth is! What do they know about *mole*?"
she laughs. "I don't know, maybe they think it's cranberry sauce."
She pauses.

"You know, Dears, I'm such a lucky woman, and I know it. I
thank God every night. I had a wonderful husband and am so
grateful for my four children and six grandchildren."

At night, we hear Lobo, raising her veined hands above us in
blessing, "*La cruz más grande del mundo, sobre su cuerpo se extienda.*"

I dream my father, my young father wearing a green, cotton
plaid shirt. He begins to fall, and I catch him, realize he's dying.
In a clear, tearless voice, I am able to say what I could never have
said without crying. "Daddy, you are such a wonderful father.
We all love you. Do you know that? We all love you." I know I've
said what we all wanted to say, this, one of life's great fears: have
I conveyed my love sufficiently to those I cherish? Have I made
my love solid for them, dependable, like a tree? Looking at my
sick father, the words caught in our throats fearing if we cried, if
he cried, the tears would never stop. Somewhere in the house I
dreamed, we put the body.

My father's right. The dead of this house have no use for
cemeteries, staying underground. They drift through the rooms
like incense, like a prayer, a melody, a breath.

Maternal great-grandmother, Mamá Cuca is busy in the
kitchen rolling the dough for apricot *empanadas* she's making for

my daughters' saints days, this woman who loves the young. She rolls out the pie dough into circles, spoons cooked apricots from our fruit trees into the centers, folds the dough, seals it with the tines of a fork dipped in flour. Soon the kitchen, dining room and living room smell like a bakery, the smell drawing us as Mamá Cuca planned.

She hands out holy cards and small silver medals, November nineteenth, Saint Elizabeth, *Santa Isabel*, Queen of Hungary, pictured with bread and roses; November twenty-second, Saint Cecilia, the Roman martyr playing an organ accompanied by an orchestra of angels. She gives holy cards of other November saints, Saint Martin of Tours, patron of tailors, to paternal grandfather, the tailor, Lázaro; and of Saint Catherine, patron of nurses, to Stella.

Since we have two Cecilias in the family, Mamá Cuca invites us to a night of music, brings each of her great-great-grandchildren to the piano to play for the family gathered in the living room hearing the music and the crackling voice of the fire. Mother plays Chopin's "Fantasie Impromtu," "Prelude in A," and Schumann's "Scenes from Childhood." Mamá Cuca serves foamy hot Mexican chocolate made with plenty of cinnamon and her warm *empanadas de chavacán*.

Another year is ending. Mamá Cuca savors the warmth of the family watching the faces of her daughter, Amelia, and her grandchildren, her great-grandchildren, her great-great-grandchildren.

I look around the comfortable room and through the window to the porch and garden, its bare trees. "*Whoo, whoo, whoo,*" the owl calls. Wind rattles doors and windows. November, the month when the living and dead ponder one another. I think back to the beginning of the month, to the *altares* we built selecting objects and scents as lures.

For maternal grandfather, Eduardo Luis Delgado, son of María Ignacia Barragan and Ignacio Delgado, law books, newspapers, a smoldering cigarette, cookies and steaming coffee, a small, *calavera* of a judge in a black gown pounding a gavel.

For maternal grandmother, Amelia Sotero Landavazo, photographs of her parents, Refugio Rochín and Juan Domingo Landavazo, statues of San Martín de Porres and San Rafael, a novena to Our Sorrowful Mother, a bottle of mezcal with the worm at the bottom, bottles of Bayer aspirins, bowls of Big Hunks.

For paternal grandfather, Lázaro Mora, son of Simona Porras and Gregorio Mora, a photograph of him with his sons in his tailor shop, good cloth for making men's jackets, needles, measuring tape, a radio playing classical music, beer, a plate of *mole*.

For paternal grandmother, Natividad Pérez, daughter of Tomasa Monárrez and Brígido Pérez, crochet needles, yarn of many colors, a *metate* and *molcajete*, dried chiles, a cassette playing, "*Ay, ay, ay, ay, canta y no llores,*" boxes of Kleenex for her tears.

For maternal aunt, Ignacia Delgado, our Lobo, daughter of Dolores Prieto Yrigoyen and Eduardo Luis Delgado, coconut-cream pie, bottles of perfume, her missal, pictures of the four of us and of our children, all of us, her children, and ten brooms.

For my father, Raúl Antonio Mora, son of Natividad Pérez and Lázaro Mora, a sandwich of Texas barbecue, *dulces de calabaza*, a photograph of him and Mother with their children and grandchildren, a picture of Our Lady of Guadalupe, the last roses of the year, a *calavera* of an optician with a wild toupe arranging optical eguipment—frames, lenses, rulers; a replica of our house at 704 Mesita, the house of houses.

My children and I placed votive candles in foil and at sunset took them down to el Río Grande, watched a lone aspen and its shadow shiver in the fading light. I watch the river, its surface tension, and think of parallel universes, unknown realms, on either side of eyes, mirrors, water, how we see through these reflective surfaces, how they reverse images, how the surfaces conceal and reveal.

Other family members follow us, curious. We light the candles and say the name of a deceased family member as we send a candle floating down the river—Anacleta Manquera, Gregorio Mora, María Ignacia Barragán, Tomasa Monárrez. We light extra candles for names forgotten. The living and dead gather on the edge of the river watching the flickering flames drift into the desert night.

On the way back to the house, Bill notices Abuelo Gregorio, at his nightly ritual, walking slowly from old tree to old tree near the river, stroking the bark with his hand, whispering.

"*Abuelo*, what are you doing?" Bill asks in a low voice so as not to startle the pious man, taking his arm. Abuelo Gregorio pats his great-great-grandson's cheek. "*Diciéndoles buenas noches a las almas ancianas de estos arbolotes, hijito.*"

"Did he say he's saying good-night to the old souls of these huge trees?"

"*Me esperan*," his Abuelo Gregorio says.

We walk back slowly seeing the mountain's silhouette as behind it the moon rises.

Diciembre, mes viejo que arruga el pellejo. / December, old month that wrinkles our skin.

W E SHAPE OUR DWELLINGS and afterwards our dwellings shape us." I read Churchill's words in a book by Clare Cooper Marcus who says that like our dreams, the places we shape send messages. Our house speaks, *fíjate, fíjate.* In our creations, the unconscious surfaces, becomes visible, and in reflecting us, lets us reflect on who we are, offers epiphanies.

So much intellectual weight for this home rising through and from generations. I stroke a rounded adobe mantle above a snapping fire, feel protective of this house that grows naturally in the Chihuahua desert, protects and mothers me, lets me listen, shed the layers I wear outside.

How much does our body know that we know not. Can it be cajoled to reveal its secrets?

I shape what I inherit into what I need, shape what shaped me, a place not mine physically, and yet a space in which I dwell, a body of stories large enough to hold the family, an earth blanket like Abuela Elena's long cloth, composed of useful scraps, never finished, with faith, *santa fe*, an unexpected home cure.

Why in my fifties did I decide to explore this house and its garden? I needed a place to put the stories and the voices before they vanished like blooms and leaves will vanish on the wind outside, voices which, perceived as ordinary, would be unprotected, blown into oblivion. Since the family isn't together geographically, using the tools I know, I created a place welcoming to our spirits, a place for communion and reunion, no invitation necessary; a space, like all spaces, as real as we choose to make it, ample enough for the family spirits who will refer to us in the past, tense can turn to us and create with us what they need, the cycle continuing, as they have inhabited one of our bodies, inhabit the body of the house, a complex earth dwelling as we are dwellings and dwellers; the past, our present in the house and garden with its water song, daily wind-swept, transformed by light.

Mamá Cleta goes to the dining-room table with baskets of fragrant oranges, lemons, limes. She gestures to Abuela Elena, our other great-great-grandmother, and to Great-grandmothers, Abuela Simona, Abuela Tomasa, Mamá Cuca, and Mamá Nacha who gaze out the living-room windows at occasional snow flakes, to join her in the making of home-made pomanders for scenting the house for the Christmas season, this month of anticipation, rituals to counter the cold outside.

Sparrows peck the leaves below the cottonwood and the *mora*, chirp and chatter, survey the brown garden and its silent fountain from branches that like bare poems reveal the strength and grace of the lines.

The family of women drifts into the dining room, chatting, helping Mamá Cleta bring *café* and sweet bread—*campechanas y laberintos*—to the table. Picking up the juicy green, yellow, and orange citrus globes, they smell the tart fruit, settle themselves in the whispers of their long dresses.

"Once, among the wealthy," says Mamá Nacha, "*pomas olorosas* were a paste of resins and oils molded into scented balls placed in expensive holders of crystal, silver, and ivory, then hung from the neck or belt with a chain."

"We make what the family can afford," says Mamá Cleta to her daughter-in-law.

"*Qué fruta tan bonita, Mamá Cleta*," the women say. They enjoy the sound of the fire crackling and the light from the oil lamps, warm contrast to the gray sky outside. To conceal her pride in

her efficiency and orderliness, Mamá Cleta busies herself sup-
plying needles, a bowl of cloves, streams of ribbon, says, "*Por
Navidad, dichoso el que en casa está.*"

Abuela Simona agrees that they are fortunate to be in their
home at this season, makes the sign of the cross, "*En el nombre del
Padre, del Hijo, y del Espíritu Santo,*" and all join her in asking
blessings, dedicating the work of their twelve hands *a la gloria de
Dios.*

Because it's December, Abuela Simona opens her missal to
read a special prayer to Our Lady of Guadalupe, *La Virgen
Morena,* whose feast day is December twelfth, the woman of
quiet strength, an aura about her, who in 1531 appears on Juan
Diego's *tilma,* the woman who protects them and their children.
In the formal bishop's chamber, while men of power frown at an
Indian who dares bring a message from the Mother of God, red
roses tumble out with the image of the brown woman cloaked
in stars.

"The roses tasted round," Mamá Cleta says nodding her head
with conviction, as if she were saying, "They were red," or "They
perfumed the desert," or "They were smooth as velvet." The oth-
ers barely glance at one another, accustomed to masking their
confusion at the oddities of this short woman with firm hands.
Abuela Simona begins the prayer, and the women, their hair in
careful buns, bow their heads, "*¡Santísima Virgen de Guadalupe! la
más dulce y tierna de todas las madres.*"

The women talk about how quickly the year passed, how the
youngest generation, Bill, Libby, Cissy, Gil, Niki, and Christo-
pher should speak more Spanish. "*Quien sabe dos lenguas, vale por
dos,*" says Mamá Cleta, but she talks about how bright and beau-
tiful the children are.

"*Son niños lindos, lindos. Dos graduaciones este año, que orgullo,*" she
says, straight as virtue in her chair at the head of the table. All
nod, these very different women united in this, their affection
for their shared descendants.

Mamá Cuca, who loves the soft warmth of little hands in
hers, sighs, "*¿Cuándo tendremos otro bebé en esta casa?* I'm going to
forget the lullabies." The group laughs.

"*Nunca, nunca.* We cannot forget those songs," says Mamá Cleta smiling but firm. "I hear there may be a wedding next December," she adds winking.

"*Flores.* How many cups of flowers in a wedding cake?" asks Mamá Nacha. The women humor the poetic questions of the woman who as a girl was lost in wheat fields and poetry.

Abuela Elena who saved her old hanging crib, four smooth rods, four long ropes, and a soft sheepskin says, "We could hang it like I used to in my kitchen." She remembers pushing the swinging crib as she chopped and stirred tomatoes, chiles, onion, *cilantro*, sees the shepherd's bed above the small hearth, the rafter on which she hangs herbs to dry, the wood boxes for flour and vegetables.

Such a different life *en el rancho* than in this house. So many conveniences here, even smooth pink bars of rose-scented soap she slips under her cool pillow at night to help her drift to sleep. She feels the heat again from the black pot in which she'd make her own soap outdoors in México having leeched the lye from wood ashes with rainwater, slowly stirring the rendered animal fat with lye water until it thickens like oatmeal, pouring it into wood molds, scoring the soap while it's warm, storing it to age, her face steamed for years by huge pots and ovens, the face caressed by her babies. She begins to hum and soon the group joins her,

> Rru - rrú - que - rru - rrú que, tan, tan, tan
> que le - che y ato - le para San Juan.
> La Vir - gen la - va - ba, San José ten - día,
> El ni - ño llo - ra - ba, San - ta A - na lo dor - mía.

"*¿Qué es esto?*" asks Mamande looking in at her relatives, perplexed at such hardy lullaby singing with no baby in sight. The group gestures for her to join them in their aromatic task, pricking the citrus skin with the needle, inserting cloves into the holes, tying ribbon around each spice-studded fruit.

"*Señoras,*" says Mamá Cleta, "I've begun gathering twigs that resemble trees and grass that resembles hay for putting up *el nacimiento*. When you walk in the garden or out back or down by *el río*, be looking for what else we could add, what might be helpful if we're inventive this busy month *del año, el mes más anciano*. The children need to see the manger and all the figures we've collected through the years. I know these younger generations like decorating in flowers from some florist blooming out of season, but you know I'm old-fashioned. I like fresh roses in July not December—unless they come from heaven, of course. The seasons should be respected and savored for what they bring, just as we savor the liturgical seasons, *el año liturgico*, like Advent, these four weeks of anticipation."

Her daughter-in-law rolls her eyes discretely.

"*¿Qué dices, María Ignacia?*" asks Mamá Cleta straightening her already straight shoulders.

"No, *nada, nada, Mamá,*" says the younger woman we call Mamá Nacha.

Mamá Cleta continues, "I've saved some dry herbs to scent the resting place *para El Niño Dios*. We'll send someone to buy *flores de nochebuena* that grow into bushes in México, the bracts turned red by the tears of a devout boy with no gift for the Christ Child."

"I was wondering if we might try the wreaths I see people buy every year," says Mamá Nacha. "Some even put that new material on their door, plastic I think it's called. With your wonderful supply of dried flowers—probably the best in the region, Mamá—I thought we might make our own *coronas*. I took the liberty of clipping some dried honeysuckle and grapevines and have been experimenting with winding and bending them. I would trust your artistic eye, of course, Mamá, for covering them with flowers from our own garden. Maybe some of your prize blue hydrangeas."

"*Ay, María Ignacia*, always wanting to try something new. Why can't you feel the beauty of tradition in your bones? *Bien, bien*, bring a wreath or two to my room later, and we can look at what flowers are left. I do want to make a few arrangements for the house though I'm not sure anyone will notice."

"Mamá Cleta, don't say that," says Abuela Elena. "Of course the children notice, but they are busy. We cannot understand the lives they live now, driving and flying. We will do what we've always done so they have a home and garden to rest in, the comfort of the familiar."

Lobo and I enter the kitchen, see the group busy with cloves and conversation. We decide to sit at the blue kitchen table while we look at a book on nativity scenes from Mexico, read that it was Saint Francis of Assisi in 1223 who's credited with beginning the custom in Greccio using a live ox and donkey for his first scene in a grotto.

I pour Lobo coffee, and we bite into the flaky *panecitos* our relatives have been eating. Mamá Cleta listens to us as she prepares finger bowls with rose geraniums and lemon verbena for the citrus-sticky fingers of her helpers. She bruises a few of the leaves and brings her fragrant fingertips for us to smell. "Like clouds at dawn," she says, "delicate pastels."

"On Christmas Eve, when I was little," Lobo says, "we went to *misa de gallo*. I remember that moment when the *monaguillos* would ring *las campanillas*, and we'd rejoice that *El Niño Dios* had again been born. If we received a little gift, it was from relatives or maybe *El Santo Niño*."

Estrella, Belén, oro, incienso, mirra. I love to feel the Christmas words for star, Bethlehem, gold, incense, and myrrh in my mouth in Spanish. I like reading them since I did not hear the stories in Spanish that often.

Lobo begins, "*To - dos los pas - tor - es va - mos a Be - lén,*"

"*¿Quién canta?*" Aunt Chole asks in her high sing-song touching the kitchen counter, the backs of chairs.

"*A Belén, a Belén,*" the crazy parrot squawks.

"Lobo's singing a Christmas carol in Spanish," I say frowning at the bird.

"Ah, *un villancico*," says Aunt Chole.

Lobo clears her throat, releases her voice again though it refuses to slide, quavers.

Unable to resist the carol, Aunt Chole smiles, and when Lobo returns to the refrain, Aunt Chole joins her, a gray-haired duet, "*To - dos los pas - tor - es va - mos a Be - lén.*"

"What's that sound?" Aunt Chole asks. I whisper to her that

it's her grandmother, Abuela Tomasa, stealthily wrapping *pan dulce* in a napkin.

"*Ee-ee*," Aunt Chole laughs, "she's taking the bread to that man on the radio, isn't she? *¡A que mi abuelita!*"

Mother comes in proud that she's dressed and has on her make-up by early afternoon. "We're talking about Christmas," I say. "Want some coffee?"

"*Buenos días*," she says to the aunts.

"*Buenas tardes*," we respond, an admonitory trio.

Anticipating her pastry, she waves away our scolding, this woman who savors sleep. "Thanks, Dear," she says when I hand her a cup, "and a *campechana* and a *laberinto*, please. I'm hungry!

"Christmas is a beautiful time when we're little. One year my father gives my brothers air rifles. You know, BB guns, and he gives me a silver mesh bag. It's really an evening bag for an adult. I think it's the most elegant thing I've ever seen in my life. My parents see to it that we have all that we want. That's before my father gets sick and the Depression hits, of course. What a double whammy, 1929. Know how I found out there was no Santa?"

"What! There's no Santa?" my son asks walking in and pretending surprise.

"One Christmas Eve, I couldn't go to sleep because I'm so excited. I'm about five or six, and I want to stay up. '*Por favor, Mamá*,' I say. Mamande says, 'Just stretch out here on our bed.' I do, and I hear her going in and out, in and out. Since my eyes are closed, she thinks I'm asleep, but I'm sly. I open my eyes just enough to watch her. She looks at me and looks at me, but I don't move a muscle."

"Ms. Possum," I say. The three women look at me quizzically, but Bill smiles on his way out, the private language of families within families.

Mother continues, "I see Mamande go to the closet and take out three tricycles and a big doll. Oh am I happy! There's the Bye-lo Baby I want. That's the year I learn about Santa Claus, but I don't say a word. I probably think: what if I say something and then I don't get anything?"

Aunt Chole sniffs the air, smiles at the scents of citrus and cloves. "Another year ending. *Mi Diosito*, is so good to me. He guides me. The Holy Spirit lets me struggle, but He knows He has to guide me. Sometimes I'm pretty rude to him. When I can't find something, He says to me, 'Why don't you look in the kitchen?' And it works."

Lobo leaves to begin her sweeping, *sw, sw, sw*, and Mother slips away.

"I saw something the other day, *reina*," Aunt Chole says. "Don't worry. It didn't scare me. You know how I get up early? Well, first I pray for the family in El Paso. That's when I saw Him. I'm praying, and I see a frame about four feet square. A child is in the frame. It isn't a baby. It's a child. He is dressed in a dry green, and I can see His pretty pink face and curly hair. I'm not scared. I can't see, but I can see the pleats in His robe. Suddenly, He disappears. '*¿Qué te parece eso?*' But my sisters don't believe me, of course."

"What do you say when you pray?" I ask. "Prayers you learned a long time ago?"

"*No, no,* I don't like those novenas or prayers in books. I pray my way, and no one is going to change that. I say, '*Mi Diosito*, help me to stay here in our home until the last days of my life.' *El Espíritu Santo es tan lindo conmigo.* He helps me with everything even when I'm fixing something with a hammer. He knows I don't want to go to one of those nursing homes. I just talk to Him like that. I just say what comes out of me, *lo que me sale.*

"I'm fine, *corazón.* Everything is wonderful. I sleep well, I eat well, I feel well. Everything is perfect. *Estoy ciento por ciento.* I even sleep until six now. I'm not getting up at three like I used to. And my sisters *ya están perfectas.*"

Mother returns to put her cup in the sink. "*Ay, Estela,*" my aunt says. "Your granddaughter, Libby, *es una criatura encantadora.* She and her young man have their college and all that. I feel insecure because I'm dumb, *tú sabes,* but they treat me so sweetly. They even kiss me on the head, and she's going to be a lawyer, from *ese* Stanford, imagine? *Me vienen del cielo.*

"You sound better, Estela, I can tell by your voice. I gave those two, *mi Libby y mi Roger,* some instructions, *consejos y unas cositas.*

I told her, 'You'll meet other men. You may like them. No, no, stay with Roger.' I gave her my recipe for pineapple upside down cake and my special pan. I told her to make *ese quequi de sorpresa*, for Roger.

"*Ee-ee*, what do you mean he does the cooking? Well, I pray for them every day. I blessed them and told her, '*Que Dios te ilumine, que te guíe en tu carrera. Encomiéndate al Espíritu Santo. Que Dios te llene de bendiciones.*'"

Lita, my paternal grandmother, enters the kitchen, begins mumbling the ingredients she'll need for making her *tamales*, *buñuelos*, *menudo*. No rest for the living or the dead this month, she thinks.

In the evening, my father, grandfathers, great-grandfathers and great-great-grandfathers sit around the kitchen table on which the Christmas cactus blooms its fragile pink blossoms. The talking stops, and the men in their pajamas and robes slurp hot *te de manzanilla*, listen to the fire and the wind. My father begins to hum, and in time, his grandfather, Abuelo Gregorio, to drum on the table. Papande begins to play a guitar, and the men smile wistfully, talk about how, with the exception of Papande, they never had the time or the money to learn to really play a musical instrument. The joking begins, lines tossed out like *serpentinas*.

"We could be a mariachi group."

"Dressed like this?" one says pulling at his well-worn robe.

"No, I'd like to play *música clásica*."

"Pero somos Mexicanos."

"*¿Y qué? Mexicanos* play all kinds of music from *rancheras* to *operas*."

"Ay, México, México. Como dice el dicho, como México no hay dos."

"No hay, no hay," the parrot agrees.

As my father intones the Mexican national anthem in a deep, false bravado, the men straighten in their chairs and sing with him, "*Me - xi - ca - nos al gri - to de gue - rra.*"

"Adelante, compañeros," says Lito. "Let's form a singing group. We're dead so what's stopping us. We may even be angels . . ."

"*Noooo, ni modo,*" the group laughs.

"Let's try. It's too cold to sit outside in the *portal* now. We can practice in here every night."

"Good idea to be near the food," my father says, "but let's not practice the night the fights are on."

"Señor Delgado, since you seem to be the only one of us who knows how to play," says Lito, "would you be kind enough to lead us? One advantage to being dead, and there are many," (All nod.) "is that I can be right back with some instruments. I'll bring violins, trumpets. Those are easy, but perhaps I can find a *guitarrón* too, and maybe my son would sing, *¿eh, Raúl?* This is a holy season. The wind howls, the garden sleeps, and the family needs to hear and feel *algo alegre, algo de esperanza.*"

"You know Esperanza too? Some woman."

"*Ya, ya,* let's not start your joking. The women will fill these rooms with the sweet smells of flowers and of *tamales* and *buñuelos,* so let's surprise them with a good concert . . . or at least *una serenata.*"

"And what is this?" asks Mamá Cleta entering the room and filling the teapot, lighting the stove.

"Mamá Cleta," says Abuelo Gregorio, "we were practicing a bit of music and talking about hope."

"*La esperanza no engorda pero mantiene,*" she says smiling and bringing a plate of *pan dulce* to the table. "Tomorrow evening we'll begin *las posadas* I know you'll each have your rosaries ready, *¿verdad, señores?*" She looks hard at the group and decides to offer them *copitas de vino de capulines,* the chokeberry wine that's said to strengthen the blood. It could be good for them these cold months.

"Now we'll really make music!" the men laugh clinking their wineglasses.

"*¡Borrrrrachos, borrrrrachos!*" The *guacamaya* is talkative tonight, well taught by the master tease.

As the twin flame tongues of the lantern listen, the men munch their *marranitos* and *semitas.* Papande begins to tune his guitar, nods to the others to select their instruments. He leads, shakes his head at the many false starts and laughter, "*Gracias a Dios* that we don't have to support this family with our music."

"*¡Se morirían de hambre!*"

But Papande in his gentle, serious way leads the group on through the music, explains the treble and bass clefs, whole, half, and quarter notes; sharps, flats, chords, harmony. By midnight, the men grin knowing that with practice they'll send music, their *música*, drifting through the walls, round the *portal*, round the *jardín*.

In the living room, Mamá Cleta hands the younger women orange rinds and the herb stems she's tied in small bundles to scent the fire. The women of the family relax in their soft nest of books and conversation.

"Who's taking care of the *luminarias* this year? I don't mind helping, but I don't want to be in charge," Libby says.

The youngest generation in the room, my children, niece, and nephews, carefully assist Mamá Cleta in creating the manger scene, such scenes "*fantasías deliciosas*," in the words of Mexican poet Carlos Pellicer. Gently, the young people pick up the tiny angels and shepherds, some made of wood, some clay, the tiny animals, camels, horses, even elephants climbing the hills to pay homage to the Christ Child.

I hear the wind, begin dreaming with one eye, think how good it will feel to pull the comforter over me later and fall asleep in the desert's voice. "Good sleeping weather," I say thinking this is the month of the full Long Nights Moon. "High in the mountains of Northern New Mexico, there was a custom called *los abuelos*. Have you heard of it? On nights like this, as snow fell and the wind blew, children were told, 'They're coming. The *abuelos* are coming.' Safe in their warm homes, the children would shiver in fright at the thought of the ragged, whip-cracking mountain ogres. The custom allowed the teaching of rules, of course: 'Behave or the *abuelos* will get you. Don't play near the *acequia* or the *abuelos* will get you. Be in before dark . . .'"

". . . or the *abuelos* will get you," my three say in unison, getting the drift.

"Study your catechism,"

". . . or the *abuelos* will get you."

"Say your prayers and mind your parents," my children pretend bitter frowns at the notion of minding their parents,

". . . or *los abuelos* will get you," they intone in deep, firm voices, laugh enjoying their antics.

"Then one night in December," I continue taking my son's hand, "for this was a winter custom, the men of those remote villages would go out and build roaring bonfires, called *luminarias* in New Mexico, and the little ones would know: the *abuelos* really were coming. The children would look out their windows, up at the huge black sky alive with stars, look up at the silent mountains, and then they hear them, a howling, 'Oooooo.' Down from the mountain come *los abuelos*, sooty and pig-faced, hairy and ragged, cracking *chicotes*, squealing, 'Oooooo.'

"The children shriek and run outside hoping not to be caught by the old men of the mountain and their long, tangled beards and their long, loud whips, ogres who were, of course, people from the village. They grab the youngsters demanding that they say a prayer or sing a song, and they know whom to grab. Often there's a dance at the end of the evening, and then the *abuelos* disappear."

"Sounds scary," Cissy says, goes to the piano and begins to play, "O Come All Ye Faithful." Lobo hums along as she reads her favorite part of the evening paper, the obituaries. I watch Cissy's long fingers, this Cecilia named for her aunt who was named after the patronness of music, the young Roman martyr who miraculously filled her bridal bower with roses and arpeggios, whose body was said to be soft as a flower eighteen hundred years after her death.

"Just look at those fingers!" a nurse said, handing me this last baby in the delivery room, the room of light. "She's going to be a pianist."

"My turn next at the piano," Bill says. "Why is it I never practice? I really like the piano. Why is it I never practice?"

We hear the older men around the kitchen table punctuate their music with laughter.

"In a few weeks they'll want to give a concert," Mamá Cleta says. "*Gozo comunicado crece.* What can we add to the occasion?"

"I'll make my *buñuelos*," Abuela Elena says.

"I'll make my *bizcochos*," says Lita.

"I know," I add. "Why don't we make some *papel picado?*"

"Can't we buy it?"

"Maybe. But we'd have to go to Juárez, and you know what the lines at the bridge are like during the holidays. Anyway, I think it would be fun to make our own cut-paper designs, shaping light and shadow. We could string some across the garden and some in this room and maybe the kitchen."

"What if it rains? Won't the paper be ruined outside?" Libby asks.

"We could make some out of plastic or oilcloth."

"Mom and her little family projects," my three say, shaking their heads.

December nights the music practice continues. Days, the baking begins, the house scented with red chile, anise, cinnamon. Lita mutters her recipe as she prepares to make her cookie *animalitos* without measuring cups or spoons.

"*Pero Lita*, some of this and some of that won't work for us," I say trying to get her recipe. She frowns, pushes her glasses back with her floured hand, annoyed at women who have to write everything down, who can't trust their hands, who don't know the feel of dough. Firmly beating her bowl of lard with her favorite wooden spoon, she dictates her recipe:

> ¾ *libra manteca, que es taza y media*
> 3 *yemas de huevos*
> 1 *cucharada de espauda, Uds. le dicen levadura*
> ½ *cucharita de sal*
> 1 *cucharada de canela molida*
> 1 *taza de azúcar*

½ taza de vino o jugo de naranja
4 tazas de harina

Se levanta bien la manteca, luego las yemas de los huevos, en-
seguida la espauda, canela, y sal. Se bate bien. Después le ponen
la azúcar y vino o jugo. Poco a poco le van batiendo la harina,
hasta que esté lista para hacer los bizcochos.

Lita's youngest daughter, Aunt Bori, short for her beautiful
name, Aurora, watches me write her mother's recipe. "You have
to beat it by hand, *m'ija*," my aunt says. "Then just roll it out and
make your designs. Mama does animals; I make stars and trees
and Santas at Christmas for my grandkids. Bake them at 350°
for ten minutes or until they're light brown."

Lita looks up at her baby, the tall daughter who towers over
her, then Lita looks at us, wrinkles her nose to push the sliding
glasses back. "*Saliendo calientes, se bañan en azúcar y canela molida.*"

"Do they realize what lard does to your insides," Cissy whis-
pers. "I don't mean to be rude, but can I just have a bagel when
you all eat these? I don't mind helping her cut them out, but I
just don't want to eat that stuff.

"Did you see the snowmen *and* women Bill and Lib and I
made out of tumbleweeds? Next we're going to decorate one of
the big cactus. Come look out at the garden."

I look out the window thinking of the rolling word for
tumbleweed in Spanish, *Rodadora*. We watch the poor pea-
cocks taking a brief afternoon stroll in the cold. *Aaayyy,*
AAAYYY.

Did I read or hear the story years ago of a giant who wanted
his huge garden for himself alone. When he locks the gate, the
sun stops shining there. Winter suddenly arrives, remains for
years as children peek through the locked, iron gates. One day
the giant sees a child sitting on a tree limb. Furious, the giant
strides out to banish the child with a halo round his head, a
child even the giant can't move, too heavy even for his huge
arms. At each visit, the child talks to the giant, but then disap-
pears, the next day appears and then disappears until the giant

daily begins waiting for his visitor. "Unlock your gates," the Boy finally says, "the gates to your heart, and your garden will again flourish, green and lush."

"Tonight's our cutting night," Cissy says the following evening, the night of the winter solstice. She hands scissors and sheets of colored tissue paper to the women and young men who come to the dining-room table.

"Maybe these young men should go join the older men," Mamá Cleta says.

"Gender division of labor," Libby whispers.

"Nothing like a sexist family," Cissy says, both girls wanting to keep their brother and his humor with us.

"I want the pink sheet," Libby says.

"Okay," Cissy says, "I've been practicing. Want me to show you?"

"¿Qué están haciendo?" Aunt Chole asks.

"Papel picado," I say. "Banderitas, Tía. The colored strings of cut papel de China. Did you know that, kids? That tissue paper in Spanish is papel de China because this kind of paper came from China as did this custom of cutting designs in colored paper?"

We fold, press, re-fold the thin rustling paper, begin to press our scissors into the multicolored sheets, constructing patterns of light and shadow, trying to imagine the shapes we're creating. What designs will our hands reveal when we carefully open the delicate sheets?

"This is good therapy," Libby says.

I finish a few sheets and then skim a newsletter on historical gardening and heritage roses, thumb through flower catalogs, show Aunt Carmen and Uncle Lalo pictures of tulips, burgandy lace and parrot. We hear the men in the kitchen, repeating songs, hear my father's pleasure in booming out, "Te trai - go se - re - na - ta, a - mor de mi vi - da," hear the laughter as the men serenade the macaw,

> Pobrecita guacamaya ¡ay! qué lástima me das
> Ay qué lástima me das, pobrecita guacamaya.

No one speaks for a while. The young people who have been gluing the *banderitas* onto the string with purple glue stick, stand and stretch out the cut paper and plastic for us all to admire our creations.

The night of the family serenade, we light *luminarias* in the garden, hang a few tin *farolitos* from bare branches, string the cut plastic flags between the cottonwood and the honey locust, then the cut paper in rows across the living-room and kitchen ceilings. Mother is putting the books she wrapped for each of us under the Christmas tree. "Are you sure you want to give your books away, Mom?" Stella asks.

"Yes, yes, yes. I want the pleasure of seeing you and Cecilia and Anthony and Pat enjoy them. I'm not going to read them again."

By the tree, Uncle Lalo and his nephews arrange folding chairs for the family musicians. "I wouldn't mind being part of their group mind you, boys, but I'm not quite ready to pay the price. The auditions aren't held on earth, you've noticed."

Hearing the men tuning up in the kitchen, the rest of us gather in the living room, find a place, then start to clap. Our musicians enter shyly, dressed in white shirts, ties with crooked knots, transparently nervous, accompanied by the *guacamaya*. Perched on my father's shoulder, the bird squawks, "*Pobrecita guacamaya, pobrecita guacamaya,*" a phrase we'll hear often in the New Year. Papande, the leader in this musical venture, nods to us, then nods at his group squirming in their stiff chairs. The squeaky music begins, and my father sings like he always wanted to sing, before an audience, like Caruso and Pavarotti. The family saints slide into the back of the room, San Rafael, San Martín, La Virgen de Guadalupe, and Santa Cecilia who's unable to resist directing, her long fingers gliding through the candlelight.

The men, the *papel picado*, light and shadow from the *luminarias* and *farolitos*, the bare tree branches, and even the very house sways in rhythm to the music that drifts through the rooms, slips under wood doors and circles the *portal*, weaves through the tress, the notes opening like blooms in the winter garden.

"Time for bed?" I ask trying to nudge my three after we've clapped and clapped, eaten white cheese with slices of *jalea de guayaba*. "It's like eating cheese with thick slices of fruit leather," Cissy says. "Not bad, but kinda weird."

We sip the fruity, sugary *ponche navideño*, joke about sending the group on the road with names like *Las Almas Santas* or Them Bones Gonna Rise Again or 2MR: Musical Magical Realism.

"Would it be a copyright infringement if we called them The Grateful Dead?" Bill asks enjoying his question.

"Why even go to bed?" Libby asks. "I'll just lie there fretting about all I have to do, meetings, law papers due. I always have trouble getting to sleep."

"Me too," Bill says. "All these people muttering their prayers at night. Who can sleep?"

"I can," Cissy says. "And Mom. Heck, Mom has trouble staying awake. Just look at her. She's trying to pretend she's awake right now. One day she's going to be killed by a book. She lies back on a cushion, holds a book up, and before she finishes a paragraph, she's in dreamland, but she pretends she's reading though her eyes are closed. POW! One night the book is going to hit her smack in the face."

"You know what I do when I can't get to sleep?" Stella asks. She takes my father's hand. "I go back to our old house, the house we grew up in on Mesita, and I go through it room by room."

I look around the living room at six generations of desert dwellers now gathered in this dream house hovering near el Río Grande between El Paso and Santa Fe, between the pass to the North and holy faith, a treacherous pass, the route to faith, all of us immigrants. Made of earth as we are, this nested adobe house, its body inherited and temporary, like ours, is protected by exterior walls we create and construct around the fertile interior, layers of vulnerable beauty. Within the body of the family dwell the homes of the next generation, another nesting, and within each of our bodies, all the selves we've been and are, held together by skin, fragile yet sturdy; a paradox, like the house that's green yet in the desert, visible yet private, unique yet organic, old yet new, open yet closed, imagined yet real, a retreat, private yet communal.

Growing up, communion meant consuming the body, "my spi - rit healed shall be," and part of me wants to absorb a thin bit of the adobe, to bring its natural and rounded beauty infused with weathered wisdom, with light and shadow into me, into us. I think of the parrots in Peru's rain forest, a thousand blue, red, yellow and green macaws whose bodies know. Within, they know to congregate on a mud bank in the morning sun to consume the earth that both detoxifies and actually nourishes their bodies.

Those of us in the room who knew and loved the house my father had built in 1939, return to it with Stella, her words, as words can, transporting us—Mamande, Lobo, my parents and siblings—to *nuestra casa de casas*, our house of houses.

"I walk across the front yard," Stella says, "look at the two Italian cypresses Daddy liked, look at the big arched window, the one Roy threw a baseball through once, and we didn't tell. I walk up the two red steps to the front porch that we'd pretend was a swimming pool, open the screen door and unlock the front door. I walk by the sofa and chairs, watch Mom playing "Clair de Lune" at the small grand piano, look at the fireplace with the fake logs and the gold screen, stop at the bookshelves, read the titles, *Vanity Fair, Far From the Madding Crowd*, Mom's books.

"I walk into the dining room and look at the chubby bride and groom in the china cabinet, look at the record albums, begin playing my old favorites, singing along, of course, since I know the words to every song, 'O - o - o - kla - ho - ma,' 'I could while a - wa y the hours, con - ferr - in,' 'The hills are alive . . .

"I walk into Mom and Dad's room, look up at the crucifix and at Our Lady of Guadalupe, walk down the hall into the room Roy, Lobo, and I shared, the room that was my sisters' before my parents added on to the house. I read the old rhymes on the linoleum, sing them really, 'Jack and Jill went up the hill,' 'All the king's horses and all the king's men,' 'He put in his thumb and pulled out a plum.' "

"You really sing yourself to sleep, Aunt Stella," Bill laughs. "Beats counting sheep, but I'd have to know a lot more songs."

We hardly hear him, too busy looking at our storybook and Madame Alexander dolls in that room on Mesita Street, at stubborn Jo in her long, blue dress, dark brown eyes and hair, and at shy Meg and her long blonde hair, her pink dress with its full net-covered skirt, the "Little Women" we played with on our beds. We look at the blue and red *World Book*, open favorite volumes of the orange-bound *Childcraft*, linger over the sketch of the rabbit who wanted wings, the giant lifting the roof of his house, and Stevenson's,

> The friendly cow, all red and white,
> I love with all my heart.
> She gives me cream with all her might.
> To eat with apple tart.

"I see all of Pat's albums of holy cards in the next room," Stella says, "and step on the green linoleum of Mamande's room, the room that had been our TV room before she got sick. I look at her chest of drawers with her novenas, Saint Raphael, Bayer aspirin, and Big Hunks; at the wooden, wide-armed chair she'd sit in when she prayed, at the big leather chair where we'd sit and watch 'Six Gun Playhouse' and 'Have Gun, Will Travel,' laugh saying to one another, '¡Ay, Cisco! ¡Ay, Pancho!'

"I walk into the yellow breakfast room where we ate all our meals except on holidays when we'd eat in the dining room and use the flowered China and the Fostoria cut-crystal. I sit at the breakfast table where Mom would sit for hours helping us with our homework, asking us '12 times 12' and 'spell *onomatopoeia*,' asking us questions from the *Baltimore Catechism*, 'Why did God make you? Can you see grace?'

"I walk into the kitchen and see Mamande making us a peanut butter and jelly sandwich. And then if I'm still awake, I open the door and go out to the back yard, smell the fresh cut grass. Lobo's sweeping, Daddy's watering his roses, our dog's asleep, my sisters and brother are playing on the slide and merry-go-round. I walk out and climb on my swing, push myself with my toes as hard as I can, and I start to sing, 'Shall we dance, *pum,pum,pum,* shall we dance,' and I sail right into the sky."

Drifting up from the river, the wind weaves through the cottonwood and *mora,* gathers voices from above and below the surface into its song, *el canto hondo.* The full Long Night's Moon chants its white blessing on the house, the garden. Deep in the earth turtles sleep; the parrot and peacocks nestle into themselves as do we. Gradually, our breaths become one.

Dichos / Sayings

In Spanish, as in any language, countless sayings, *dichos* or *refranes*, exist that enrich the language and are a means of perpetuating communal wisdom and values, also humor. *Quien habla con refranes es un saco de verdades*, who speaks in sayings is a sack of truths. Often the phrases of layered meaning rhyme and delight ear, eye, and mind with word play seldom completely conveyed in translation.

Each chapter or month in this book of family memories begins with a *dicho*. Others are also found in the text and are listed below in the months they appear. Enjoy!

House of Houses

Ut rosa flos florum, sic est domus ista domorum. / As the rose is the flower of flowers, so is this, the house of houses.

p. 9   *Como siembras, segarás.*
        As you sow, you will harvest.

Enero el friolero / Chilly January

p. 22   *Hacer de tripas, corazón.*
        From intestines, making a heart.

p. 28   *Ya se le fue el pájaro.*
        The bird (mind) has flown away.

p. 41   *No hay rosa sin espina.*
        Every rose has its thorn.

Febrero loco / Crazy February

p. 49   *Lo traigo entre ceja y ceja.*
        He lives between my eyebrows.

p. 53   *Amor viejo, ni te olvido, ni te dejo.*
        Old love, I neither forget nor leave you.

p. 58   *Algunos nacen con estrella y otros estrellados.*
        Some are born star-blessed and others star-bonked.

p. 60   *No es desgracia ser pobre, pero es muy inconveniente.*
        It's not a disgrace to be poor, but it's certainly
        inconvenient.

Marzo airoso / Windy March

p. 77   *Este mundo es un fandango, y el que no baile, es un loco.*
        This world is a dance, and only fools don't join in the
        music.

p. 97   *Panza llena, corazón contento.*
        Full stomach, happy heart.

Mayo / May

Enero friolero, febrero loco, marzo airoso, abril lluvioso, sacan a mayo,
    floreado y hermoso.
Chilly January, crazy February, windy March, rainy April bring
    on the beauty of flowering May.

p. 140 *Sólo lo barato se compra con dinero.*
        Only what's cheap can be bought with money.

p. 143 *Al que madruga, Dios le ayuda.*
        God assists the early bird.

p. 143   *Echando a perder se aprende.*
        We learn by making mistakes.

Junio / June

Huerta sin agua, cuerpo sin alma.
An orchard without water is like a body without a soul.

p. 145   *Lleva la música por dentro.*
        She has the music inside.

p. 146   *No hay rosa sin espina.*
        Every rose has its thorn.

p. 148   *Donde hay amor, hay dolor.*
        Where there's love, there's sorrow.

p. 162   *Para el amor no hay edad.*
        Love is ageless.

Julio / July

Al que buen árbol se arrima, buena sombra le cobija.
Seek shade under a worthy tree.

p. 168   *Le corre la sangre muy despacio.*
        Her blood runs slowly.

p. 168   *La memoria de la niñez, dura hasta la vejez.*
        Childhood memories last a lifetime.

p. 170   *Como pez en el agua.*
        Like a fish in water.

p. 176   *De tal palo salta la estilla.*
        The splinter resembles the wood.

p. 182   *Mala hierba nunca muere.*
        Weeds never die.

p. 182   *Las flores contentan pero no alimentan.*
        Flowers please but appetite they don't ease.

Agosto / August

Goza del mes de mayo que agosto llegará.
Revel in May, for August soon arrives.

p. 189 *Mientras en mi casa estoy, rey soy.*
   In my house, I'm king.

p. 209 *Cada chango a su mecate.*
   Every monkey to his string.

p. 210 *Lo bailado, nadie te lo quita.*
   What's danced, is always yours.

Septiembre / September

De lo hermoso, hermoso es el otoño.
To speak of lovely, speak of autumn.

p. 229 *Cada cabeza es un mundo.*
   Each mind is a world.

Octubre / October

La que anda entre la miel, algo se le pega.
Honey clings if you're surrounded by it.

p. 238 *La que canta, sus males espanta.*
   Singing, we frighten away our trouble.

Noviembre / November

La primavera se hace ligera, el invierno se hace eterno.
Spring breezes by, while winter seems eternal.

p. 255 *Cuando Dios quiere, el agua es medicina.*
   When it's God's will, even water is medicine.

p. 257 *Llegando al camposanto, no hay calaveras plateadas.*
   No silver-plated skulls at the cemetery.

p. 262   *El muerto a la sepultura, y el vivo a la travesura.*
            The dead to the grave, the living to mischief.

p. 262   *No hay mejor salsa que un buen apetito.*
            A good appetite is the best sauce.

p. 266   *Un lugar para cada cosa, y cada cosa en su lugar.*
            A place for everything and everything in its place.

Diciembre, mes viejo que arruga el pellejo.
December, old month that wrinkles our skin.

p. 274   *Por Navidad, dichoso el que en casa está.*
            Blessed, to be home for Christmas.

p. 274   *Quien sabe dos lenguas, vale por dos.*
            If you are bilingual, you count twice.

p. 276   *Diciembre, del año, el mes más anciano.*
            December, the oldest month of the year.

p. 280   *Como dice el dicho, como México no hay dos.*
            As the saying goes, there's only one Mexico.

p. 281   *La esperanza no engorda pero mantiene.*
            Hope, non-fattening and nourishing.

p. 284   *Gozo comunicado crece.*
            Shared joy grows.